To Helen and Tom —
   Page 171 — We were
there!
   Barb and Bill
December, 1989

# BIG TEN COUNTRY

BY BOB WOOD

DODGER DOGS TO FENWAY FRANKS
BIG TEN COUNTRY

# BIG TEN
## COUNTRY

### A JOURNEY THROUGH ONE FOOTBALL SEASON

## BOB WOOD

WILLIAM MORROW
and Company, Inc. New York

Library of Congress Cataloging-in-Publication Data

Wood, Bob. 1957–
Big Ten country : a journey through one football season / Bob
Wood
p.    cm.
ISBN 0-688-08922-4
1. Intercollegiate Conference of Faculty Representatives.
2. Football–Middle West.   3. College sports–Middle West.
I. Title
GV958.5.I55W66   1989
796.332′63′0977–dc20                                         89-35052
                                                                CIP

Printed in the United States of America

1 2 3 4 5 6 7 8 9 10

BOOK DESIGN BY RICHARD ORIOLO

*To everybody who rocked the Spartan Stadium
student section back in 1978.
Especially, to Sheck and Benny C., to Waldo, Hor, Trink, and
Scotch-man.
To my brother, Drew.
And to my Eden Roc roommates, Brennan, Frank, and
Kearls.
To you all—a "Red Pop" toast for
"Smith to Gibson and 24–15."*

# ACKNOWLEDGMENTS

To Lisa Drew, my editor, a real live Badger grad in New York City. Thanks for all your help, for taking on *Big Ten Country* in the first place, then making it better. Now, maybe others besides Wisconsin fans will know the crazy things that go on inside Camp Randall . . . after the final gun.

To my brother, Drew, who is about as good a Spartan fan as there is. Thanks for the title. And for the inspiration. If you hadn't kept telling me, "You can do it," I wouldn't have done it.

To Murph—it's bad enough you're a Pirates fan, but the Washington Huskies too? Geez, what's next, the Miami Heat? Regardless, thanks for all the read-throughs—on both books. You helped a ton. And you're a good friend. Good luck bringing the "Black Hole" to South Kitsap football.

To my agent, David Black—thanks again for that *Dodger Dogs* phone call back in '86. Thanks for sticking with me, for all your hard work—despite my not so hot dollars-per-hour payoff ratio—but no, you'll never get the Kirbster!

To my Midwest–to–New York connections: David Means, for keeping your boss from killing me; Bob Shuman, for keeping in touch; Bruce Giffords, for keeping the flavor of the tailgates; Paul Greenhalgh; for your couch. Thanks, guys.

To my only real hometown ever—Kalamazoo, Michigan, in the heart of Big Ten Country. Thanks for all the *Dodger Dogs* support.

To Mom and Dad (two more State fans)—thanks for helping me out along the way. I love you both very much. And I promise, next time I stop by, it'll just be for dinner and not for the whole year.

To Amy, for planning the chapter title pages. Nice job, Sis!

To J.D., for titling the chapter title pages. Good luck with Doris Day!

To Andrejs Kregers and to all the other Baker Brothers at Players Pub (Kazoo's best bar). Thanks for teaching me the difference between gin and tonic.

To Bill, Mary Jo, and Billy Abbe. Thom too! Thanks again for the office. It's still the best one in the world.

To Bruce Demming, for your words of encouragement back when I really needed some. And for introducing me to the "girls" at the UW barns.

To the Red Roof Inns of America, and particularly to Mike Agee. You've put together the world's finest motel chain. Remote-control TV, free coffee, and *USA Today* . . . who needs Tom Bodett?

And to Kinko Copy Center in Kazoo, for my daily visits. Sorry about all the "No, that's not quite dark enough yet's."


While I was roaming the Big Ten, a lot of people took time out to visit with me. To all of you, thanks. And to the following people, a special thanks:

Michigan State: Bill Wiedrick, Dede Goldstein, Keith Williams, Martha, Julie, Chris, and Leanne "with the tired feet."

Minnesota: Steve Lorinser, Doug Cornelius, Peg Pederson, George Hudak, Joyce and Roger Betin.

Wisconsin: Mike Leckrone, Bob Leu, Hank from Mickie's, Bob and Sue in Section O, Arlie Mucks, Andy Katts, Margaret McCormick.

Michigan: Herb Wagner, Al Renfrew, Jeff Long, Don Lund, Jerry and Bill (the barbers), Bud and Hanky Van De Wege, Rick Peitras, and Joel, the State Street ticket daddy.

Iowa: Mark Jennings, Rich Wretman, and Andy Piro; the Hawkeye marching beer band. Rosemary Lyons, Anna Murphy; all the friendly folks in Hawkeye tailgate land.

Illinois: Walt, Ann, and Nicki at the Union info desk; student employees at the Illinois Library Archives; Don Dodds and Gary Smith; George Wenthe and the Minsker tailgate clan.

Indiana: Jeff Jones, Doris Seward, Curtis D. Aiken, Stephen Pratt, the Bones, David and Courtney Everson; Alice, Bob, Ron, and Larry at Nick's; my campus tour guides, Brent and Theresa; Jim Lenahan and Dick Barnes.

Purdue: Bob DeMoss, Dr. William Daniel, Bob Weisenberger, Joe Manfredo, Ray Brown, Dave Guarino, George Owen, Dawn Beck, Kim Radcliffe, Lani and Bibi Barnes.

Northwestern: Sharon Miller, Margaret Akerstrom, Northwestern Crew, Verna of Theta Chi, the Purple Hazers, Mike Baum, Bob Voight and Walter Paulison.

Ohio State: Archie Griffin, Steve Snapp, Jim Kinney and Dave Rencehausen, Jacques Taylor, Dave Wieble and Bob Nelson.

To the Big Ten offices, particularly to Mark Rudner—thanks for your cooperation and for allowing me to use the Big Ten name.

And last, but certainly not least, thanks to all those good folks that welcomed me into their tailgates last fall. Thanks for the Bloody Marys, the brats and the beer, the Arkansas Razorback chants, the "Purple Haze" days reminiscing, and for just being nice people. You all are the heart of the Midwest and the real reason Big Ten Country is the best place on the globe to see a football game.

# CONTENTS

# INTRODUCTION

I pretty much live for three things: summer nights in the bleachers (preferably with the Sox in town), Frank Sinatra's voice (preferably alongside Billy May's band), and Michigan State football (preferably on a crisp Saturday afternoon in Spartan Stadium). *Dodger Dogs to Fenway Franks,* my book of travels through the major-league baseball world, calmed one urge. Mr. Sinatra hasn't yet dropped me a line about writing his life story. That left the Spartans. So this book's about them and the other nine teams in the Big Ten. It's about my trip through Big Ten Country.

I'd like to think of myself as a normal human . . . at least a seminormal one. And of course a Big Ten football fan—of the green-and-white variety. Well, like any other normal Big Ten football fan's life, mine revolves around my school's colors. Apartment walls ooze loyalty— sandwiched between your basic family shots hangs a whole host of green and white: a bunch of pennants, a big block S State flag, and a shrine to one of the greatest days of my life—an '88 Rose Bowl poster. Plus, there's my most prized possession. The only one in recorded history. A personalized, autographed Lorenzo White action photo. Number 34 dancing through a hole in the middle of the Western Michigan Bronco line. Signed courtesy of my brother, Drew, who knew somebody, who knew Lorenzo: "To Woody"—that's me—"dining on a little Bronco meat, Lorenzo White." What a prize! Only it could rate a hang over my desk—alongside Sinatra.

The Spartan logo finds more than just walls, however. My car's covered with green-and-white "Go, State" decals. And the key that kicks her into gear hangs from an "MSU #1" key chain. Kitchen cupboards overflow with Spartan coffee mugs, the late-model ones dotted with red roses. Block S champagne and wine glasses, usually reserved for champagne and wine, but milk on occasions when the sink's filled, find a home in the kitchen too. Front-hall closets are wadded with green stuff, spring and fall jackets, a big, gray, 100 percent cotton MSU hooded sweatshirt, and at least one umbrella that opens to a school colors kaleidoscope. But it's in the bedroom that my greatest Spartan virtues lie. And without a doubt the biggest drain on a battered Visa card. T-shirts by the billion—featuring everything from a Magic National Championship to a prehistoric Cherry Bowl, all in 100 percent cotton and categorized by sport.

If you didn't guess already—I am a State grad. The year was 1980. Not a Spartan by birth, I was indoctrinated in green and white those five years I partied through . . . and the colors just seemed to stick. Probably the same way it happens in Champaign with orange and blue, or at Indiana in the crimson and cream shades. Something even tells me that Northwestern grads end up wearing a hell of a lot more purple than they would've if they'd gone to school someplace else. The colors, the dedication, the four or five or six years that you spend at a place like Michigan State or Illinois or Indiana, prime you for life and provide a place to come back to and pop the hatchback on fall Saturday afternoons. Plus, they take away the need to ever hire a wardrobe color consultant. You just end up in the school shades.

Most Big Tenners, however, upon graduation stick somewhere

close to home. Usually the Midwest. I did not. I left in '81. In an effort
to find myself, I threw a dart and ended up in Seattle. There I lived
life as a misplaced ex–Big Ten junior-high-school teacher, in Pac Ten
land, a place where people go to college football games only if there's
nothing else to do. Worst of all, they never really care who'll win on
January 1, then they never seem to lose.

It's tough to explain the difference between the two conferences—
aside from the Rose Bowl record. Sportswriters define it by the forward pass: "They use it. . . . We don't! That's why they usually beat
us." Weathermen say that Pacific Coast weather's ideal for football.
While the Midwest is buried in Christmas snowstorms, and teams are
practicing in the local drift or indoors in some aluminum gym, it's sunny
and 70 in the land of the mellow. Guys are taking off their helmets and
soaking in the sunshine. Some West Coast studies even claim California high schools turn out a higher-quality teenage athlete. Which I'm
sure is horse crap!

All I know is that compared to folks in the Midwest, Pac Ten fans
milquetoast their way through football season. ABC cameras at Husky
Stadium in Seattle never miss the chance to zoom in on boats tailgate-
docking at the stadium's open end on the shore of Lake Washington.
Ahh—a lovely sight indeed! What they don't feature is scalpers taking
a weekly bath because anyone can get a ticket for cost, regardless of
who's in town. USC and UCLA, it seems, always play before corner-of-
the-end-zone empty seats, unless they're playing each other for the
conference championship, while the two Oregonian teams, the Ducks
and the Beavers, draw about as well as an Ohio state high-school
semifinal playoff game. Although the Pac Ten's ruled the Rose Bowl
for the most of the past couple of decades, when it comes to the
important stuff—the marching bands, the tailgating, the cold crispy fall
sunshine—there's really no comparison. Big Ten football is God's gift
to Saturday afternoons in October.

Football in the Big Ten is magic. It's sunny, blue, crisp autumn
afternoons freezing your rear off—nipping on some schnapps and hot
chocolate. It's tailgating for five hours talking football, munching dogs,
brats, burgers—anything, really, that'll stuff its way onto the grill. It's
cruising the bookstores to pick up just one more red-and-white Bucky
Badger T-shirt, or another black-and-gold Hawkeye version just because Herky's on the lapel. It's that explosion, that roar of the crowd
that greets the opening kickoff, and the marching-band fight song that
blasts out a celebration of each home team's score. It's loyal alums

head-to-toed in their school colors, and crazy, screaming end-zone student sections. It's anticipating that public address update of the Iowa-Michigan game, and wondering who'll kick the winning field goal this time. Big Ten football is passionate. It's friendly. It embodies the good things that college football is all about. And as career decisions go, I'll bet you I'm not the only one who's moved back home because of it.

You see, after six years of Pac Ten land, of my only ABC Big Ten football coming in half-time updates during some West Coast double-header, and after six years of begging the bartender to turn his satellite dish east just so I could home in on a MSU-vs.-Iowa Big Ten Game of the Week—I moved back home. Back to Spartan Stadium Saturday afternoons and great marching bands and five-hour tailgate parties. Back to a land where the pregame's as important as the game itself. Back to the Big Ten, the football conference that year in and out leads the world in the most important stat—attendance. And as a reward, in '87, my first fall back home since the days of Muddy Waters, the Spartans rose up from the doormat to take home the roses. I found my paradise!

Then I got to thinking—a lot of folks are just as passionate about the Big Ten as I am and never leave their living rooms. Some leave their living rooms but not their campuses. So I figured, why not find out about Big Ten football on the road! The college football season's eleven weeks long. There are ten stadiums in the conference. I'd just go to one a week. I'd watch the biggest games, the games that figured who would be in Pasadena come January 1. Michigan vs. Michigan State, in Michigan Stadium on October 8, that would be priority one. I'd catch Iowa and Indiana against a decent opponent—maybe each other. And Northwestern in a game they might have a prayer to win. I'd get to finish up with *the game* down in Columbus. Best of all, wherever possible I'd catch the Spartans in their white road unies.

Along the way I could do all the things I do best. Eat, obviously. And in the finest style. I'd tailgate where folks really knew how to tailgate— at Illinois, at Ann Arbor, and outside the gates of Camp Randall in Madison. I'd traipse about college campuses that have been traipsed about for over a hundred years. And I'd do it during nature's finest show—autumn. I'd sample food, not only in the parking lots but also in town. For survival's sake, I'd have to find the best burger and best breakfast. Because there, along with the best tavern, I'd probably find the most interesting folks. Being a stadium groupie, I could walk through places erected before anybody cared where CBS'd hang its TV cameras. And maybe if I worked it right, I'd actually see the Little Brown Jug and the Indiana-Purdue war memorial—that Old Oaken Bucket. Marching bands—the best, no doubt, in the world—would be performing for me on their home turf. I'd interview them. The kid that dotted the *i* at Ohio State—and Purdue's gorgeous Golden Girl. What a way to spend the fall! A dream vacation filled with food and sunshine and crisp blue Saturday afternoons. And Big Ten football.

So that's pretty much how this whole thing came about. That, along with a few little events that fell neatly into place. *Dodger Dogs,* my baseball book, got me a summer appearance on the David Letterman show. Once you're fried by Letterman, you're famous for life and anybody'll buy your story. William Morrow graciously agreed to. I decided I'd upgrade my on-the-road living conditions and vowed never again to live in a place that didn't have remote-control TV. That bagged Motel 6. So I set up a reservation string of Red Roof Inns across the Midwest. I added a couple of Nat King Cole "Best of's" to my case of Sinatra tapes. I applied for a third Visa card. And I hit the road, in search of all the good things that make Big Ten Country the best place on the globe to watch a football game.

### BIG TEN COUNTRY TOUR, FALL 1988

| | |
|---|---|
| September 17 | Notre Dame at MICHIGAN STATE |
| September 24 | Northern Illinois at MINNESOTA |
| October 1 | Michigan at WISCONSIN |
| October 8 | Michigan State at MICHIGAN |
| October 15 | Michigan at IOWA |
| October 22 | Michigan State at ILLINOIS |
| October 29 | Iowa at INDIANA |
| November 5 | Michigan State at PURDUE |
| November 12 | Purdue at NORTHWESTERN |
| November 19 | Michigan at OHIO STATE |

# 1

# MICHIGAN STATE UNIVERSITY

## THE SPARTANS

| Michigan State University East Lansing, MI | Spartan Stadium |
|---|---|
| Best Breakfast | Bagel Fragel |
| Best Bar | Dooley's |
| Best Burger | Dagwood's |
| Best of... | |

### The Best in Big Ten Country

#### BURGER

| | | |
|---|---|---|
| 1. | Dotty Dumpling's | Wisconsin |
| 2. | Dagwood's | MSU |
| 3. | Hamburg Inn #2 | Iowa |
| 4. | Crazy Jim's | Michigan |
| 5. | Annie's Parlour | Minnesota |

**M**ost of *Big Ten Country* was to be an exploration into territories where I'd never been before. Exotic, out-of-the-way places, like Bloomington, Indiana, and Iowa City, Iowa, and Champaign, Illinois. You see, much as I live for Spartan Saturdays, and much as I love getting out on the road, I never really put the two together. My Michigan State football road trips were limited. To two, actually—the first one back in '78, when my roomates and I headed over to Ann Arbor. There, blasted by a constant flow of vodka and apple cider, we cheered Kirk Gibson and Eddie Smith to a 24–15 upset win over Michigan. But because of the cider, or maybe the shock, I didn't have a clue to what the campus, or the town, or even what much of the game was like. My second voyage came in '87, when Michigan State was rolling to the Big Ten title. I joined my sister, Amy, in Chicago. We took the El from her place up to Northwestern, and watched Lorenzo bury the Cats. It was an ugly day, though, cold and wet. The trip was short: the El to the game and back to the El. No roaming in between. Two conference road games in twelve years! That's it! Still, my lack of Big Ten road work allowed an edge to this journey. Aside from Ann Arbor and Evanston, where I figured to have a few déjà vu flashbacks, every other *Big Ten Country* place I'd visit would be a fresh experience. Every campus I'd stroll would provide the excitement of a first date!

As for State, the best parts are locked away in my head. Memories of an ex–college student! So no matter what happens to future Spartan football teams, no matter if someday down the road State turns out the absolutely greatest football team on earth, even if we finally beat Bo two times straight, to me the green-and-white glory year will always be 1978. The Eddie Smith to Kirk Gibson, to Mark Bramer, and to Eugene Byrd year. The season the Spartans beat up on Michigan in Michigan Stadium. With *me* sitting in the end zone! That's Michigan State football. That and Saturdays in the Spartan Stadium student section just being a typical student.

Being a typical college kid revolves around a few standard necessities. Things that I doubt have changed all that much in the past ten football seasons. At least for students' sakes I hope not! College kid standard number one is, and always will be, life in a continual state of bankruptcy. Which is good, because it builds character. A second important basic—a part-time job for weekend beer change—I fufilled in '78 at the local sub shop. A class schedule that, although it lacked a major for the longest time, adjusted quite well to Spartan football games and my intramural games was my third covered necessity. And finally, an apartment with a balcony. That was the real key to college life—an apartment with a balcony. 'Cause then the burger cookouts, the hours spent with your feet propped up and the music cranked, the sun going down, all of that with the right balcony, and you could live the stuff that Old Milwaukee beer commercials are made of. And you knew for a fact that "life just doesn't get any better than this!"

Apartment 305 at Eden Roc housed *the* balcony. It also housed me and my three roommates, Brennan, Frank, and Kearls. After a couple of years in the dorms, we'd moved to 305 Eden Roc because of, well, primarily the balcony. The rest of the place came with it! A typical college kid apartment, it was the greatest place I ever lived. Five rooms for four guys; a kitchen that only two of us could fit in at a time, with a sink constantly filled with all sorts of floating growing things; cable TV and three stereos (one in each bedroom and a family-room model). Best, though, was that balcony. A balcony that hung out over a parking lot and faced a building full of other balconies . . . always, it now seems, crammed with gorgeous women. A balcony that looked west and caught those orange East Lansing sunsets full force, through the telephone wires. A balcony that turned warm spring nights with Sinatra, a beer, and a burger into an absolute heaven. And a balcony, three floors up Eden Roc, that on Spartan Saturdays in the fall exploded in a football celebration.

Our Spartan Saturday morning routine was a simple but dedicated one. And always the same! Lunch was provided courtesy of the Golden Arches. Usually a couple of Quarter Pounders with cheese, fries—tons of fries—and a couple of big Cokes. We were convinced that McDonald's fries had a chemical added to them that reconstructed dead brain cells. They must have, cause we always seemed to handle the day's two big questions—"Who's got the tickets?" and "What are we gonna drink today?"—without a hitch. Balcony music was another necessity that required a vote. Sinatra was vetoed on game days. Usually it was the Cars, or the Raspberries, or sometimes Bob Seger. Always something loud. Always something we knew the words to. We'd open the sliding glass doors, turn the speakers out to the balcony, and blow away the parking lot. Meanwhile, tickets and borrowed student IDs for visiting friends were rounded up by a barrage of phone calls. As for the day's alcohol consumption—group votes were tallied; important decisions, based on who drank too much of what the night before, were made. Usually the game-day bar menu came down to "schnapps and something" or "vodka and something." Or just plain beer. Anyhow, collections were taken, and a beer run made.

Then it was kick back and have some fun. And watch the parking lot wake up. All sort of folks got into the act. Alumni came back to check out their old stomping grounds. Parking places evaporated, sucked up by visiting Spartan fans. More kids making more beer runs were out and about. Our balcony was the best place to watch from. And best—leaning back in a living room chair with the feet propped up on the rail, and a cold Old Mil in hand. Spartan talk and Spartan chants rolled, with folks inside, with kids across the lot, and absolutely anybody down below. The fight song would get an every-other-album-side turn. And was always joined by a full chorus of balcony singers. No matter how out of tune, we always knew the words. After a half hour of filling flasks, meeting friends down from Central or over from Detroit, of yelling or singing across to next-door neighbors or folks in the lot, it was time to head out for the game.

The Spartan Stadium walk, from almost any direction, is a treat. From the apartment complexes on the east end of campus, on a cool blue day, it might be the best in the world. Sidewalks ease over onto campus, and roll along the Red Cedar River. Trees cover the banks and splash fall colors. By noon streams of green, pumped and well oiled, were on their way. Dorms, Shaw Hall at the middle of campus in particular, always cranked on game day. Like a strobe light on the concrete sidewalk dance floor, music, all different kinds from all different stereos in all the open dorm windows, belted out in one long continuous stream of noise. And that fight song, always the Spartan fight song, usually on the biggest stereo in the place. The closer you got to the stadium the more intense the green, and the crowds of people. Old folks, parents and kids, students, some throwing Frisbees on the way, some throwing footballs, others passing the flask. Program sellers and souvenir vendors. And ticket scalpers holding up a pair. The whole walk was a celebration.

Usually, we'd make the game about a half hour before kickoff. When warm-ups were still rolling. Brennan liked pregame warm-ups. He may have been all through playing, but Brennan still thought like a linebacker. And ate and slept and looked like one too. He loved to watch the bodies crunch. And ate up the pregame drills. A 3–0, smash-'em-in-the-mouth, kick-'em-when-they're-down game was a Brennan game. To him, all quarterbacks wore dresses, and Jack Lambert was the greatest football player that ever lived. Brennan was an abnormally good fan for a student. Frank and Kearls and I were like most of the other end-zone students, there for the good time as much as the game. And we spent the pregame, like everybody but Brennan, roaming the student section, looking for friends. The routine wasn't much different than at the Friday night taverns. You get there early, find your buddies, since nobody checks tickets you decide where to sit, and then sock in for the celebration. And somewhere in between you pull the beers out of your socks and belts and coat pockets and start popping tabs.

Kickoff exploded the end zone! One mass of energy, with a band down below to bring a little rhythm to the madness, every event was a happening! Passing things, anything, up through the stands, was a game-long occupation. Missed field goals or made ones—the ball would end-over-end into the end zone. And then start climbing up the section. Within five passes, the ball would be up, up, and gone—over the stadium edge to a roar of end zone cheers. Girls got passed up too. Some would fight to the death before being uprooted. Others would just give up and go, like a wooden plank—hand to hand to hand to the top. Unlike the footballs, girls did not get tossed out of the stadium. Although once, I remember, after one had reached the top, somebody tossed a dummy dressed like a Spartan fan over the edge. The usual crowd roar was tempered with a gasp, from the folks too far away to tell the difference.

The band too rocked the student section. A live fight song, always right in front of us, cranked the whole game long. And in the second half, band sections would split up and do all sorts of crazy little numbers. Drums put on their drum show, and the trumpets put on theirs, and best of all a squad of baritones played the "Faygo Red Pop" song. Everybody knew the words. And while the baritones would play, we'd sing and sway. Second-half TV time-outs and kickoff breaks were always filled with slow swaying, and the whole Spartan end zone singing about red pop.

Center stage, though, belonged to the Spartans, and the absolute intensity of college football. Nothing in those college years, not even studying for midterms, got us more fired up than the Spartan football team. Plastered right up against the field, in our end zone seats, you could actually hear the pads pop and feel the bodies break. Goal line stands were electric, because you sat on top of the play. If the ball was at the other end, you might as well be in another world—human forms were barely visible. But then again, that was the best body-passing and flask-passing time. And the noise! The entire game was one deep roar—swelling and ebbing, just waiting to explode to a good stick or a long, winding, dancing Spartan run. And always there stood before us that unwritten challenge, that which proved what we, the end zone student section, were made of, the challenge of backing the other team's quarterback off the ball. When the quarterback was a Wolverine, the challenge became a manhood test. . . . It was our duty to screw up Bo's offense. Best of all though, were the touchdown celebrations. The high fives and rolls of flying toilet paper and jumping up and down. Those were my very favorite college football days. Back in '78. Those mad afternoons in the end zone. With "Faygo," and body passing, and fight songs, and flasks full of schnapps.

Nowadays, as a creaky old alum, I go the mellow route. About all my body can handle from the student Saturdays is the Golden Arches and an occasional shot of schnapps. Even so, I still get the satisfaction. Still love the stadium celebration. Still enjoy watching the student sections let loose. Especially that first game of each season. Every year it's like a rebirth.

Well, my big-time rebirth came in '87, the year before *Big Ten Country.* USC was in East Lansing for a Labor Day national-TV night game. It was my first game back home in Spartan Stadium in eight seasons. And I was as pumped as if I'd been blasting the Cars and singing the fight song at 305 Eden Roc. We'd gone to the game early— me, my brother, Drew, and a few of his friends. With the hatch popped, we grilled burgers down by the Red Cedar. They ate. I roamed and reminisced.

All the old feelings came rushing back. The sensations of the walk to the stadium. The Red Cedar, the changing colors, the streams of green and white. The Frisbees and footballs and flask passing. Spartan Stadium, across the road from the river, stood as stately as ever, and even wore a halo. Portable lights, in for the game, rose up and cut the twilight. Behind it, still standing, still identifying Michigan State College, that old red-brick smokestack. MSC, one letter under another, was plastered down the brick. Out beyond, on the IM fields, acres and acres and acres of tailgaters. The butterflies were swarming. Like a high-school kid on his first date, I'll never forget that night. I'll never forget walking the end zone ramp up into the seats. And that explosion of color! All at once the bright white lights, and an endless sea of green. Upper-deck overhangs, both of 'em crammed with people, a packed house of Spartan fans. Down on the field, running plays into the end zone, Brennan's pregame plays, was the football team. Coach Perles in the middle with his arms folded. I'd clicked my heels three times. . . . Like the ruby slippers, my white Nikes had spun some Spartan magic.

One other Spartan memory really sticks with me. A moment that I relive over and over again. And it whirls in my head whenever I hear the Michigan State fight song. The story goes back to '84, at the first Cherry Bowl, that two-year disaster bowl that just happened to hit Detroit during its coldest, snowiest Decembers. State played Army. I'd flown in from Seattle. My first Spartan game since graduating. Brennan and Drew picked me up at the airport. We fought the traffic tie-ups and the subzero cold, and reached the bubble-topped Silverdome an hour before kickoff. It felt good to be back! Green was packing the stands, and we were in place for Brennan's pregame drills. I even think we sneaked in a couple of beers, just like in the old times.

But something just wasn't right. The roof kept out the icy cold. It was the middle of December and I wasn't wearing a jacket. No sky. No wind. No sun. Although it was my first State game since college, I felt out of place, even kind of bummed out. Then the Spartan band hit the tunnel. The first time I'd seen them in four years! The drum major, chest back and baton thrust up, kicked out of the tunnel and across the middle of the empty green. Double-timing, the Michigan State Marching Band followed. The MSU fight song shook the place. State fans roared. Shivers ran down my spine. Eden Roc, the end zone days, all of it came back. They were playing my song! I jumped—and sang along! As loud as I could sing. Now every time I hear it, every time I jump and sing along, the image of that drum major sprinting across the empty Cherry Bowl turf whirls. And since that time, marching bands have changed for me.

The marching band, when I was a student, was an end zone necessity. It did the "Faygo" song; it kept us rolling on the "Banks of the Red Cedar." It basically did its job. But I didn't know where it came from, how it got into the stadium, or where it went when the game was done. And I didn't much care. Not a lot of kids did, really. Marching bands, at least to students, lived the life of Rodney Dangerfield. On-stage they got their cheers; other than that, though, "no respect."

But from the Cherry Bowl on, I changed. I started following the Spartan band. All college bands. Watching them in pregame, and instead of heading under to grab a dog and a Coke, I stayed in my seat at half time. I even started sticking around for postgame shows. Postgame shows? Good Lord—when I was a student I thought *everybody* went home and celebrated. The band included.

As for prestadium stuff, as a student I never thought much about it.

When we got there, the band got there. I kind of figured they just assembled in the tunnel. Not true! Bands, like football teams, put on a pregame show. I saw my first in '87. On a sunshiny 70-degree day, Indiana dropped in for the Big Ten championship. I spent the hour before kickoff up at the Landon Hall Field and watched the band warm up—instead of the football team! The Michigan State Marching Band had finally reached a level equal with the Michigan State football team. So I told myself, this trip, if I was really gonna feel the heart of Big Ten Country, I'd have to catch other bands' practices. I'd listen to other bands' postgame shows. I'd become sort of a marching band groupie. It'd be both a pleasure and a duty, but something that I had to do. Because, you see, college marching bands play a big, big part in that Saturday football fanfare explosion.

Well, Michigan State was stop number one. A great place to start visiting bands. I didn't really need to explore East Lansing. I already knew where to find all the State game-day color. Instead, I spent most the week hammering my Visa at the bookstore and sitting in the grass out at band practice. Finding either wasn't much of a chore. The State bookstore owns me; I know the route as well as my own driveway. And my Visa number I'm sure is on their most preferred list. As for the band, all I had to do was open my ears. My first cruise through campus on Wednesday morning, I turned off Frank and rolled down the window. A distant version of the Spartan fight song drifted across campus. The Cherry Bowl flashed in my memory.

I found the band under the shadow of Spartan Stadium, in a big grassy field out in front of Jenison Fieldhouse. Sparty, the Michigan State statue, the guy that drops his helmet should ever a State grad virgin walk past (which, by the way, has never happened), stood at the street intersection. He was getting a facelift. Scaffolds and a chain-link fence locked him in. A big SAVE OUR SPARTY sign stood alongside. Why, it was time to clean him up, and how the contributions were going was spelled out on the sign. Behind Sparty, between the roads that intersected there, in front of the old hockey arena, lay the band practice field. It was limed, all one hundred yards, just like a football field. Bleachers, some thirty rows' worth, were pulled out and set up on the sideline. Next to them, a giant temporary scaffold. A guy with a bull-horn stood on top of the scaffold and barked orders below. Looking up, hot and just plain pooped, stood the Michigan State Marching Band.

" 'Attention' is very, very cheesy!" the guy with the bullhorn reprimanded the squad. I found out a little later he was Bill Wiedrich, State's rookie band director. He had a hell of job ahead. School hadn't started yet. No students, other than those that played horns and those that played football, were back. And in three days he had to get a group of kids whose "attention" was "very, very cheesy" ready for a national TV game. Saturday was Notre Dame! And more important for the band—ABC!

"From the gut," he demanded. "From the *gut!*" The kids, close to three hundred of 'em, rectangled together below, waited for three sharp whistle blasts, and answered, "Atten-hut!"

"Still too cheesy! Again. *This time from the gut!*"

*Tweet! Tweet! Tweet!* "Atten-HUT!" The response was a little deeper. It snapped a little quicker.

"One more time!"

"ATTEN-HUT!" The group was crisp.

"Better!" You could tell he was trying to toughen the troops.

Band practice continued. And would continue Wednesday, Thursday, and Friday, from eight in the morning till eight at night. For the freshmen, even longer. And Saturday morning in the stadium it'd start up again at 7:00 A.M. This was cram week; three days to get it together. Those normal three-hour, season-long practices ballooned to twelve hours. And not just for the marching band. Other parts of the package were putting in time as well. The flag corps worked out across the street in front of Landon Hall, at the old band practice field. The twirlers hung around and stretched and twirled. And the drum major, the band photographer, and various other band people roamed between the two fields. I never realized all the band groups that actually came together on Saturday afternoons. I certainly never figured they had a three-day deadline for game number one.

A deadline and kids . . . not a great combination. Nothing is more nerve-racking than cramming stuff into a teamful of kids with an hourglass guillotine dangling overhead. I know—I coached junior high football for six seasons. Only adults worry; pressure just bounces off kids . . . whether they be a team of fifteen-year-olds getting ready to play football in two weeks or a marching band of eighteen-year-olds getting ready to play trumpet in three days.

Actually, once you get done passing out shoulder pads and helmets, none of which fit till the fifth exchange in three days, and documenting just exactly how to form a plastic mouth guard to your lips, the two—

band and football—are a lot alike! Group work, all sorts of group work, dominates both of them. At football practices it was the linemen who got to spend all fall out at the blocking sled. Running backs practiced running and receivers practiced receiving. Meanwhile quarterbacks, like drum majors, stood around and got their confidence up. State's band practice was headed in the same direction. Sousaphones split into squads of four and marched in step. A group leader would lead. Three followers would follow. Other squads, trumpets and trombones, flutes and saxes, broke into fours and did the same. All split up all over the practice field, in some sort of organized manner, and all were working on parts of the State fight song. Starting and stopping, and pivoting with the horn swings.

After twenty minutes of the groups, it was back to the giant rectangle, the boss from the tower having found more things wrong than just the "cheesy" atten-hut. Same as football scrimmage. Seemed like we'd finally get the line blocking at one end of the field. Get the QBs stuffing the ball into the fullbacks' guts at the other. We'd bring 'em together and fumble five of the first six center snaps. So what do you do? Go back to basics. Practice the huddle, work on the snap count. "Set—blue—hut, hut, hut!" over and over again. What does a big-time college marching band do? Assemble in a rectangle and practice the "atten-hut, atten-hut, atten-hut" over and over again!

I'm sure Bill Wiedrich was hoping that Saturday's Spartan marching band performance could at least fire off an "atten-hut" that wasn't "too cheesy"! I used to pray we'd get through the first game without twelve fumbled snaps.

Friday afternoon I held my first interview. I bribed four tenor sax players out of their first ten minutes of dinner. The price, a cold Coke apiece. At five o'clock they dragged their saxes over to the end of the field, and plopped into the grass. Two seniors—Martha, the squad leader, and Julie, a second-year marcher—along with two brand-spanking-new freshmen—Chris, over from Charlotte, and Leanne, "whose feet hurt"—made up one of the umpteen million four-person squads that had been marching up and down the practice field all afternoon. We just sat in the grass, downed a Coke, and talked MSU Marching Band.

"So," I asked, looking at the two worn-out freshmen, "is it any different than high school?"

Typical question from a nonband guy, met with a round of band guy laughs. All four of 'em got a kick out of that one.

"A lot," Leanne with the tired feet popped up. "A whole lot different."

Chris, the most serious in the group, documented how. He leaned back on his saxophone and thought deep freshman thoughts. "The horn swings, we didn't do horn swings in high school." He thought again. "Or at least we didn't do 'em anything like they do here."

"Yeah," Leanne echoed. "The horn swings are tough."

Horn swings are the Spartan marching band trademark. As they march and play, every fifteenth count is followed by a deep dip, as they swing their horn or sax or whatever the instrument down from the playing position, almost like they're paddling a canoe with it. Then as quick as a flash it's back up high again. Gives the band a great ID mark, and it makes their march to the stadium the best of any band in the land.

Martha explained the band setup. What they tried to get done in three days, and what the chances were for freshman survival. She took on her leadership duty zestfully.

"As a squad leader, it's up to me to make sure the freshmen know their fundamentals."

"We're trying. We're trying." The freshmen laughed.

"I know you are . . . and you're doing well." Martha was a nice squad leader. "I also have to get them prepared mentally to go through the tunnel. It's scary the first time."

"It's scary every time," quiet Julie peeped.

"It's gonna be something like they've never seen before. I know I can still remember my first time. A nonconference game, I think." You could tell she was excited just thinking back. Her voice got a little higher, and her eyes brightened. "You kick through the tunnel and you see all those people and it's just, *wow, all those people!*" She caught herself.

The freshmen laughed. A little in fun—a little in nervousness.

Chris worriedly mentioned something about his biggest crowd being a filled Charlotte High School football stadium. A whole two thousand.

Martha laughed. "Not Saturday!"

"There's a lot of pride here too," Julie noted. "That's what I like. That's why I did it in high school. You play in the band and you just feel about eighteen feet high. And it's a great feeling."

Chris, for a guy who'd been on the job for only three days, summed things up pretty well: "You just do the best that you can do—so that the band is the best that it can be. And we make Michigan State look even better!"

"Right!" Everybody—Martha, the squad leader; Julie; Leanne with the tired feet—agreed.

"You know," Leanne tossed in as the four kids were getting up, "Mr. Wiedrich told us this morning that *USA Today* picked Notre Dame to win by four points. Now that they found out the Michigan State band is gonna be at the game, he said they've called it even. I think that's great!"

"You know," I said to Leanne, "if the band's playing tomorrow, I'll bet you *USA Today* ends up making Michigan State a touchdown favorite."

"Yeah!" She smiled. "I'll bet they do!"

And the squad walked off, in step, to eat a little, work a little on those horn swings, rest some tired feet, and dream about marching through that tunnel on Saturday. Plus recharge for another three hours of Friday night practice!

# NOTRE DAME AT MICHIGAN STATE

*Spartan Stadium,*
*East Lansing, Michigan*

| Standings | Big Ten | | | All Games | | |
|---|---|---|---|---|---|---|
| September 17, 1988 | W | L | T | W | L | T |
| INDIANA | 0 | 0 | — | 1 | 0 | — |
| OHIO STATE | 0 | 0 | — | 1 | 0 | — |
| IOWA | 0 | 0 | — | 1 | 1 | — |
| MICHIGAN STATE | 0 | 0 | — | 0 | 1 | — |
| MICHIGAN | 0 | 0 | — | 0 | 1 | — |
| MINNESOTA | 0 | 0 | — | 0 | 1 | — |
| PURDUE | 0 | 0 | — | 0 | 1 | — |
| NORTHWESTERN | 0 | 0 | — | 0 | 1 | — |
| WISCONSIN | 0 | 0 | — | 0 | 1 | — |
| ILLINOIS | 0 | 0 | — | 0 | 2 | — |

Notre Dame at Michigan State, what an opener! For me, at least. For the Spartans, the Rose Bowl glow had already been blotched by Rutgers. The week before they'd stumbled out of the blocks, beaten by a field goal by the Scarlet Knights! The Scarlet Knights?! Still, it didn't make much difference. Nobody, not the coaches, not the players, certainly not the fans, needed to worry about getting up for Notre Dame. Since Lou Holtz has taken the reins, Notre Dame's resurrected from the dead. And when ND is rolling, like it does a lot nowadays, most anybody that isn't Notre Dame nuts can't stand them. An endless barrage of Fighting Irish TV appearances does that to otherwise normal people! With State, though, it goes a little deeper. Back to '66, the national championship showdown—Duffy and Ara. The one where Ara had 'em fall on the ball, to salvage a 10–10 tie. The one that killed the chance for a Spartan national championship. Since then, and since ND weathered the Gerry Faust bumbling years, the rivalry's intensified. Notre Dame usually wins, but always the old 10–10 story revives, the traditions kick in, ABC or CBS or NBC shows up, and the game's a good one. Saturday would be no different. Spartan Stadium would be hopping.

Game day in East Lansing, as at most Big Ten towns, provides a tasty menu of activities to pick from. For me, choice number one's a time machine drop back to the balcony at 305 Eden Roc. The Japanese, unfortunately, have yet to come up with a reasonably priced time machine. Still, between the bars and the tailgates, and the campus to roam, there's plenty to do. Good memory-making stuff! And a lot of it rolls around Grand River Avenue.

Grand River, the main drag, runs east-west, alongside campus. At the center it's about a ten- or fifteen-minute walk from the stadium. A little longer if it's a sunny day and you browse along the way. The Ave, and the blocks that fan off it, are loaded with bars and T-shirt-crammed bookstores and other game day hangouts. Places where you can dig up something other than a beer and handful of pretzels. Places where not everybody in attendance carries a fake ID. Places that catch the excitement of college football, but not the end zone atmosphere.

The best of the bunch is Dooley's. Two levels, with a downstairs dance floor, Dooley's was and still is State's student show-off piece. It's the place where, when Mom and Dad came up for a birthday visit, you'd catch an early Saturday burger. Then after you saw 'em off, you'd come back at 9:30 and wait in a two-hour line, just to squeeze inside. Dooley's gets all kinds of State crowds, the Greeks and the geeks, and the otherwise normal college student. It gets the young kids trying to pass off fake IDs and a ton of returning alums. It's sharp, sleek, and sophisticated . . . but still has Miller on tap. Along with a half-dozen other brews. It covers all its bases pretty well. Pool tables and video machines fill one upstairs corner, while at the opposite end, thick wooden booths and clear-coated tables provide spots to sock in, pound brews, and talk Spartans. Downstairs, bands and crazy college kids boogie the nights away. A Dooley's specialty is Spartan sports photos: Lorenzo and Scott Skyles and Magic decorate the inside walls. Out in the doorway, it's Mr. T. A quote upside his Mohawk-shaved head kind of tells the Dooley's story: "I pity the fool who gives me a fake ID." It's a college feel, packaged in a classy flavor and soaked in sports stuff—all of it green and white.

Flip side to Dooley's is Dagwood's. Unlike most college towns where alums gravitate to a single favorite place, the Spartans get two. And Dag's is the home bar version. From the street it looks like somebody's house. From the doorway, somebody's living room. Across campus from Grand River, it sits on the border between college kids and Lansing towns folk, a mile or two from Spartan Stadium. One of those places that you'd never find in the AAA directory, Dagwood's glows with a hole-in-the-wall Midwest warmth. The booths look like they've been yanked out of the front seat of a '57 Chevy pickup, while the barstools probably could be tossed into the truck bed and trashed. The jukebox selection is Dagwood's at its best. Guy Lombardo plays alongside the Cars. Patsy Cline next to Jefferson Airplane. Elvis and Rod Stewart share a letter. A little Frank, a little Bing, the Spartan fight song, and at Christmastime a whole lot of added "Jingle Bells"–type extras. Good for kids or alums, Dag's is a shot-of-Jack-Daniels-with-a-beer-back hangout! Plus it grills, without a doubt, the best burger in town . . . and maybe the best homemade fries in the world. On game day, before and after, it's packed!

Either way you can't lose. Flashy or homey, or one of the dozen other versions along Grand River, bars are a great way to prepare. But there's more! Lots more!

Michigan State's campus is gorgeous. Especially in the fall when yellows and reds and oranges splash all the green. A pregame drift through the old part of campus is like strolling about a national park. Ivy-covered Beaumont Tower solemnly chimes the quarter hour. Old red-brick dorms, green ivy climbing the windows, sit nestled under sturdy oak and pines. Old-fashioned lampposts stand off in the grass. Walkways roll right off Grand River and wind down to the Red Cedar River and over it to the stadium. It's nature's little addition to college football Saturday. And if you catch rush hour about forty-five minutes from kickoff, with all the green sweaters and green buttons and green jackets and T-shirts, it looks like National Park Service rangers have been replaced with a flood of campus bookstore employees.

But the best place to get that pregame hype is in the parking lot. And all it takes is a hatch or a trunk, a hot grill, a filled cooler, and a good heart. As students we never thought of it, driving the car across campus, opening the trunk, and bringing the balcony to the game. But for ex-students Friday night is spent dreaming about it! Tailgating—the absolute best way to prepare for any sporting event ever created. Folks pull up and unload, then sock in for four or five hours. Better than balconies or living rooms or back patios, it's a parking-lot home away from home. Green vans and green station wagons and big block S flags. Card tables covered with green tablecloths and Spartan chairs. Grills, ice chests, bad-weather awnings, and all sorts of good hearty eats. Tailgating is a Big Ten football specialty. And the Spartan Stadium lots hold their own with the best of 'em.

Probably State's most tempting tailgate offering is all the room! Little concrete lots stretch out under the stadium. Those get filled up with the motor-home-type crowd and a few private tent parties. Some cars and vans too. Other small lots across Harrison Street, a few blocks from the stadium, provide more spots. Best, though, are the grassy intramural fields. And the best one, State's finest place to park and eat and dig up extra tickets . . . is the Munn Arena lot. Out in front of Munn hockey stadium, it's where the normal nine-to-five, station-wagon, van, sock-in-for-a-full-five-hours-before-game-time folks end up. With good food, good folks, just an oval track away from Spartan Stadium, it's the place to load up for the Fighting Irish.

For three hours, from eight to eleven, I roamed the parking lots. I ran into Spartan fans from all over the state. I visited; I drank Bloody Marys and listened to Spartan stories. I munched most anything offered my way. I took a look into the real heart of Big Ten Country. This time a green-and-white one.

Early in my roaming, I ran into John and Nancy Rogers, famous—at least famous in their hometown of Kalamazoo, Michigan—for a second-place finish in the 1987 Great State Tailgate. To kick off the '87 season, Michigan State sponsored a tailgate contest. Spartan tailgaters from all over the state put on their best show. Each featured a different theme. Judges filtered through the crowd, checked them out, and voted on a winner.

"It came down to two groups . . . us and some other guys," Nancy Rogers, major architect of the Rogerses' setup, noted. "The other guys won and got eight round-trip tickets to Europe. Europe," she said again, like she still couldn't believe it. "We came in second." The second-place finish still hurt a little.

"What'd you win?" I asked, expecting a massive vacation to Mexico or Hawaii or some other exotic retreat. Something that would measure at least a close second to eight round trips to Europe.

She sighed. "A weekend getaway to"—she sighed again—"to . . . Grand Rapids." She bounced back: "But we had fun putting it together."

Dick and Carol joined Nancy and John and a lot of other friends in putting the Great State Tailgate thing together. It was kind of like a little icing on the cake for hanging around the Spartans so long. Since '65 the foursome had tailgated together. Usually at the same spot. Usually about the same time, four hours before kickoff. Good spot! Munn lot, up in the corner, next to the stadium sidewalk.

Nancy and Carol grabbed some scrapbooks off the table. A table that was green-and-whited up for the Notre Dame game and filled with dips and veggies and all sorts of little Michigan State paraphernalia things. A table that had a big Great State Tailgate second-place trophy sitting in the middle of it.

"Our theme was 'I'm Dreaming of a Green Christmas.' We had all sorts of green Christmas things here." As they paged through the pictures, the ladies provided a "Green Christmas" tour presentation. It was like hitting up the old high-school yearbook.

"We invited Santa Claus." Nancy did most of the filling-in. Instead of red he'd appropriately worn green. From his picture, he was a pretty good-looking Santa. Definitely department store material. "We had a tree with all sorts of Michigan State ornaments on it. And a Dickens singer in a green top hat. That was John." John is an ex–high-school football coach, a 1962 Spartan grad, and the gas grill chef. In addition, of course, to being an occasional Dickens singer.

"Let's see, we had a generator to run everything. There was a woodworking bench for Santa's toy shop, and some of the kids dressed up like elves. We even had an electric piano for Christmas carols."

"Nancy played it," Carol revealed.

"Sing the song," John prodded the ladies. "Come on, pleeease!"

They didn't actually need a lot of prodding. The two had it memorized. They'd probably sung it a few thousand times since the Great State Tailgate. So they sang. A duet rendition of Irving Berlin's classic "White Christmas," spiced, of course, with all the rearranged Spartan lines. Whites turned to greens, and touchdowns and Rose Bowls and field goals took the place of sleigh bells in the snow and glistening tree-top stuff. They even sang in tune . . . Der Bingle would have been proud. It was a cute song. Something sweet, something for all of us to clap at and toast with a Bloody Mary.

"Never in a million years did we actually think we'd go to a green or red or any other kind of Rose Bowl," the singer-songwriter explained. "I mean it was great. The Rose Bowl! And then to win it!"

"Fate," John laughed. "It was that song that did it!"

The Rogerses invited me "in." We sat and talked Spartan football, and the difference between Grand Rapids and Europe. They let me in on all the other best Big Ten tailgate hangouts. Illinois, John told me, was a must. Good tailgating there. They'd even seen a couple married a few years ago at the Illinois version of the Great State Tailgate. Preacher and gowns and tuxes, all right there in front of a blue-and-orange van. The bride, apparently, was loyal to Illinois and wore orange as well. Together we tried to figure how the defending Rose Bowl champs had bellied up to Rutgers last week, and then reminisced about better, rosier times. Still, we were optimistic. Good tailgaters always are. John Rogers finally revealed their real reason for such a tailgating obsession. I'd asked him if one team more than any other inspired the liveliest parties. I wondered if they grilled a little more intensely or tipped 'em a little more frequently if, say, Michigan or Notre Dame was in.

"Our philosophy," he told me, "is we wanna win every game. Every single one! We'd love to go undefeated each year!" He looked at his buddies and smiled. "But we've never lost a party."

Notre Dame games are good roaming games. Plenty of tailgaters. Plus the sun was out. The shorts and T-shirt weather made the lots a little more festive and put fans in a story-telling mood. And not just green-and-white fans either. I found out, by way of a Notre Dame couple up for the game, that it was Knute Rockne's one hundredth anniversary. They never really said what it was Coach Rockne's anniversary of, but they assured me that it was plenty enough to ensure a Notre Dame victory. Outside another van, tending another grill, was a guy who'd actually played for State back in '66. He never really did play a lot. He was just a second or third teamer. But standing on the sidelines he'd had a great view of the 10–10 tie. Unlike most Spartan fans, the ex–Spartan player revealed that State had been lucky to get out of the game even. He didn't say why, or how come, or even toss in a what-if, but he did say that 10–10 wasn't as bad as everybody thought. Still, he found time to fire a parting shot at Ara for not taking a gamble on the win.

Over by the stadium, some Dixieland jazz musicians were doing their thing. The Geriatric Six—Plus One, a group of seven football fans/jazz banders, have been serenading the Spartan game-day parking lot since back in the seventies. These, however, are not mere football fans. Nor are they mere musicians. The group's average age is sixty-two. That's where you get the "Geriatric." The "Plus One" is Don Thornburg, the fifty-five-year-old "kid" trombonist. "Plus one" does not, however, refer to Don's age. It refers to his job. He's the only one of the seven who isn't a Michigan State professor. The rest are! It's probably the best-educated jazz band in the world.

Dr. Maurice Crane, a sixty-three-year-old Spartan professor of humanties, is the band's founder. "We may not be the finest musicians in the world," Maurice popped. "But we're a gang. Our main feature is whoopee. It's to have a good time!" And they do. So do all the tailgaters who gather around their bandstand.

As for the gang . . . try a string of full-fledged Ph.D.'s. Dr. Bill Faunce, sixty-one, on the trumpet is a professor of sociology. Dr. Waldo Keller, sixty, a prof of veterinary medicine, was the first American ever to perform a cataract operation on a Bengal tiger. Now he does a little research during the week, and on game day weekends plays the trumpet. Jim Smith, a retired music professor, another kid, is the fifty-seven-year-old bass violinist. Dr. H. Owen Reed, seventy-eight years old, who, Maurice confessed, "plays circles around the rest of us," has written operas and symphonies famous all over the world. Dr. Owen Brainard, sixty-six, is an artist and a prof and a drummer. And occasionally Doug Weaver, Michigan State's athletic director, will even hop onstage and pull out the ole banjo.

The gang kicks out everything from "When the Saints Go Marching In" and "Tom Dooley" to a nifty jazzed-up version of the Michigan State fight song. Sometimes the band members wear green sweaters; sometimes they wear white. They don't wear white shoes because Waldo just won't wear them. And hats are out because Dr. Bill, according to Maurice, is a "crotchety old fart who won't wear a hat." But the seven have a great time. On game day Saturdays, they play for nothing. The rest of the time, all bucks go to a scholarship fund for kids to come to State and play jazz.

"The price is right. We're free!" Maurice acknowledged their new-found success. "Well, not really free," he corrected himself. "They took us to the Rose Bowl. And what more could you ask for? Every Big Ten musician dreams to someday play at the Rose Bowl."

Back up on campus, while the Rogerses mixed their Bloody Marys and sang "Green Christmas" songs, while the Munn Arena lot filled with smoking brats and the Geriatric Six—Plus One cranked out Dixie-land tunes, a couple of stadium marches were taking place. One of them, early in the morning, was led by George Perles. Coach Perles, as apple pie as coaches come nowadays, has revived an old Duffy Daugherty tradition. In fact, George's six-year reign has been a six-year Duffy revival. "Work hard and keep your mouth shut and good things will happen to you," that's Perles's motto. With it and an iron-fist defense, Michigan State's risen out of the "mud." One of the reasons Perles has been so successful is the tradition thing. One of the traditions is "the walk to the stadium." There's not a lot of fanfare to the walk. A couple of hours prior to each home game, the team leaves Kellogg Center. Across the river, a half mile from the stadium, Kellogg is where the players stay on the eve of home games. George and his assistants and the football team, decked out in ties and green blazers, walk over together. No playing around, no games, no interviews. It's where they put on their game faces. It's simple. It's traditional. It's nice for players' family members who come and watch. And it's kind of a classy thing to catch.

The other pregame march starts up at Landon Hall field about eleven o'clock. Landon Hall field, a big grassy open area, is where the band warms up. It's sandwiched between the old brick "Virgin Island" dorms and the women's IM, just up the street and around the corner, a couple of blocks' swing from Spartan Stadium. From the concrete tailgating back at the stadium, you can hear the State fight song warm-ups, drifting through the trees and across the river. The tunes add a little more excitement and anticipation to the parties. And provide tailgaters front-row seats to the greatest pregame parade in the Big Ten, the Spartan marching band's stadium march!

Before the game, Landon field buzzes with Spartan green. Band members warm up, flag carriers adjust their flag harnesses, and twirl-ers bathed in green sequins stretch out. Fans warm up too. Mostly band fans. Moms and dads and little kids. Tailgaters roam over from the lots. Some patrons of Dooley's and Dagwood's leave the bars a little early and slide over too. And families strolling the campus grounds get lured over by the music. Like a gigantic musical magnet, the warm-up attracts green-and-whiters from all different directions.

I strolled up just in time to hear three whistle blasts echoed by a very noncheesy "ATTEN-HUT!"

The kids had aged since Friday afternoon. With stern faces (that's the military march style), decked out in green-and-white unies, a big block Spartan S on each lapel, they looked ready for ABC. So did the alums.

You see, Saturday was alumni band day. Alumni band is a strange but happy sight. Once a year, usually the day of the first band game, band grads come back and give it another shot. It's just for fun! Well, a little for pride too. Old players and fat players, and players just out of school, all of 'em with their instruments stood grouped together. Most wore something green. But usually it was only a T-shirt or an old "Marching Band Alumni" jacket. Shorts were pretty standard. The two rectangles, the young professionals and the out-of-shape oldsters, stood at attention, side by side.

Together the two ripped off one last rendition of the fight song, and the march began. Alumni led the way. All the old mannerisms were there, the horn swings and the timing—even the playing was still up to snuff. They were into it as much as the kids. The only difference was the alumni smiled—they were allowed to. Behind them stepped the modern-day Michigan State drum major and the Spartan twirlers. The girls' bright green sequins glittered in the sunlight. Next came the flag corps, ten guys, each with a Big Ten flag anchored in a harness. Color guard girls followed with green-and-white flags. And finally, stepping as smartly as a Roman legion on its way to battle, the Michigan State Marching Band brought up the rear. Clapping fans flooded in front of, alongside, and in the wake of the band.

The march was full of fire! Stepping to the drumbeat, down Circle Road and across the river, the band bore down on Sparty. Still surrounded by his face-saving fence, still with helmet in hand, he had the best view. A lot of people, hanging on the fence, joined him. Marching ten abreast, the band took up the whole street. It strung out like a slinky, back to Landon Hall field. And while the trailing end was still stepping in time, the alumni end hit the fight song. Folks following cheered. Tailgaters turned and waited. Sparty, I think, but I can't be sure, nodded his approval.

At Sparty, the band takes a hard left! It hits Red Cedar Road, which hugs the river! And the rest of the way to the gates of Spartan Stadium, the Spartan marching band cranks out the State fight song. Tailgaters, waiting and buzzing, cheer and clap along. Ticket scalpers offering up their final rock-bottom sales pitch take a quick break and watch. The Geriatric Six—Plus One shift from Dixieland jazz to a Dixieland State fight song. The two fight songs mix together somewhere in the middle of the lots. Amid cheers and Stroh's toasting, and little kids tugging on Dad's shirtsleeves, the marching band's parade down Red Cedar Road and into the stadium tunnel is electric. It's a confidence builder too. Nobody, but nobody, at the moment it passes would bet against State.

It seemed like nothing could go wrong! Inside Spartan Stadium the mood was jubilant. Roars greeted the band's arrival, and the football team's dash from the tunnel to sidelines. Roars greeted the fight song—all twenty prekickoff renditions of it. Roars greeted the coin toss and the opening whistle and the kickoff. After that, though, the roaring subsided. It matched State's play! A good, crisp, hard-hitting first half turned into a second-half rout. Notre Dame proved that the Rutgers fiasco had been no fluke, and that the old Gerry Faust days were long gone. It also unfortunately proved that as long as Lou Holtz was around, there were gonna be plenty of chances for some heavy-duty Notre Dame hating. The Fighting Irish rolled, 20–3. And it really was a lot worse.

As for the Spartans, I wondered if they'd score again the rest of the season. I'm sure a lot of other State fans did too. Oh sure, there were a couple of moments. Plays that got the place rolling. There always are on college football Saturdays. At least three times Percy Snow nearly separated a ballcarrier from his head. And a reverse from ole conservative George got a healthy round of applause. Not because it gained anything, not because it didn't, but because it wasn't tailback left or tailback right, like everything else. As for the rest of the game, unless you enjoyed watching Notre Dame put on a how-to-run-the-option show, it was Rutgers on instant replay. Still, the bands rolled. Both of 'em. Chris and Leanne-with-the-tired-feet and a hundred other freshmen had marched the tunnel for their first time ever. It was a new season, a rebirth of college football. And if nothing else, Notre Dame was off the schedule till next fall.

As for me, I survived the loss. I hate losing, especially to Notre Dame or Michigan. But roaming around campus, talking to the kids and the tailgaters, I didn't feel like the loss was life and death. We were still undefeated in the conference. Spartan Stadium was still the best place in the whole world to spend a Saturday afternoon and I still had my Eden Roc memories. We still were, and would always be, the only 1988 Rose Bowl champs in Big Ten football history. And like Paul Rogers said, "We've never lost a party." I figured if State lost eleven straight in '88, and never scored another touchdown ever (which, by the look of the offense, seemed probable), I'd survive. I was just gonna enjoy cruising the Midwest, and enjoy running into other marching bands and other tailgaters. There'd be other games for Notre Dame pounding. Maybe if we all prayed hard enough, they'd bring back Gerry Faust. And if nothing else, Wisconsin was last on the schedule. So at least a tie was certain. With all that in mind, I figured I'd make it.

Besides, on Friday I'd bought three more green and white '88 Rose Bowl shirts. On sale for half price. I was set for life!

# 2
# UNIVERSITY OF MINNESOTA
## THE GOLDEN GOPHERS

| University of Minnesota Minneapolis, MN | Metrodome |
|---|---|
| Best Breakfast | Al's Breakfast |
| Best Bar | Stub + Herb's |
| Best Burger | Annie's Parlour |
| Best of ... | |

| The Best in Big Ten Country | |
|---|---|
| **BAR** | |
| 1. Nick's | Indiana |
| 2. Stub + Herb's | Minnesota |
| 3. Varsity Club | Ohio State |
| 4. Harry's | Purdue |
| 5. Dooley's | MSU |

Remember when *College Football Report* appeared only on ABC—because only ABC showed college football? Remember when Keith Jackson covered all the biggies and Jim Lampley read his postgame scores to the beat of the Notre Dame Marching Band? Those were the days before ESPN, back before Beano Cook became an expert at something, and before college games were taken apart, sized up, and spit out like the pro version. Maybe best of all, it was an era when Brent Musburger worked only on Sunday. Remember those good ole days?

Well, TV bigwigs would like to think that times have changed. They'd like to think that just by flooding the airwaves with college football, they've brought the Saturday game up to Sunday's standards, and that now, finally, the NFL and NCAA are clones. And you know, because of strategically placed cameras, the unending evaluation by all sorts of experts, and the Chevrolet commercials filling the breaks, they almost convince us that they're right. At least from the living room couch they almost convince us. But in person it's a whole different story! Pro football and college football are not the same! They exist in entirely separate worlds. In fact the only real connection between the two is that CBS now pays a bundle to show both.

Pro football is All-Pro Superstar drug updates . . . lately on a weekly basis. Pro football is Brent Musburger droning on and on and on about what the Giants have to do to the Steelers on Sunday in order to get into the playoffs. It's Brent Musburger droning on and on and on about the ultimate importance of the game, not only for the franchise but for the good people of New York and Pennsylvania. And it's only week number two. Pro football is the officials' sixth on-the-field meeting in the first half, checking with the guy up in the booth to see if Eric Dickerson stepped out on the thirteen-yard line or if it was actually the eleven and a half. It's that automatic one-point kick after a touchdown and a punt on each and every fourth down. Pro football is on-the-field predictable, and off-the-field scandals, drugs, and contract crap. It's overpriced, overhyped, and overblown. It's a game made for TV commercials.

I know! I've actually sat in the stands and suffered through two whole pro-football games. Much more than enough to catch their full-flavored excitement—and to declare expertise. The first was a few years back in the Kingdome, with free wedged-against-the-roof tickets for the Seahawks and Browns. The second was a more recent rendition down in Cincinnati.

My Bengal game happened during the 1987 strike season, after the regulars groveled back. The Steelers were in town and both teams were out of it. Ticket scalpers were taking a bath, it was a crisp sunny day, and I didn't have a thing to do. So I took a bus downtown, shelled out five dollars for a seventeen-dollar ticket and strolled inside for my first-ever outdoors pro-football game. *Bowling for Dollars* would've been more exciting! Riverfront Stadium, nicknamed the Jungle in 1988 only because the Bengals won a few games that year and fair-weather fans packed it, was stone-cold dead in 1987. And since it's a plastic-grassed, three-ring multipurpose circle, it wasn't split into separate sections. No school-colors-covered alumni groups, no marching band firing off a song that everybody knew from the heart, and no squirming, screaming student section. Just the haves up in the luxury boxes, and the have-nots everyplace else. And everybody, whether admitting it or not, was bored to tears.

The biggest reason for the boredom was the players. Pro players really don't give a rip, at least not enough to hustle. At both games, both teams spent all four quarters just walking around, I guess because they were too "cool" to run. In high school you broke the huddle, you sprinted to the line, you ran on and off the field, because as Coach used to say, *"You can hustle, goddamn it,* or you can *sit!"* College players still hustle, because coaches still yell at 'em. But in the pros, where the lowest-paid running back probably makes twice as much as the head coach, and where unions dictate working conditions—players walk. Everywhere. On and off the field. On the sidelines. From the locker room and to the locker room, from the huddle to the ball, and from the ball back to the huddle. And TV just skips around the walking, like it doesn't even exist. The laziest stroll of the game, the one that really captures pro superstars at their hustling best, the one I'd never caught on the tube 'cause CBS was always selling something at the time, was the quarter change. Pure pro football! The gun would sound—and from one 20-yard line clear across the field to the other 20-yard line, twenty-two helmets unsnapped and came off, and while Chevy ads filled living rooms across the country, twenty-two superstars dragged their butts across the "Jungle" turf.

Spontaneous emotion—it's not pro football's finest feature, but it's what the college game thrives on. I swear to God, every college football game I've ever seen starts with a tailback running left. About three yards from the line of scrimmage, and two from the quarterback, defensive guys bury the kid. They just hammer him! Then the whole defense piles on—not on the ballcarrier, but on the guy who made the the first pop. Fists thrust into the air, they pull him up and slap his helmet, the whole stadium rocks, the band fires off a fight song for the first of probably six hundred times, cheerleaders bounce up and down as much as the TV cameras, and if things are all in place and every-thing's right with the world, Keith Jackson's firing off some line like "Oh—what a hit!" For touchdowns, the celebration intensity triples. The kid that crossed the goal line disappears under mounds of stuff—

teammates and mascots and cheerleaders, and rolls of toilet paper tossed from the student section. The home team's whole stadium goes bonkers! On the road a single visiting-team-colored end zone section—a tiny island—erupts in celebration. At the "Jungle" after a Bengal TD, everybody's gotta step back so that Icky Woods can do his "Icky Shuffle." Everything in the pros seems so planned, so uninspired.

College football also provides a fan-to-school loyalty that the pros can't. A loyalty that exists between the two and creates a group of diehards who live for their alma mater's football team. It's a strange kind of prize, but just because you're an alumnus you can sit there on Saturday afternoon in your school-colors-covered clothes and feel like it really is *your* team taking on Notre Dame! Pro football's different. There are owners and there are fans. One group has the big bucks and the luxury boxes, the other overpriced season-ticket bills. And there's nothing that remotely resembles a pro-football alumni office. Nobody went to Houston Oiler University for four years and tried to figure out what the hell to do with his life. Nobody almost flunked out as a freshman, finally picked a major, and learned a career on the campus of the Seattle Seahawks. Nobody anywhere on earth is hanging a Philadelphia Eagles diploma on his bedroom wall! But for those who went to school at Iowa or Indiana or Northwestern, part of them will always remain there, and they get to relive a little of it each time they go back.

It works the other way around too. College football thrives on franchise loyalty, a history of loyalty down through the generations. You don't see the University of Wisconsin football team hopping on a plane and transferring to Nebraska because fan attendance is down. Correct me if I'm wrong, but I don't think that the Ohio State football program's ever packed up and headed off to Indianapolis. I don't even think they've come out in the newspapers and threatened to. College loyalty is safe for all time. You know today, you knew yesterday, and you will know a hundred years from now that your team will be playing at the very same stadium, on the very same campus, in the very same school colors . . . until—well, Super Bowl 2525.

Even the stadiums are different, especially on game day. Most Big Ten stadiums are architectural wonders, the very best technology can provide—impractical, uncomfortable 1920s technology, that is. Even so, they ooze character. Aside from Chicago's Soldier Field and icy

Lambeau up in Green Bay, the pros have sacrificed character for comfort. Clean, accessible bathrooms and big parking lots have replaced World War I memorials. And none of them provide those special collegiate game-day accessories. No student sections, no band, no time-tested fight song. They don't have dumb-looking mascots roaming the sidelines, a campus to scout before the game, or a homecoming that brings loyal alums back year after year. No, they've got high-priced guys out on the turf, walking around with their helmets off. And on the sidelines, luscious cheerleaders with big boobs, whom nobody but the front-row fans gets to see.

Why talk about this now? Why bring up Brent Musburger while on a tour of the Big Ten? It seems almost sacrilegious! Well, there are a couple of reasons, really. Most important, to make sure nobody ever accuses me of being a pro-football fan! Second, the Golden Gophers are the Big Ten's lone team that skirts that college/pro division, because in a way Minnesota football has abandoned its college traditions. It's the only Big Ten team to play each week on Saturday night instead of Saturday afternoon, the only Big Ten team that doesn't play its home games on campus, and the lone conference school where most of the kids drive to class, then don't bother to come back on the weekends. Worst of all, the Golden Gophers play inside a dome—a bubble, to be more specific—the Hubert H. Humphrey "Metrobubble."

It's not that Minnesota football comes without tradition. That's what I thought when I hit town! Like most non-Minnesotan college football fans under the age of sixty, to me the Golden Gophers were the guys up north with the funny team name, the guys who always lost the Little Brown Jug, usually by a whopping score! They were a team that finished down the ladder near Wisconsin. A team that squared off with somebody each season, usually Northwestern, in the battle for the Big Ten basement.

Let's just say I was a little uninformed!

"Minnesota's collegiate football history is a little less colorful than Michigan or Yale. But it's rich! Real rich!" Steve Lorinser, the *Minnesota Daily* student editor, a walking library of Golden Gopher football, revealed to me. You see, at each campus I tried to find the student-paper sports reporter, somebody who felt about his school football program the way I felt about the Spartans. That way I figured I'd get at least one biased, heartfelt view of each team. Well, in Lorinser's case I found the Golden Gopher football archives department. Steve Lorinser lives and breathes and writes all about University of Minnesota football. He can tell you about Bronko Nagurski like he was suiting up and lining up across from him on Saturday. A sixties-looking radical type who's replaced a Vietnam War obsession with Golden Gopher football history, he's hung around the U off and on for fifteen years. And he couldn't wait to fill me in on the Gophers! He dug up old articles on old traditions. And he gave me stories hot off the press. He found a 1987 article that he'd written, telling all about Minnesota's twenty-three greatest players, two finest coaches, and ten biggest games of all time. Almost all of his choices were pre–World War II. But best of all, he gave me the inside story of three of college footballs greatest trophies—the JUG, the AX, and the PIG—all part of Golden Gopher football lore.

The Little Brown Jug trophy—awarded to the winner of the Michigan-Minnesota contest since 1903—is one of college football's oldest and most famous traditions. Steve told me the story, and spiced it with the little emotional things that only Bronko Nagurski fans would care about. He knew the two 1903 teams involved by heart. One was Fielding "Hurry Up" Yost's point-a-minute Michigan squad, which ended the season 11–0–1 and outscored its opponents 565–6. And the other was the Golden Gophers they met in Minnesota, a 14–0–1 football team that, by the end of the season, would outscore the opposition 618–12. He knew all about their defenses and defensive strategies, and their offenses and offensive strategies. He knew about why both dominated college football, and how the game really worked way back then before facemasks and forward passes. He could even play-by-play that first Jug game–that historic 6–6 tie.

As for the Jug, Steve told me about that too. The Jug was just some brown thirty-five-cent water crock that the Michigan team picked up at a corner hardware store. It wasn't important really, at least not until the Wolverines, who'd left it behind after the tie, wrote to Minnesota asking for its return. Minnesota suggested that if Michigan wanted its jug, the Wolverines could "come back and win it." A couple of years later Michigan did just that, and Minnesota gave it back! After a few years' layoff, the rivalry resumed, and in 1919 the Golden Gophers crunched Michigan 34–7. This time the Wolverines sent the Jug packing. A trend had set in; the press caught on and fanned the flames. At a banquet following the 1920 game, Fielding Yost, the Michigan coach, suggested the old water crock be painted half maize and blue, half maroon and gold—to signify the two schools. It was. And after every game since, the score gets recorded on the side and the Little Brown Jug goes home with the winner.

The Paul Bunyan ax trophy is one that Minnesota's won a little more often, which only stands to reason since the Golden Gophers share it with Wisconsin. In fact, four years running heading into '88 it had stayed at Minnesota. A Wisconsin W Club donation in 1948, the five-foot-long woodcutter's ax lists Gopher-Badger final scores down the handle. It adds a little flavor to the schools' rivalry. I figured in 1988 the ax might get a second use as well. As lousy as the two teams had been playing, it looked like the winners could use it to chop their way out of the conference basement!

The last of the three, the Floyd of Rosedale trophy, the one that Iowa and Minnesota share, was Steve's favorite. "It's the one," he told me, "that matters most to Minnesota football fans."

Floyd's story went back to 1934, when the Bernie Bierman teams were plowing through their five national championships. That in itself shocked me. Sure it was fifty years ago, but hell, I never figured Minnesota had won five Big Ten titles, let alone five national championships! Well, 1934 marked the middle of the Gophers' Golden Decade, and a season in which, among others, they creamed Iowa, 48–12. But the game was controversial. Injuries and insults ran a four-quarter course and erupted in the stands. The whole state of Iowa was hot! It set up a bloodthirsty rematch the next season. "Iowa newspapers," Steve said, "whipped Hawkeye fans into a state of frenzy. Not only that, but the '35 game was Iowa's Homecoming." The Iowa governor, Clyde Herring, made things even worse when he issued a warning to the Associated Press: "The University of Iowa football team will defeat the University of Minnesota tomorrow [November 9, 1935] . . . and if the officials stand for any rough tactics, like Minnesota used last year, I'm sure the crowd won't." Coach Bierman took notice. Infuriated by the threat, and a bit leery of Iowa football fan mobs, he didn't hold a practice at Iowa. Instead Coach Bierman took his team across the Mississippi River. There, guarded by Illinois state troopers, the Golden Gophers held their final pregame workout.

Meanwhile, Minnesota newspapers jumped on Governor Herring's statement and whipped up emotions on the Minnesota side. Team members' parents demanded that Minnesota Governor Floyd Olson call out the National Guard to protect their boys. Olson acted. He promised worried parents that their kids would be safe, and had the Gophers' train met in Iowa City by federal agents and twenty-two Iowa City police officers. Then he defused things more by offering a bet to Iowa and the Iowa governor. The bet was a Minnesota prize hog for an Iowa prize hog. Winner take all. He ended his challenge with "The loser must deliver the hog to the winner in person. You are getting odds because Minnesota raises better hogs than Iowa. My personal regards and condolences . . . Governor Olson." Herring took up the challenge and the game was played with a pig at stake.

Well, the '35 Iowa game, like the first Jug game, was a classic. And Steve knew it by heart. A come-from-behind 13–6 Golden Gopher win—he hit all the highlights. Four days after the win, Governor Herring personally presented Governor Olson with a 220-pound prize hog—Floyd of Rosedale. Floyd, however, wasn't just any pig. He was, as Steve said, "a full-blooded champion brother of Blue Boy—the famed porker who starred opposite Janet Gaynor and Will Rogers in the 1933 movie *State Fair.*" Soon after the bet was paid off, a St. Paul artist bronzed Floyd into a fifteen-inch-tall sculpture. And since 1935, the Floyd of Rosedale sculpture has been the prize of every Minnesota-Iowa football game.

"It's the last game of each season. It'll probably be the only sellout this year. It's still a really big deal to folks up here. Just ask around," Steve suggested. "People will know about the pig."

Besides Steve Lorinser's trek down memory lane, I rounded up a few traditions of my own. In fact I found all the necessities any school could ever want to put on a good hard-core college football show. The campus itself is a beaut. Up above and across the Mississippi from Minneapolis's skyscraper-covered downtown, it's the Big Ten's only real big-city school. And still it's splashed with old ivy-covered brick halls, and white-columned buildings that've stood on site for almost a century. It's got that Big Ten campus standby too. Right off Washington Avenue, in front of Northrup Auditorium, stretches a big beautiful oak-lined quad. It's great place to relax and people-watch, and if you ignore the kids' fashions, you can pretend it's still the Bernie Bierman days.

The U-district also buzzes with a good college feel. Shops and bars and bookstores run for two blocks alongside the campus. A few hole-in-the-wall taverns are great places to catch the college sports crowd. Best of the bunch is Stub & Herb's. On the corner of Washington and Oak since 1929, it features a library archive array of old black-and-white photos: facemaskless players, team shots, and action shots of football when it still resembled rugby; there's even modern-day stuff. Basketball photos too, old ones from way, way back, line the walls. No pub in the Big Ten displays a more classic selection. Roaming Stub & Herb's with a draft in hand is a twenty-minute trip through college football and basketball history.

The university's finest college football tradition, though, stands just a "twenty-yard down and out" from Stub & Herb's. Memorial Stadium, erected in 1924, is a wonderful old place. From the tavern's front door all you see is the stadium facade, a red-brick shell dotted with a 1920s touch. Small arched windows run in rows above the entrances. Small, arched, almost single-file entrances are sealed by heavy wooden doors. Outside in front a plaque proudly proclaims: "This stadium was erected by members and friends of the University to honor the men and women of Minnesota who served their country in time of war, A.D. MCMXXIV." Quietly hugging the University Avenue sidewalk, Memorial offers a quaint, almost Wrigley Field air. It's the perfect place for that Saturday afternoon Golden Gopher college-football explosion!

Memorial's the final touch. An old Big Ten stadium smack-dab in the middle of a Big Ten campus. With city streets knocking on its door, with fans spilling out of the corner taverns just across the block, with that hard-core Golden Gopher football tradition to draw on, Memorial ought to explode with excitement. Like a long, loud tribal drumbeat, on football Saturdays the Brick House ought to send a battle cry throughout all the campus. Throughout the whole state of Minnesota! The Bernie Bierman days, when the Golden Gophers ruled the country, must've been electric! Especially when Floyd was on the line.

Now, though, there are a couple of catches. First of all, it's a commuter campus. Depending on whom you listen to and what your criteria are, anywhere from 60 to 90 percent of the forty-five thousand students drive to the U from someplace else. Consequently, the place doesn't have that college campus lived-in look. Kids don't carry ratty backpacks around and look like they've spent the year living off leftover bar change. Instead, they dress sophisticatedly. They fight for parking spots and stroll to class. They don't live, eat, and breathe the University of Minnesota. Most just come and go according to convenience and their downtown part-time work schedules. As a result they don't seem to possess the undying loyalty that four years of living at a school creates. The complacency stretches to football too. Students, for whatever reason, just don't show up.

But the biggest reason Gopher football has lost its zip sits a couple miles across the river. Far enough away to take a bus to reach, but close enough so its air-blown bubble roof catches the horizon, the biggest dud of all is the Metrodome. In 1982 it trapped the Gophers. University officials opted for big-city lights, comfy seats, and warm inside Saturday night temperatures. Memorial Stadium was abandoned, its red-brick shell bordering the campus sidewalks gone to seed. Pretty soon it'll be bulldozed. And with it the spirit of a long, long line of Golden Gopher traditions.

After the "old Brick House" turns to rubble, Gopher football fans will have to turn someplace else to recapture the good ole days, to Steve Lorinser columns, or the trophy case over at Bierman Athletic Facility, or the black-and-white photos hanging on the walls at Stub & Herb's. Or maybe they can just peek inside their own memories, if they ever knew the thrill of Golden Gopher football, outside on the grass, at Memorial Stadium.

# NORTHERN ILLINOIS AT MINNESOTA

*Metrodome,*
*Minneapolis, Minnesota*

| Standings September 24, 1988 | Big Ten | | | All Games | | |
|---|---|---|---|---|---|---|
| | W | L | T | W | L | T |
| INDIANA | 0 | 0 | — | 2 | 0 | — |
| OHIO STATE | 0 | 0 | — | 1 | 1 | — |
| MINNESOTA | 0 | 0 | — | 1 | 1 | — |
| PURDUE | 0 | 0 | — | 1 | 1 | — |
| IOWA | 0 | 0 | — | 1 | 2 | — |
| ILLINOIS | 0 | 0 | — | 1 | 2 | — |
| MICHIGAN STATE | 0 | 0 | — | 0 | 2 | — |
| MICHIGAN | 0 | 0 | — | 0 | 2 | — |
| NORTHWESTERN | 0 | 0 | — | 0 | 2 | — |
| WISCONSIN | 0 | 0 | — | 0 | 2 | — |

N ow, don't get me wrong! It's not that I don't like Minneapolis. How can you not like Minneapolis? It's a wonderful city. People are friendly. Riding the bank of the Mississippi, it's in a gorgeous setting. And it seems like it's expanding everywhere. I'm for any big city that keeps getting bigger but still holds on to tradition, especially one tucked away in the cold North. No, Minneapolis is lovely. It's the Metrodome that sucks! I'd already seen the summertime job it did on major-league baseball. Saturday I was going to watch the autumntime job it'd do on college football as well.

But how could I complain? I had my Red Roof reservation a few miles south of town and, with a 8:00 P.M. start, the whole day to get ready for the game. Plus, the Spartans were gonna be on the tube that afternoon. So, even if it was the Metrodome I had to face, after a little caffeine, a cruise through the sports section, and some Saturday morning cartoon-channel flipping, I was pumped for the Gophers. Well, sort of. I didn't really know what to do with myself. I mean, college football at most normal colleges happens when the sun's out. You always have that chance that punts will be floating up into a beautiful blue sky and that sunlight will be sparkling off tubas and skimpy sequined baton-twirler outfits. And maybe, just maybe, if you're sitting in the right place, even layered in frost-fighting clothes, you'll leave the game with a rosy-red sunburned face! At the Metrodome, though, all the sunlight is fake.

To combat Dome-itis, I improvised and planned my own little fantasy. My plan: Instead of 1988 in the Dome, I'd pretend it was Bernie's bunch playing Iowa, for Floyd, at Memorial Stadium. Even if nobody else was around, I'd do what Gopher fans in the thirties did. I'd roam the campus. I'd visit the bookstore. I'd stop by Stub & Herb's and end up over at Memorial for a make-believe 1:00 P.M. kickoff. After that, since MSU was going to try to score again, this week against Florida State, and since ESPN was carrying the game, I'd just find a place to tune in. After the Spartans were officially 0–3, I'd head down to the Dome and 1988's 8:00 P.M. inside version of college football.

Good plan! The morning was a bright blue sunny one, the campus empty—but pretty. I headed over to the bookstore and dug up a Golden Gopher T-shirt. It didn't take long—shirts were plentiful and lines were short. I popped in at Stub & Herb's and drifted through the black-and-white photo archives. Aside from the walls, it was empty too. Finally I made my way over to Foul Play, a bar with four TVs on the other side of campus, down University Avenue in an area called Dinkeytown.

Foul Play's a more modern version of your standard college sports bar. Video games and a basketball hoop shoot take the place of Stub's black-and-white oldies. Still, a couple of taps, ball games on the tube, and a college sports crowd are the main draws. At least college sports crowds on basketball (Wednesday) nights are a main draw. At noon on a football Saturday, there weren't many more than a dozen folks hanging around. A couple of tablefuls watched the Buckeyes trying to salvage some Big Ten pride against LSU. A couple of other tablefuls were eating lunch. I bellied up to the bar and tried to get the word on Gopher football. The thirties or the eighties or any decade in between!

Not a hot topic! I guess Northern Illinois in town on a Saturday night didn't raise goose bumps. But after I'd mentioned that I was roaming the Big Ten, and that this was my first trip ever to Minnesota, the bartender offered a suggestion.

"George Hudak, the night manager, that's who you gotta see. He's from the Golden Gopher golden days." The bartender chuckled about his unintentioned tongue twister, and pointed to the wall at the end of the bar. "There's an article down there about George. He'll be in, in few minutes. Stick around, he's the man!"

I slid down the counter and looked up at the article. It was from the *St. Paul Press* a few years back. The guy in the picture, the focus of "Football Hasn't Changed for Hudak," looked hard, old-school hard, as if a smile was something reserved for a gridiron victory, not some newspaper photographer. A two-way back, three-year player for Minnesota in the forties, Hudak was tough! You could tell by what he said. All his quotes followed from a "keep your mouth shut, work hard, and good things will happen to you" attitude. And you could tell by how he played too. Hell, you could tell what he was made of just by all the injuries he'd gutted out. "He played with four cracked vertebrae, he played with a partially dislocated shoulder, he played with a sprained ankle and a broken finger, he played," as the *Press* so eloquently put it, "with bruises and colors Picasso never heard of." One hundred seventy-three pounds of steel, George Hudak was tough, all right. He was two-way, old-school, before-facemasks-and-plastic-and-rib-and-hip-pads-and-Isotoner-gloves tough. He was the classic Bernie Bierman warrior.

"Hear you wanna talk to me," a voice cracked from behind. "Come on back." It was Hudak. He was a wiry guy, not real big, but still two-way old-school tough. And with a hell of a handshake too. He just about broke my fingers.

By the time I'd scooped up my backpack, hustled back to his office, and knocked on the open door, the ex-Gopher already had the night receipts out and was counting them.

"What can I do for you?" His voice was gruff. Hard and direct. He sat hemmed in between the wall and receipt-stacked table. The office, a renovated closet, was crammed with everything the bar needed but didn't have room for. Bottles, books, tons of stuffed boxes, a few waiters' shirts hanging on a hook.

I told him that I was on my way across the Big Ten, watching college football. And that I was just out roaming before the Gopher game. "I was told you were the man to see."

He smiled. "Where'd you go to school?"

"Big Ten," I answered. "Michigan State." I like telling it to people that way. He seemed to like it too. He nodded and mentioned the Spartan '88 Rose Bowl win. We were on the same track! While he figured totals and shook his head about the "damn women" who couldn't get their time cards straight, we talked a little Michigan State football. Some of it the old days, back when he'd played. Some of it the new version, and of course the Rose Bowl win.

We'd only exchanged a few Lorenzo White thoughts, and talked for a couple of minutes, and already I admired the guy. For his thoughts as well as his history. He was the old school personified, the type of guy who'd call a spade a spade, no matter what the consequences. He must've been a hell of a football player. He probably hit like a Mack truck, and the list the *Press* tallied was probably only half the injury story. I'd bet the house George Hudak never spiked a football or did an "Icky Shuffle." But he loved the game! That fact was clear. And at my request he did a little reminiscing. He thought back, way back to when he'd been a kid, in the Gopher Golden era, back to the middle thirties and the Bernie Bierman national championships.

"There was a different atmosphere over at Memorial." He nodded down the street toward the old stadium. "Up here everybody was a part of Gopher football. Not just the kids, but the city, the whole state of Minnesota. Hell, back in the thirties you said you were from Minnesota, people were proud to meet you. Damn proud!" He paused. He thought back to those old days. "Back then just to see a game in Memorial Stadium was a highlight of your life. On a day like today, you had so many people up here. Some never attended the university, but you came over at nine, ten o'clock. You strolled around. You had lunch somewhere. You went to the game. It really meant something then. It was nostalgic."

"Did you go and watch after you were done?" Hudak seemed like the type of guy who would've given an arm to get the Jug from Michigan or Floyd from Iowa. I just couldn't see him graduating and not coming back. The bond was too strong.

"Never missed a game." He stopped and added, "At Memorial."

"How 'bout the Dome?" I wondered, although not really. The Dome wasn't George Hudak. How could it be? He was facemaskless, dirt-and-grass-and-mud-under-gray-skies football. I knew the answer before I even asked the question.

"Uh-uh." He shook his head. "Two times—that's it. That's enough!

Downtown it's more of an attraction to the community. Like any . . . like any movie theater or any concert that comes to town. Today the game's just something to do from seven to ten o'clock. Something to take up three hours on a Saturday night."

He thought back to the Brick House. Seemed like whenever we got talking about the Dome he'd end up bringing the conversation back to Memorial. "But up here . . . up here it was a feeling of tradition. It meant something to people. It gave you a feeling of respect."

Respect is what George Hudak is all about. It's the very basis of him. It was, I'm sure, when he played for Bernie Bierman. It is now, I'm sure, as he manages the bar down the block from his old stomping ground. And he learned a lot of it wearing the maroon and gold of Minnesota.

"I read the article out front. You were pretty good!" George brushed it off—I'd have been disappointed if he'd done otherwise. I asked him what it'd been like playing college ball, what he got out of it. I wondered if it was worth all the injuries.

And he answered, straight from the heart. "Football's a great learning process. . . . It teaches you about life. The simple principles, the good things in life. That's what you learn! You learn that if you lose . . . you keep getting up. Life's not over just cause you get knocked on your butt once or twice. If you lose one somewhere—so what! The guy was better than you. So what! You don't shoot yourself, you get up and keep moving. There's always tomorrow.

"And you gain friendships," he went on. "You get to know the real person by season's end. You find out if he's a bullshitter or if he can play football too. You find out how he handles himself in pressure time!"

Unfortunately, the George Hudak times are long past. Times have changed. Football, or at least the way kids look at it now, has changed too. And that bothered George. He told a couple of simple stories, the kind that marked the end of the old-school era. Two of his ex-teammates, guys like him who used to leave it all out there on the field, now coached high-school football. Both had to deal with the new kind of kid. George admitted he'd never coach today.

"I could never put up with it. Kids just don't have the dedication."

What he was talking about wasn't a life-sacrificing dedication either, just simple team loyalty. He couldn't understand how a star running back on his buddy's team could tell the coach he wasn't gonna make a Friday night game—because his dad was taking him deer hunting. He couldn't figure out how another kid, a kid who besides carrying a football played the trumpet, could ask his coach to excuse him from the half-time locker room—so he could go play with the band. George Hudak couldn't understand that. Because to him, a guy who loved the Brick House up the block, a guy who'd busted his ass two ways the whole game for Coach Bierman, a guy who'd probably have run into a brick wall if his coach wanted him to, to George Hudak it all comes down to loyalty. And to dedication and respect. Unfortunately, they aren't top commodities in today's world.

University Avenue runs alongside Memorial Stadium. From Foul Play to the stadium is a four-block stretch of university buildings on the stadium side of the street and frat houses on the bar side. It's the University of Minnesota's fraternity row, a blacktop carpet to the old football field. George Hudak and Steve Lorinser had talked about what it'd been like in the old days, back before the games moved downtown. Fraternity row, they both had said, was Main Street. There was all sorts of activity, people cooking out on the front porch, parties and music all the way down to the stadium. During Homecoming, the row really jumped. The frat houses were decorated, and kids would be out and about all morning long. The Homecoming floats rolled right past Foul Play down the Ave and into old Memorial. So did the band. A half hour before my imaginary one o'clock kickoff, I followed their path.

Since no real game was scheduled, my walk was quiet. Some kids were out on the porches, some were doing a little barbecuing, a few played catch with a football, but not much was going on. Sigma Chi, one of big houses on the row, had a filled-up front porch. Four guys were lounging around doing nothing. I figured I'd find out if they were Gopher fans.

"Nope!"

"Not anymore. Not since it's downtown!"

Eric and Scott did most the talking, but it was a subject that caught at least a little lazy Saturday afternoon attention.

"Why not?" I had a pretty good idea, but wondered if a frat house full of guys saw it any differently.

"Well, for one thing, you gotta go downtown to watch it!"

"It's in the Dome, and it's at night."

"And the Gophers, well . . ." A couple of guys laughed. A couple of others shook their heads.

The porch was in agreement. Students didn't go because it was inside, at night, and downtown. And at least partially because the Gophers were pretty feeble nowadays.

Eric had seen it like it was, back in 1981: "I was here the last year it was at Memorial." A couple of the young guys perked up. They hadn't seen it, but they'd heard that it was real college football. "It was intense. Every single frat had a big barbecue outside. There were about a million people cruising by. The band would go right past us! God, it was great!

"Now I've got season tickets . . . but I never go."

A guy sitting over in the rocker, who'd been listening but not talking, piped up, "They need to push it towards the students instead of Minneapolis. The city's already got the Vikes and the Twins. We don't have anything anymore. In the Dome we don't even have a student section."

"Why not keep it up here?" I motioned across the street to Memorial. All week long and I still hadn't found a single kid on campus willing to defend the Dome.

"They tried," the kid in the rocker revealed. "There was a commission to 'bring the Gophers back to the Brick House.' But you know how that is. Big bucks downtown wanted it, and they got it."

"That's why we take our road trips to Madison." A voice with a body attached strolled out of the doorway. "We have to go someplace else to catch Big Ten football!"

"And Madison is *craaazzzzyyy!*" A kid on the porch helped out the one in the doorway.

"Yeah, Madison is crazy! We try to go to Camp Randall once a fall. You get to see it right, down there!" He turned to me. "Have you ever seen Wisconsin's Fifth Quarter? Man, it is something!"

A few of the guys among the six now on the porch had gotten a little curious about what I was doing, and why anybody would really give a rip about Gopher football. So I told them.

The kid in the rocker nodded. "Show him the Bronko Nagurski portrait. He'd like it." Then he reminded me, "You know Bronko was a Sigma Chi." I shook my head and told him I hadn't known. But I'm sure a lot of other Sigma Chis didn't know either. And probably at least one there on the porch didn't even know who Bronko was.

"Can't." Scott shook his head. "We used to have Bronko Nagurski's portrait right over the stairway." He stopped. "We used to, shit . . . till somebody ripped it off."

The whole thing seemed so strange. It was as if the school and the kids were two separate groups with entirely different ideas about how things should work. All week long I'd seen it and heard it. Memorial sat there, abandoned, left to go to seed. Kids, the few that lived on campus and roamed Stub & Herbs and Foul Play, wanted it back. They hated the Dome, and the school too in a way, for selling them out. Like most kids, though, they blew it off and found other Saturday night things to do. But I wondered. Couldn't anybody, anywhere on campus, find something right with the Dome? There had to be something. I asked once more, and was barraged with answers.

"Nope. You can't even tailgate down there. It's illegal."

"Well, I guess a couple of the bars are all right."

"It's warm in the winter!"

Eric, who'd caught that last Memorial Stadium homecoming, took notice of the winter comment. "Don't be a puss." He turned to his frat brother. "Half the fun of going to Memorial was peeling off all the layers."

It's about a block from the frat porch to Memorial, still too far to see inside. In fact, for folks who didn't know, folks driving down University Avenue, Memorial Stadium probably looks like any other old U building. Hovered over by the Radisson hotel, it just very quietly fills a charming corner of an old campus. From the outside, almost all along the brick wall border, Memorial hides its real purpose. Up close, though, it cries! Like Ebbets Field must've cried. After it was abandoned, after the crowds and the Dodgers stopped coming, before they killed it, and tossed up a housing project in its place.

I drifted up to the open end of the horseshoe, to the holes of the chain-link that guarded the old stadium and waited for my one o'clock kickoff. Clouds had sneaked overhead and spattered the blue. Breezes joined them. Still it was sunny, pleasant, a wonderful day for college football. I pressed my nose to the chain-links. A quiet, empty, battered stadium stared back.

In 1924 a copper box had been laid in the stadium cornerstone. The box contained two things: the names of thirty-two hundred Minnesotans who'd died in World War I and a sprig of olive leaves from a tree growing beside the Temple of Zeus in Athens, Greece. Around that copper box arose a big red-brick memorial to the war dead and a temple to Golden Gopher football. And for fifty-seven years, on Saturday afternoons that temple shook the Minnesota campus. In 1988, I looked out at the bones that remained. From the open end, the old horseshoe swung out and back around on a single level. Small openings, from the cavern down under, led walkways up and in. But nobody walked them anymore. Old bleacher seats that had once been crammed with Golden Gopher fans, the old seats that lined the inside of the shoe, were battered. Some rotted half away, some splintered, some ripped out altogether. Aside from the bare, sandy, fifty-yard-line land, tall grass and weeds littered the field. They grew in clumps like a back lot strewn with broken glass. One skinny goalpost stood at my end. I could almost hear the old place weeping.

"It'd be a gorgeous day for a football game, wouldn't it?" A fellow drifted up behind me. He'd made it just in time for kickoff. "There used to be solid people all over here." He motioned down in front of us, the open end where the bleachers use to stand. "Wind would come in from the west, behind you if you were sitting in the bleachers. It wasn't so cold at your back. But it was a tradeoff—the other side caught the afternoon sunshine." He paused. "It really was wonderful . . . at either place!"

I could tell that the fellow hurt thinking back. It must've been like watching an old friend wither away from cancer. Still, neither of us said much; we both just stood there looking out over the field.

"Kids don't go anymore!"—he broke the quiet. "It's become an adults' game now. I don't know if it was the prices or if the students changed, but it used to be packed with kids."

I nodded. "I'll bet it was something."

He nodded back. "It was. It surely was." And as quickly as he'd appeared, the football fan drifted away. The wind blew a single plastic cup out across the weeds.

Downtown, the Dome buzzed. Cops blowing whistles and redirecting traffic, people heading inside, starting to fill the place. It was kind of like a Hollywood movie premiere. I'd shuttle-bused over. Set up by the U for students or anybody else on campus, the buses kept cars from complicating things. And since you can't tailgate, why bring a car? With tailgating out, for entertainment folks roam the bars. Humphrey's, named like the Dome for Hubert H., seemed to be the most popular. It was crammed with patrons, a constantly changing flow. Some stopped and waited for friends on the corner out in front. Some, drifting from the parking garages a couple of blocks uptown, slowed and peered into the windows. They gave the corner cop a headache but livened the Dome some.

Humphrey's isn't a Stub & Herb's. Not nearly. Photos of modern ballplayers in modern uniforms dominate the modern walls. Some are Golden Gophers, but mostly it's Fran Tarkenton and Kirby Puckett. The Vikes and Twins—Humphrey's is their bar. Saturday nights in the fall, Gopher fans get to borrow it. But even then, the Saturday night renters didn't look collegiate. Gold-and-maroon Gopher wear spattered the place, but didn't saturate it, not like Dooley's game-day green in East Lansing. TVs hung overhead, some tuned to CBS, some to ESPN, almost all blaring football games. People drank and talked and yelled; some kept track of the games. But the Spartans had about died, so I wasn't really in the mood. I stepped back outside. Clouds had brought some rain. It'd started to drizzle.

They try, they really try to prepare the Metrodome for college football. Program vendors out in front wear maroon and gold. Ticket booths, even if by accident, once upon a time got a gold finish. The marching band, bused down from campus, circles the Dome. Two times. It blasts the fight song; band parents and diehards follow and get into the Golden Gopher mood. The band members even stop at an outside gate and put on a little pregame concert. But since the drizzle had picked up, the concert this time only lasted for a couple tunes and they disappeared inside with everybody else. By kickoff all that was left, sight or sound, that even hinted of Minnesota football was a tiny alumni band. It consisted of a dozen or so out-of-shape but dedicated ex–marching band players. They stood with their backs to the Dome, wedged under a lip in the concrete that kept the drizzle off. Everybody was wearing maroon.

The band was made up of a tuba, five trumpets, a couple saxes, one flute, other assorted brass instruments, and a small lady, barely twice the size of her drum, keeping time. That was it. And nobody seemed to pay much attention to them. If you were deaf, they'd have blended back into the stadium wall. Undaunted, they kept cranking out the tunes—the "Gopher Rouser" and other football fight songs that usually ring around a college Saturday football field.

"We're the picnic band!" Carol Rosendahl revealed on one of the few and very far between picnic-band breaks. I'd walked up, stopped in front of them, and stared as though they were a group of street musicians and I didn't know where to toss the quarter.

"Been going for about twenty years or so. Isn't that right?" she asked one of the five trumpeters standing alongside.

"Yeah, I think we started back in 'seventy."

Carol Rosendahl, picnic-band spokesman, was a 1975 graduate. She was a bit older than most seventies graduates, since '75 had been her second time around. Or was it her third? In 1955 she first started at the U, and played sax in the Minnesota band. But girls couldn't march back then. So in 1975, when they could, she came back and finished up. And she marched too!

"There's an alumni band and then there's us. . . ."

"But somebody's almost got to die to get in this one," the trumpeter added.

"We've got a lot of family here. My son's playing with us, just today though."

"The gal on the end"—she pointed to the squad's lone flutist—"that's her mom over there. And next to her mom is her dad. A couple others are related too. We've got a lot of family."

"Why 'the picnic band'?" I was curious; I didn't see a picnic anywhere.

"Because of the tailgate playing up at old Memorial. We do a few parties and some weddings, a dinner here and there, and all the Gopher games. But we got our name from the tailgates. Those were the best times—tailgates up at old Memorial."

A couple of the picnic banders nodded.

"She's right," one added.

The piccolo player, who'd been listening, jumped in: "I loved playing up there. Even when it was cold. I'll never forget one game we played in the snow." She turned to another player. "Remember that? I think it was California. They put straw down so we could play—I guess so we wouldn't fall down." She turned back to me and burst out in a grin. "God, that was fun."

"Yeah, but it's sad now." Carol shook her head. "Memorial Stadium is heartbreaking. It's falling apart, no football field. I can't even look at it, it's so sad."

A stray Gopher couple, a pair who hadn't quite caught the crowds and were cruising in the drizzle, stopped. "The 'Rouser,' let's hear the 'Rouser.' Carol excused herself, dropped back into formation, and the picnic-band dozen struck up the "Rouser." I nodded and headed for the Dome's revolving doors. I was sucked through and left nature behind.

I might as well have left college football behind too. It's not right, it's just not right! You buy a sixteen-ounce beer, you grab a bag of peanuts, you find a cozy plastic seat, and like George Hudak said, you kill three hours on a Saturday night. The man up at Memorial was right too—hardly any kids. Adults were everywhere. Even the Sigma Chis were right. Student sections, for what few students had shown, just happened to be wherever you could find a pocketful of students.

I found an open end-zone seat. There were thousands to choose from. I draped my coat and backpack over the one next to me and sat the draft down on the concrete floor. I shelled some peanuts and tried to imagine the fanfare and excitement and Mother Nature surprises that we were missing. No bright blue sky or sunshine. No clouds or gray or even freezing rain. As long as the roof stayed inflated, nobody'd ever again get to catch a Gopher home game in a snowstorm. The picnic band would never need straw to cover the field. Minnesota would never have to invest in its own Goodyear blimp. And planes would never zoom by dragging BUY BOB MURPHY'S USED CARS banners behind them.

I looked at the quiet people sitting around me and tried to figure out how it was better for them. Clothes, I guess—they didn't need to layer like Eric had up at Memorial. It was a pretty safe guess they'd never have to bother with umbrellas popping open in their faces and blocking their view. They'd never have to worry about student section Frisbees or beach balls or passed-up college co-eds headed their way. Mother Nature would never get to screw things up either. It'd never get really cold or wet or hot or foggy or cloudy or rainy. The band could always perform in ideal plastic conditions. Goldie the Gopher would never slip and fall, and crunch his cottontail because of a slippery turf. And the football team would never have to blame a loss on anybody but themselves. Ideal college football conditions—70 degrees and bright plastic lights.

As I sat there wondering about all this, the roof shook. Outside, thunder rumbled. We could hear it through the Teflon. The morning-long blue skies finally gave way to Minnesota's fall. A finely dressed lady, looked like she was filling a Saturday night three-hour block, turned to her husband. They were sitting next to me, in a place where most colleges stick the students.

"Honey," she said. "Listen to that. I'll bet it's pouring out!"

He nodded. "Good thing we're inside."

I didn't have the heart to tell them that earlier in the day up on campus, the sun had been out. That a slight breeze was rolling in from the west, through the bleachers, and that bright warm sunshine was finding a closed end of a tired horseshoe. I didn't mention that that afternoon would've been a wonderful day for a football game.

At about one o'clock up at the Brick House.

Up at Old Memorial.

# 3
# UNIVERSITY OF WISCONSIN
## THE BADGERS

| University of Wisconsin Madison, WI | Camp Randall |
|---|---|
| Best Breakfast | Mickie's Dairy Bar |
| Best Bar | Jingle's Stadium Bar |
| Best Burger | Dotty Dumpling's Dowry |
| Best of... | |

✱ tied for best

| The Best in Big Ten Country |
|---|
| MARCHING BAND |
| 1. Wisconsin ✱ |
| 1. Ohio State ✱ |
| 3. Michigan State |
| 4. Michigan |
| 5. Illinois |

The year: 1978. The place: Spartan Stadium, East Lansing, Michigan. State had just finished pounding Wisconsin, 55–2. My roommates and I were basking in the victory. We circulated in the Spartan student section, checking with friends, figuring out where to celebrate. Down in the other end zone, way down at the Wisconsin end of the field, while green herded toward the exits, a bunch of folks dressed in red hadn't bothered with planning—their celebration was already rolling. The Badger band cranked tunes out across the empty field. Wisconsin fans were singing and clapping; some were even out in the end zone, polkaing. You'd have sworn they'd just won the Rose Bowl! Red bodies attacked the goalpost. A few guys shimmied up it. The post started swaying. Unsuspecting cops rushed over to save it. The goalpost swingers saw 'em coming, gave up, and drifted back in among the polka dancers. We all stopped gloating and looked at each other. What the hell was going on? They'd just lost by fifty . . . right? They were carrying on like they'd won by fifty . . . right? We looked at the scoreboard. It still said, "Home, 55; Visitors, 2." A little confused, we stumbled up to the cleared exits. I took one last glance over my shoulder. Behind me sat a quiet, empty Spartan Stadium. All except for that far corner of the Badger end zone. Everybody, even the band, was out on the field and dancing.

That was my first brush with the Madison spirit. My second was a little later that night. Dooley's, State's best postgame bar, replayed the football games. If we won, we'd go and watch. Particularly if the final was 55–2. Well, as on most Spartan Saturdays, Dooley's was green. This time, though, with a heavy red tint. The red clustered together at booths alongside one of the TVs. It'd gotten there before us. We arrived just in time to catch the opening kickoff. Just in time to see a Spartan trapped in the end zone. A safety and a 2–0 Wisconsin lead. The Badger fans erupted: "WE SCORED FIRST! WE SCORED FIRST! WE SCORED FIRST!" Their chanting rocked the place. It rocked the place all night long. Every time State scored—every single one of those replayed fifty-five points—Wisconsin fans, bolstered later by the end-zone polka dancers, chanted, "WE SCORED FIRST!" They closed down Dooley's singing the Wisconsin fight song!

That's the Madison spirit. And I was finally going to the source— Madison, Wisconsin. Or as folks who frequent the place call it, "Mad City." Surrounded by cow barns and rolling farms, Madison is where the Wisconsin state government comes to order and where, out on the capitol lawn, the annual Midwest Marijuana Harvest Festival tokes out. It's a loud liberal twang set in the middle of a good ole conservative part of the world. A city and a university in one—just talking about the place can get confusing. Ask people if they've ever been to the University of Wisconsin, they'll say, "Oh, you mean Madison." Ask if they've ever been to Madison, they'll say, "Oh, you mean the university." But ask if they had a good time, they'll just smile, shake their heads, and tell you something crazy!

Crazy reputations are founded on crazy stories, and the U of W's got tons of them. It's the school where back in the late seventies a group of students ran for the student government on one promise: "If elected, we will bring the Statue of Liberty to Lake Mendota," the big lake behind the school. Well, they won, and that winter when the lake froze over, the new government emptied the student treasury. They commissioned a gigantic replica of the liberty lady—her head and torch, anyhow. Then they plopped her on the ice out behind the school. She looked great! It was as if they'd flown to New York, hijacked the real thing, and plunged her up to her nose in Wisconsin ice water. Madison's the place where that same group, once the treasury plumped back up, reemptied it on a second project. They got ahold of thousands of plastic pink flamingos and planted them all over campus. Pink plastic flocks greeted enrolling freshmen, and also got the ticket reelected. Wisconsin's where in the mid-eighties, a slate swept all thirty-eight student government seats on the controversial issue of eliminating "threeks" (forks with three prongs) from the Union cafeteria. The big coup that landslided the election took place two football seasons ago. Government officers road-tripped to Notre Dame, posted signs, and announced to South Bend radio stations that they were on a mission from Madison. Their goal to take over the University of Notre Dame and make it an extension of U of W. While Notre Dame students crammed the football game, the Badgers headed to the Union, reeled down the ND school flag, and replaced it with a big red one. A big red one with a white W in the middle. Oh, yeah, they also sneaked inside and stole all the cafeteria forks.

Stories are nearly as strange when it comes to Badger football. Crazy road trips, band polkas, and 55–2 loss celebrations are standard Badger folklore, and it transfers over to the other sports too. Back in '82 the UW hockey team headed out to Providence, Rhode Island, for the national championship. They didn't win the tourney, but they did win the heart of Providence. The following hockey season, the Providence Chamber of Commerce flew a representative back to Madison. He brought a trophy with him and made a special presentation to the university. The trophy said: "To the University of Wisconsin—'The World's Greatest Hockey Fans.' " In '86, in the midst of a another horrible football season, Badger fans hit the road for the University of Nevada, Las Vegas. As usual Wisconsin lost, this time 17–7. But so many Badger fans showed up that Nevada had its biggest-ever home football crowd. It's like a University of Minnesota student told me the week before, up in Minneapolis: "Mad City—now those are real fans! My brother went there. He told me the stories. He told me that back in '81 when they beat Michigan, kids were naked swinging from the lampposts." Why not? Everything else happens in the Mad City.

Students call it the country club. It sits on the banks of big, beautiful, blue Lake Mendota. It has a theater, a beer hall, homemade ice cream, a cafeteria (now with four-pronged forks), and some great home cooking in Sunday dinner portions. It's got an outdoor terrace to kick back on and catch the lake breezes. It's got sailboats, canoes, and pontoons that you can get with a student ID. It's where in the winter of '79, the Statue of Liberty stared back into the cafeteria windows. The Wisconsin Student Union—it's pure Madison!

Most normal Student Unions at most normal colleges are actually kind of boring. In four years I don't think I wandered into State's more than a couple times. And those were just by accident. Usually you got your basics—first and foremost a plastic cafeteria, serving—of course—plastic food. You have your study rooms, rooms for student government to meet in, one-dollar movies on the weekends, and lots of TVs where kids can catch the afternoon soaps. Noontimes during the week are normal Union peak hours. At night the place turns into a backup library or a morgue, if there's any difference. And on the weekends, most Student Unions might just as well shrivel up and die. Not so at Madison. The Union probably provides more entertainment than 90 percent of the cities in Wisconsin.

The setting's wonderful. Lake Mendota, the biggest of Madison's three city lakes, washes its shore. Filled with lake smells and sounds, it's so big and blue you can't even see across to the other side. Seagulls and ducks hang around the concrete pier begging for bread scraps. Anchored out in the water, about a hundred yards off shore, sailboats sit and wait for the weekends. Where the lake bumps the shore, at the foot of the Union, boats pile up. Kayaks and canoes, sailboats and wind surfers—there's always some sort of activity going on, be it class or leisure. Townsfolk even get in on the act. "Good bass," I was told by an old guy casting out in front of the Union. "That is, over in them weeds. That is, if you got a boat." As for the perch, "Well, they ain't biting too good this fall. The school cropped one of the fins. Had to tag 'em for some study they're doing." He shook his head and fired the line again. "I don't know if that goofed 'em up, or maybe just the hot summer. But they sure as heck aren't biting."

The four-story Union building, built back in the twenties, is a beaut. The view's great—from the cafeteria, which offers all sorts of good home-style eats, or from the Rathskeller. Modeled after an old German beer hall, the Rathskeller serves up brats, popcorn, and a hearty assortment of brews. Discussing politics, working on crossword puzzles, highlighting a text with a big fat yellow marker, or just nursing a beer and listening to tunes, kids flock to it. The front lobby provides more pleasant surprises. Info boards point the way to all sorts of activities—everything from the billiards room to the live theater schedule to what's the free Thursday night band. There are stacks of the two student newspapers to reach for as well—that's right, two! The conservative *Badger Herald* and the liberal *Daily Cardinal.* Madison kids get more political views than most folks across the country. And there's always a lineup for Babcock Hall ice cream, which according to students is the best ice cream in the world. It's made on campus by food science majors, who get the on-campus cream from dairy science majors, who milk the campus cows. And the tastiest flavor? Without a doubt, caramel nut cluster.

But the best part of the country club is back outside where Union meets the lake. A three-tiered patio slopes to the water. Thick green vines spill over the building and onto the red brick. Fat maples shade it. All sorts of round tables and chairs and students and faculty sit outside and soak up the sunshine. Or breathe in the fresh lake breezes, or listen to the screeching seagulls and quacking ducks. It's a great place just to relax.

In fact the whole campus is. Madison's a real sleeper! It's one you never hear mentioned when the "What do you think are the prettiest schools in the world?" question pops up, but one that ought to be! The Union's the center. To the east is downtown and the state capitol. The other direction provides rolling hills and trees and old campus buildings. Long sloping Bascom Hill, the place all those flamingos invaded a decade ago, is usually packed with backpack-toting kids on their way to class. Observatory Drive, which sits high above and parallels Lake Mendota, provides a view that reminds you of Appalachian foothills, not the "Dairy State." Art classes meet daily, sit on the grass, and try to re-create it with paintbrushes. Students use it to celebrate the first snow by "traying"—taking on the snow and the hill, at the same time, atop a cafeteria tray. Come fall, tree tops below dot yellow and red and orange. Along the water's edge, from the Union some three miles around to Picnic Point, runs Lakeshore Path. Joggers and bikers and students mosey along it. A thick run of woods buffers it from campus. Mendota splashes the path's other side. Concrete benches slide off to the water's edge—it's a place for kids to go and dream. Or alumni to come back and reminisce.

Off Observatory Drive, past Elm Street, just before you head into the intramural and band practice fields, at the center of one of the biggest campuses in the country, is where the "girls" live—eighty to one hundred of them. At 4:00 A.M. every morning, and 4:00 P.M. every afternoon, they get milked. Guernseys and Jerseys, with those big sad eyes, live in the Wisconsin cow barns. There are horse barns, poultry barns, and pigs and goats and sheep in their own barns too. All of the buildings look like they've been pulled right off Old McDonald's farm. And all sit right in the middle of campus. But the cow barns, they're something special. The "girls" plod up in line, get milked, plod back out of line and wait to get squeezed again. Kids in the dairy school cover a chunk of tuition by taking care of them. Kids in the food science school pay their way through by turning the cream into Babcock caramel nut cluster. The girls just plod back and forth twice a day. It's kind of sweet, in a way. You can actually stand there on Elm, watch a city bus plow past, hear a sharp whistle signal "touchdown" on the IM fields, catch some practice bars of "On, Wisconsin," and listen to those long, low, lonely moooos.

"Alumni, hey, alumni, we love to have you here! Really appreciate you showing up! But SHUT UP!" the guy in the big red tower boomed out over a loudspeaker. It was alumni band week. Probably three hundred band grads would show up on Saturday. Thirty or so were hanging out at the Friday afternoon practice, and they were having a grand time. Giving the players shit, pounding beers from the two kegs they'd dragged along—their old bandmates, their old coach, all of 'em hard at work—the beer-guzzling grads on the sideline were in heaven.

"Thank you, alumni!" The guy in the tower went back to frowning at his band. The alumni went back to guzzling and hooting.

The University of Wisconsin Marching Band, the liveliest in the world and arguably Camp Randall's Saturday afternoon main feature, practices west of the cow barns, just off the lake. Every fall, from three o'clock till five, the members fill the big IM field with marching band music. Mike Leckrone, their director for the past twenty seasons, stands in his tower and frowns. And yells. And puts on a mean face. In the tower he sounds a lot like the Grinch. But in person at his campus office, and probably when the alumni band isn't screwing things up, Mike Leckrone is more like a cross between David Letterman and Lou Holtz. Like the Union and the student government history and so many other things in town, he's pure Madison.

Before I hit town, I'd promised myself the Wisconsin band director was one guy I wouldn't miss. Hell, he was famous, more renowned than the football coach, basketball coach, and university president combined. You see, all season long, whenever I'd mention my Big Ten road trip, I was hit with the same first question—"You been to Madison yet?" I must've of gotten it twenty or thirty times. Before I could even answer, a second question popped: "How 'bout the Wisconsin band? You seen the Wisconsin band?" Invariably I'd get crazy stories about both the school and the band, along with at least some five-minute ramble about the "Fifth Quarter." From what I could gather, the Fifth Quarter was something the Badger band specialized in, something that fans who'd road-tripped the Big Ten named over and over again as the best thing about a day at Camp Randall. I got it in pieces, all different versions from all different viewpoints, but decided on a couple things: One, the Fifth Quarter was a lot of fun; two, it involved fans and the band, polkas and singing and dancing in the aisles; and finally, it didn't matter if the Badgers won by one or lost by fifty—the Fifth Quarter show went on. Considering what Michigan was probably gonna do to them on Saturday, that was lucky for me. And for the Wisconsin fans too.

"All the Big Ten bands have one. The Fifth Quarter is just our version of the postgame show." Maybe in Mike Leckrone's mind it was "just our version," but I'd learned enough to know that Mad City's version of anything had to be more like a weird rendition. "About seven or eight years ago, I thought it ought to be a little more fun, so I started throwing in some things. And since our fans are a little on the crazy side"—he laughed—"well, I started throwing in crowd participation. It'll give the impression of total anarchy—but there's always something happening. The kids are always doing something. Sometimes the band will dance. Sometimes they'll go and get cheerleaders. I think it's particularly fun when they go get the other team's cheerleaders. The other kids don't know what to think . . . especially if they've won!"

"I know!" I flashed back to 1978. I mentioned the Spartan Stadium 55–2 celebration. "I sure as hell didn't know what to think."

Leckrone started laughing. "I'll bet you don't remember what they were yelling that day."

"Bet I do." Together we chanted: "WE SCORED FIRST!"

"I got a Fifth Quarter story even crazier than that one." The director grinned, thinking back. "Happened up at the Metrodome. Sometimes the Fifth Quarter can last as long as forty-five minutes. And we'll do it anywhere. Well, this was after the Minnesota game. We were just doing our regular thing—I don't know how long we'd been out there, maybe fifteen or twenty minutes. It really didn't show any signs of letting up. Fans were dancing. The band was playing and dancing. And somebody in the Metrodome, they just . . ." His grin turned to laughter. ". . . they just pulled the switch. There we are in the dark. The place is empty and we're playing the Bud song. Well, we finished out the song. Wisconsin fans'd riot if we ever quit in the middle of the Bud song. There were enough panic lights for us to find the doors. So we headed to the outside plaza and finished up another fifteen minutes in the rain." Still chuckling, he shook his head. "Yeah, kids that were here then still talk about that one. They'll say, 'I was there when they turned the lights out.'

"I'm not sure if you could do a Fifth Quarter just anywhere." Leckrone got a little philosophical. "The fans here really are something else! And there's a real rapport between the band and the fans. Really something special. Like the Bud song." He started grinning again. Any mention of the Bud song all week long got Wisconsin people grinning. "We have this tune they call the Bud song—'You've Said It All.' Kids love it. And they just beg for the tune." He smiled and slapped the table. "And I make them beg for the tune. We play little games back and forth. It really is fun!

"You know, that's the best thing about Fifth Quarter. No matter what happens during the game, the postgame is celebration time. It's fun—you leave the stadium fired up."

The band director and I talked about a lot of fun things. And a few not so fun things. We talked about the problems in the Camp Randall stands. All week long I'd been hearing about them. I'd heard how a couple of years ago, the passing-up of things and the student section partying had gotten out of hand. I'd heard that the school administration had overreacted, that they'd posted cops at the top of the stands, that they'd broken up the student section with a buffer zone, and that they'd practically strip-searched kids at the front gates. Leckrone shook his head. "The word 'Gestapo' was used a lot."

Students survived by adding a new chant to their game day list. The fine for being caught in the stands with booze was $27.50, so "TWENTY-SEVEN FIFTY!" and a good round of boos rocked the student section whenever cops made a bust.

"The administration's realized they indulged in a little overkill and now are trying to put some fun back into it. But once you've lost something, you've gotta work twice as hard to get it back . . . so unfortunately you're probably not going to see this thing at its height." He grinned an optimistic grin. "But I have confidence, knowing the Wisconsin fan mentality, that it will come back."

"What about this?" I asked about the giant depth chart he had leaning up against the wall. Information about the Wisconsin band covered everything in the closet-sized office. The board listed all instruments and below them was a list of all 240 kids at all the positions. And not one single kid was a music major!

"Oh, that. It's a depth chart. I use it as a motivator. Kind of an ax I have dangling over their heads."

"Do you know 'em all?" Two hundred forty kids, I figured, were a lot to know, particularly just in the third week of the season.

Leckrone grinned. "Try me."

I pointed to a tag dangling from a nail. The coach recited, "Steve Gates is a trumpet player. Kind of a gangly kid. I think he's from Green Bay, but I'm not sure. Steve's been in the band. Let's see, this'll be his fourth year."

"Not bad." I pointed to another tag.

"John Schlick. Stands about five-three. A trombone player and a house fellow. Good kid.

"I felt at a big school like this it's a rap that you're only a number. So I made it a point to let the freshmen know by the end of the week, 'I'm gonna know your name.' It dissolves some of that impersonality. Lets 'em know, 'Hey, I'm a real person.' Also, it can be terribly intimidating. If I'm in my tower with a bullhorn and I say, 'Schlick, you're out of line,' it's a lot scarier than 'Hey, kid in the blue shirt.' "

But he's only intimidating in the tower, and not terribly intimidating there, at least not to beer-guzzling alumni. Usually Mike Leckrone's a walking, talking, laughing University of Wisconsin advertisement, whose favorite line is "Madison's a fun place! People get stuck in Madison of their own free will," he said. "A grad gets a job offer. He'll say to me, 'I've got a shot at this real good job, but I don't know, it means I gotta leave Madison.' " After a half hour in the band building, I figured one of the "stuck" ones was the university band director.

The band's crazy, the lake's a beauty, the campus is filled with all sorts of neat little cubbyholes—all that and more. State Street, the five-block swing that connects the Union with the state capitol, might be the most interesting place in town. Only buses, bikes, and people travel on State Street. *No cars allowed.* It runs smack-dab into the capitol rotunda. At night, lit up, the rotunda looks like a lighthouse beacon. All sorts of shops spatter the sidewalks—Taco Bell, pizza places, Oriental food shops, interesting hole-in-the-wall bars, record stores. Red Wisconsin T-shirts, posters, signs, and all sorts of Bucky Badgers fill State Street windows. It's a great college walkway. During the day the sidewalk's crammed with all kinds of wooden stands—fresh fruit, souvenirs, belts and belt buckles, jewelry. Street musicians play for spare change. It's got the flavor of a big-city market. At night, kids just bounce from bar to bar and provide that electric college-town buzz.

Friday night I did a little State Street bouncing of my own. I found three guys tipping beers at the Brathouse, a normal Madison tavern. No live band, no dancing, just a hearty jukebox, brats, burgers, beer, and all over the floor—peanut shells. The three were assessing Badger football problems, which were mounting after three opening losses, two to always-tough Northern Illinois and Western Michigan University.

"They've ruined it. They've just ruined it." Bob, a 1987 grad after a good six-year run on his degree, was pissed about the way the university had clamped down on the crowds. "We used to pass girls through the stands, the drinking was good, the team was pretty good too. We used to have a great time. But now . . ."

"Now," Dale, another guy who'd been around for a while, interrupted, "now it's sad. I see football players every day in the training room—they work hard every day. You want 'em to win, but you know they won't. And they know they won't. You feel really bad for them!

"It didn't used to be like that! When I went to school, Coach

McClain, he turned it around. No matter who we played, we played well. We had a good team. We even went to a couple bowls."

Randy, who'd been silently surveying the situation, put his collegiate major to work. "I've taken a sports marketing class." Dale and Bob raced to see who could roll his eyes first. "Essentially, any sporting program from the Athletic Department standpoint is a product. All right?" I nodded. Dale left to get another pitcher. Bob looked around and started cracking peanuts. "And due to the fact that they have wins and losses, it's an inconsistent product. You cannot determine what they'll do. The problem with this program is they have not been able to emphasize the social aspects. This university has three revenue-producing sports: basketball, hockey, and football. And the fact that they've put the clamps on the socializing has hurt their attendance. The fact that your team is losing, you need something else to rely on. . . ."

"What he's saying is they fucked up! They flat fucked up!" Bob was a little more to the point. "OK, so things got a little out of hand a couple years ago . . ."

"More than a little, actually." Dale plopped the pitcher down on a handful of peanut shells. "They started tearing up bleacher seats. Instead of girls, they started passing bleacher seats up. The final straw was when some kid at the top of the stadium actually threw one over the top . . ."

"Luckily, nobody was killed."

". . . but that was the beginning of the crackdown."

"They broke up the student section, put in a buffer zone. Man, it used to be great. Remember Dale? Remember? We used to sit in Section O." Bob turned to me. "It was great. Everybody in Section O would chant: *'P sucks O!'* " His chant carried across the bar. Somebody, probably an old P season ticket holder, chanted back, *"O sucks P!"*

"Yeah, I remember. And then P would chant, *'O sucks P!'* "

"And then O and P together would chant"—all three guys yelled out the O-P chant as loud as they could—*"K, K, K is gay!"* The P season ticket holder, across the bar, joined in.

"That was a riot. And the cup fights and the Fifth Quarter."

"Remember when we lost to Michigan, when Harbaugh was quarterbacking for them. They had to stop the game five times, we were so loud!"

"Those were the good ole days." Dale shook his head. "It's still a good time. But I wish the guys were a little better."

Bob agreed. "You know, though, even if the team's lousy, the fans here are great. I know every state claims to have the best fans, but Wisconsin fans, they really are the best."

"Iowa fans are good too," Randy added. "And they do make a substantial profit from their football attendance."

"Yeah, Iowa's good. And I know they make some money. And I know they win more than we do. And I know they fill their stadium every single week. But when Wisconsin fans are psyched . . . *man*—they're the best fans in the world!"

*October 1, 1988*

# MICHIGAN AT WISCONSIN

*Camp Randall, Madison, Wisconsin*

| Standings | Big Ten | | | All Games | | |
|---|---|---|---|---|---|---|
| October 1, 1988 | W | L | T | W | L | T |
| INDIANA | 0 | 0 | — | 2 | 0 | 1 |
| OHIO STATE | 0 | 0 | — | 2 | 1 | — |
| MINNESOTA | 0 | 0 | — | 2 | 1 | — |
| IOWA | 0 | 0 | — | 2 | 2 | — |
| ILLINOIS | 0 | 0 | — | 1 | 2 | — |
| MICHIGAN | 0 | 0 | — | 1 | 2 | — |
| PURDUE | 0 | 0 | — | 1 | 2 | — |
| MICHIGAN STATE | 0 | 0 | — | 0 | 3 | — |
| NORTHWESTERN | 0 | 0 | — | 0 | 3 | — |
| WISCONSIN | 0 | 0 | — | 0 | 3 | — |

**Other Big Ten Games:**

ILLINOIS AT OHIO STATE

INDIANA AT NORTHWESTERN

IOWA AT MICHIGAN STATE

MINNESOTA AT PURDUE

Seven o'clock on a gray, rainy Saturday morning and Mickie's was packed. A waitress who couldn't have been much older than eighteen was getting change. She turned to me, sighed, and shook her head. "Oh, I hope I'm doing all right. I just don't know . . . I'm kind of new."

"You're not new, you're part of the team!" Hank, the old guy working the register, the kind of guy everybody ought to have for a grandpa, reassured her. "You're doing great!" The freshman grinned and squeaked out a "Thanks, Hank." She wasn't worried anymore.

Mickie's Dairy Bar is your classic hole-in-the-wall. A bricked-front, one-room breakfast place, it sits on Monroe Street, in the shadow of Camp Randall Stadium. It's a smile on another Madison face, another Madison neighborhood, one with taverns and frat houses and train tracks—a neighborhood centered by a big old fieldhouse and a football stadium. All sorts of friendly stops branch off the sidewalk, and since 1946 Mickie's has been one of the friendliest. The menu's tacked against the back wall, up above the door to the kitchen. Prices are hanging up alongside it. Daily specials, homemade coffee cake—blueberry-, apple-cinnamon-, and pumpkin-flavored—and about a half-dozen other things get scribbled on a little chalkboard out front. Red spin-around stools belly up to the counter. Old wooden booths line the sides. And in the middle, the place where the worried freshman waitress had been scurrying about all morning, are Hamilton Beach malted milk makers, an old Coke fountain, and a thousand other things straight out of the fifties.

Saturday mornings in the fall when the Badgers play at home, Mickie's is the first place to bustle. Kids from the band stop by before heading to the stadium for practice. They hang out. They guzzle milk. They order seconds and thirds of coffee cake. They laugh and make a lot more noise than most folks do at 7 A.M. on a Saturday morning.

"Those were the glory days." Hank was talking about when he'd lived inside the football stadium. Well, actually inside Baumann-Schreiner Hall, which sat inside the stadium. It was a student dorm named after two University of Wisconsin football players, both of whom had been killed in 1945 on the beaches of Okinawa. Hank's door practically opened up to a forty-yard-line seat. "Yessir"—he smiled—"you've gotta have a good memory to remember some glory days round these parts."

Hank works the cash register at Mickie's and looks like he popped straight off a Norman Rockwell calendar. Everybody in the neighborhood knows Hank. He's the type of guy that'd probably be at his best sitting around the pickle barrel telling stories in some backwoods general store. Well, Mickie's has that old general-store spirit. It's named after Mickie, who opened the doors forty-two years ago. Those were the days when Hank was just a college kid. He'd stroll over from his dorm across the street, eat dinner, and visit with Mickie. In '48, Hank's uncle, on the advice of his nephew, bought the place. Mickie's stayed Mickie's, but soon changed from a tiny restaurant into a tiny general store. One with a good-sized pickle barrel for talking around. For twenty-five years Hank worked there. When Debbie and Mark Percy bought the store in '79 and turned it back into a breakfast place, they kept Hank on. Now he runs the till, says hello to folks, and keeps worried waitresses' spirits up.

"Been a tough year so far, hasn't it?" I wondered how Badger fans, Hank being a pretty good one, took all the losses.

"Use to it," he deadpanned, gave up, and chuckled. "It's tradition. These kids are probably the best thing about it." Hank nodded at the band kids cramming the booths—laughing and talking and drinking their milk. "More people go to see them than the games."

"Thanks, Hank."

"See ya, Mr. Peters."

The different band sections would come and go in groups. Trumpets and trombones arrived first. Percussion players, slightly heavier sleepers probably because of all the racket they make, made up most of the second wave. Their rain gear—big red capes and band hats—hung on an aluminum rolling coat rack up front, right up there alongside wooden wall cutouts of Bucky and Mrs. Bucky.

"They come in here at six-thirty or seven for breakfast. They head over to the stadium for warm-ups. They spend the rest of the morning serenading the neighborhood . . . for beers." He laughed. "Yessir, that's the modern-day band—play for beer."

Hank knows his football. "It's tough to run the veer when you haven't got the horses. This coach we got in here keeps trying. I tell ya, when you lose two yards every play, fans get a little uninterested in a hurry."

Hank knows Camp Randall. "I just found out myself how it got the name. They used to train Civil War troops over here. The vets got teed off when the state turned the land over to the university, so they made them name it after Governor Randall. He was Wisconsin governor during the Civil War."

Hank knows his waitresses too. He leaned over the register and nodded. "Now she's an extraordinary co-ed." He was talking about Lisa. Lisa'd been around Mickie's for a couple of years. "Works full-time and goes to school full-time. She's something else, all right. A real sweetheart. I'll tell you, if Hollywood was smart they'd give her a shot."

And Hank knows the not so good waitresses—of which, by the way, you won't find too many at Mickie's. A snippy waitress scurried past the register. She wasn't Hank's sweetie and she wasn't the worried freshman, just a girl who couldn't smile and handle business at the same time. We watched as she grumbled her way back to the kitchen with a last-minute toast change—white to wheat. Hank smiled and shook his head. "Yessir, you only go as far as your stuff'll carry you. Well . . ." He winked at me. "Her stuff carried her to that last rush about an hour ago."

While I was at Mickie's, the neighborhood wiped the sleep from its eyes. Gray drizzly skies brightened long enough for tents to pop up and tent stakes to spike the soggy grass. Souvenir stands layered with plastic, and stuffed with red Bucky things, hit the curb lawns. The few tiny parking lots across from the stadium started filling with cars. Some "M Go Bluers," mostly red though. After a little coffee cake, and a couple of cups of coffee, after the band kids had gone over to the stadium and Mickie's settled into its normal game-day morning mode, I slid outside and roamed the smorgasbord. Wrigley Field on a Saturday afternoon in July—that's Camp Randall in the fall. It's a city stadium surrounded by a city neighborhood. Streets and street traffic, all sorts of friendly bars, tiny burger joints, Mickie's, and the Madison specialty: beer gardens, beer gardens, and more beer gardens.

A food tent sat in the grass across the street from Mickie's.

"No, I am not—you guys cut it out." A lady, probably in her fifties, was laughing. I'd asked a couple of old fellas working the coals who was in charge.

One had pointed to Lucy. "She darn near is the foreman."

The other chuckled, "Yup, the lady in red. She's the head cheese."

The Shriners' club's been putting up a tent on the grass triangle off Crazy Legs Lane (the old guys called it Elroy's Street) for almost a dozen years now. Lucy was the head cheese.

"Oh, we have lots of fun." Lucy smiled. Madison's Shriners, like most Shriners, look like a grandma and grandpa association. "Yes, lots of fun. And quite a few Shriners stop by. Folks from Ann Arbor and Minnesota. They buy a Coke and a hot dog. Sometimes they invite us up to their school." Lucy paused. She thought for a minute. "You know, we always say we'll stop by if we make it up there, and we never go. Maybe we shouldn't say that." She beamed a big smile. "Oh I guess it doesn't matter, it's just nice to be invited."

Kitty-corner a half block from the Shriners' tent, in a small parking lot, sat the neighborhood's biggest beer garden. A temporary wooden snow fence circled the lot. Coals were glowing in the giant cookers. A big sign out front said: OLD STYLE. It was sitting next to a smaller sign that said: Exchange Club—Dane County. And below it in little letters: "All Proceeds Go to Prevent Child Abuse."

"Over here we're boiling beer." The guy in charge, an old Badger himself, took the lid off the vat. The aroma almost picked me up by the nose and floated me away. "We throw in onions and green peppers, and red peppers, and when those brats are cooked, we'll let 'em soak.

"Ohhhhh, it is good! Real good. Come on back. In about an hour we'll be packed. And these babies"—he rolled some of the grilled brats into the vat—"they should be just about right by then."

No other Big Ten stadium has so many places to suck down a beer and munch a brat, and all only a block's walk from the stadium. Corner taverns, besides bursting at the inside seams, toss up fences and roll barrels out into the parking lot. Brats, taps, tons of people—overnight beer gardens engulf the neighborhood. The Big Ten Pub, the Copper Grid, and, down the street next to a big stone arch that tells the Camp Randall story, Jingle's roll out the mat. On the outside Jingle's is just a skinny brick front painted red and attached to a tin-can army barracks. It looks like a good stiff wind would send the place tumbling down the road. Inside, though, it's Badger heaven. Stuffed with football pictures and basketball shots, and on game day loaded with alums, it's the best place to learn about Badger football from the inside out! Or, once the beer garden gets rolling, from the outside in.

If it's burgers you want, Dottie Dumpling's Dowry grills up the best in the Big Ten. It also tosses in a good portion of character on the side at no extra charge. Christmas lights hang from the beams, all sorts of weird stuff crams the walls, and the tunes are great. On request— Motown, blues, Sinatra, Beatles—just ask the cook behind the counter and you'll get your wish. Then grab a brew, relax, and chow down on the biggest, juiciest, most loaded burger in the world.

For the most part, Camp Randall's got a nine-to-five crowd, a down-to-earth beer-and-brat crowd. There are exceptions—not, however, to the craziness. Train tracks that graze the Shriners' booth run a half block down from Mickie's and across the street from the stadium, where they provide a different kind of entertainment. A group of Badger fans from Whitewater rented a train, an engineer, caterers, and the tracks, and chugged over for the game. "We do it once a year. It's a great time!" a guy tipping a brew on the back platform of the caboose yelled down to me. "And best of all," his wife added, "we get to stay for the Fifth Quarter."

Beer gardens, taverns, train tracks—the whole neighborhood bursts with college football flavor. But it's tastiest right out on the sidewalks. Monroe Street, Randall Avenue, and Breeze Terrace, the three streets that cross at Camp Randall, are filled with all sorts of salesmen from ten o'clock on. Ticket scalpers take their annual Badger bath. They round up tickets for five bucks a crack—then almost beg folks to buy them for ten. Brats, peanuts, and popcorn get hawked from almost every corner. The Bucky Badger invasion—sanctioned and unsanctioned—flourishes. The *Bucky Wagon,* a vintage red 1932 fire engine, with W flags flying, cruises the neighborhood. The running boards are crammed with cheerleaders, while Bucky—a student hidden in red stripes, a badger body, and a huge smiling Bucky Badger head—stands in the back bed and gets waves from all sorts of folks, little and big. T-shirts, hankies, coats, sweatshirts—Bucky is stitched onto more cotton, polyester, and waterproof stuff than Mickey Mouse ever dreamed of. Bucky's Locker Room, a closet-sized room off the field-house, features university-backed Bucky stuff. "Fuck 'em, Bucky," hardly an official university slogan but definitely a Mad City favorite, pops up on quite a few homemade tailgate posters. And then there's the really off-beat. Some guy in a red T-shirt, shorts, and a big white cowboy hat stood on the Monroe Street sidewalk, his highly specialized Bucky item stacked below him in a big red box. "Get lucky with Bucky," he yelled out. Family crowds strolled past—moms and dads and kids wandering happily off to the Saturday afternoon football game. "Only two bucks apiece. Two for three bucks. Get 'em while they're hot. Bucky Badger condoms! And look"—he held one up—"Bucky's picture's on the package!"

Breeze Terrace, the block that hugs the big double-deck side of the stadium, really starts hopping about eleven o'clock. Streams of red fill the narrow road. Like Addison outside Wrigley, it's a beehive of fans, of tipping beers, and of sales pitches. Only difference: Wrigley Field blends quietly into Wrigleyville; Camp Randall's old concrete facade towers over Breeze Terrace. Plus, Breeze just bursts with kids! It's the college crowd block—the U's second frat row. Front-yard beer gardens bulge with college kids. Music pounds the block—not collegiate fight songs like over at the tailgates, but hard-core rock and roll. Live bands usually grab at least one front porch, while the rest crank supersized stereos up to ten and blow the speakers out. Local FM stations roll in the trucks and deejay the event. Gigantic inflatable Old Style cans, and Bud cans, and Spuds MacKenzie things hover over the yards. On the street, fifteen or twenty souvenir tables run a continuous string of more Bucky things for sale. "Get 'em here, Bucky Badger T-shirts only eight bucks." "Peanuts, fresh peanuts, in the shell." "Hot bratwurst." Breeze terrace swirls with loud noises and good smells. The block's a red-carpet explosion of energy rolled out from the Camp Randall gates. All this at a place where the football team stinks!

Camp Randall holds seventy-nine thousand—the Michigan game drew sixty-three thousand. That's not a lot compared to a few years back, before the student section crackdown and the football team turned to mush. Back then Camp Randall was an automatic sellout. Still, with rain pelting the band's pregame show, and every single human inside knowing that Michigan was gonna bury the Badgers, sixty-three thousand wasn't half bad. The crowd rumbled like any other Big Ten football crowd. Polite cheers greeted the final note of "The Star-Spangled Banner." Polite cheers and clap-alongs greeted "On, Wisconsin." But when the *Bucky Wagon* hit the stadium runway— stuffed with cheerleaders, with flashing lights and screaming sirens, with smoke shooting out of it, with Bucky himself perched atop the bed, both arms high in the air—the student section erupted. Moments later a gargantuan fifty-foot-tall Bucky Badger was inflated and hovered over the goalpost. The real Bucky got down on his hands and knees and bowed to the giant shrine. The student section erupted again. Out on the field, on the first play from scrimmage, Michigan's halfback Tony Boles blasted straight up the middle and went fifty-five yards for a touchdown. I figured it was up to the band and the students and that crazy Mad City tradition to keep folks around for the duration. The game sure wouldn't. In fact, for pure Badger football fans, it was gonna be one of those cover-your-eyes-and-pray days.

"Absolutely nuts." Bob turned away from the on-field massacre and told me about the old days. "This place used to be absolutely nuts. You used to have to kill to get in Section O."

About five rows down and a few seats to our right, a guy stood up, raised both hands above his head, and turned into a human O. He yelled, "OOOOOOOOOOOO." It sounded like some Bavarian religious chant. Four of his buddies jumped up and joined him: "OOOOOOOOOOOO."

"In the Fifth Quarter all the stands used to shake." Bob's wife, Sue, was a Madison grad too. They were up from Chicago. "Other fans would come here, beat us, then see us dancing in the aisles, and wonder what the heck was going on."

Section P caught wind of the "OOOOOOOOOOOOs" and answered, "O SUCKS P, O SUCKS P." The chant spread. O returned the favor: "P SUCKS O, P SUCKS O." Down on the field Mike Gillete, the Michigan kicker, booted his third extra point of the first quarter.

"Boy, they really cracked down."

"They started frisking people at the gates." Bob and Sue would swing back and forth between me and the game. Section O and Section P would swing back and forth between each other and the game.

"It got really paranoid after a while. You couldn't even take a sip. They had cops all over the top of the stands." Sue turned and pointed up. "There's just a couple up there today. But the last two years they had cameras and binoculars, and if they caught you drinking, they'd come down, grab you, then throw you out."

"And ticket you too," Bob added.

Section P erupted. I looked at the field; punt teams were trotting on. I looked at P. A tennis shoe was gliding up the stands. Hand to hand to hand, it darted up the stands like Tony Boles cutting through the Badger D. The closer it got to the top, the louder the chants from below: "OVER, OVER, OVER!" A skinny kid with long hair got it at the top. A cop, not more than fifty feet away, looked right at him and shook his head. The kid looked down at turned-around Section P. P chanted, "OVER, OVER, OVER!" He looked at the cop. He stood up and winged the tennis shoe out of the stadium. Section P cheered. The cop walked over to the skinny kid. He escorted him down the stairs. Section P booed.

"The cup fights used to be incredible."

"Students bought sodas just to throw them!"

"Five at a time."

"Big plastic cups with cellophane over the top. When they hit you, they exploded."

"I got hit once right here." Sue pointed to the top of her head.

"Pretty serious permanent damage." Bob laughed.

"First they got rid of 'em. Brought in paper cups. Now they're back to plastic."

"OOOOOOOOOOOO" rang out below. Another student had turned himself into a human O. From Section P, a plastic cup barrage exploded on him. Twenty or thirty, most of 'em empty, just pelted the kid. A couple of filled ones splattered Coke all over his chest. Almost instantaneously, the Os retaliated. Cups flew back in the opposite direction. The kid stood through the entire battle, never once breaking his chant.

"FIRST DOWN, WISCONSIN." The announcement rang through out the stadium. The student section roared—its loudest roar since the inflatable Bucky had risen up over the goalpost. With 9:37 to go in the second quarter, the Badgers had finally eked out a first down. The tide, however, had no intention of turning. Wisconsin's first-down string halted at one. Bo finished the half in Bo style—calling time-outs and sideline-passing to jack the lead from 35– to 42–zip.

At most football stadiums, half time is rush-to-the-restroom time. You spend it smashed into line with all sorts of people who spent half number one drinking either too much coffee or too much beer. At Camp Randall, half-time bathrooms are empty, the stands down under like a ghost town. Up and in, the PA blared, "LADIES AND GENTLEMEN, WE ARE PROUD TO PRESENT THE UNIVERSITY OF WISCONSIN MARCHING BAND." Cup fights stopped; "O SUCKS P" and "P SUCKS O" chants temporarily halted; everybody quit not paying attention to the field, and did. The band marched onto the turf. The stadium thundered. The student section clapped along to whatever number the band decided to play. Alumni stood and watched and joined the students. Camp Randall looked, sounded, and felt like a giant Baptist church revival. And when it was over, when the teams came back after cheers for the band, and cheers for the returning Badger football team, it was back to student section entertainment.

For the second half I drifted down to the big track surrounding the field. A lot of people do that in the second half of a Badger game. The band uses it to split into sections, take the pom-pom girls around, and do little numbers all over the stadium. Frustrated Badger fans use it to hang on the chain-links, about twenty feet behind Bo, and hurl insults at him. A lot of parents take their little kids down and get a photo with Bucky. Most, however, do not actually get to talk with the famous badger. I did! Well, at least to Saturday's Bucky backup.

"I was a tuba player as a freshman. A cheerleader for two years. And I always kind of wanted to be Bucky . . . so this year I am. And it's a blast," Matt Norman, Bucky's backup, grinned. "Women's volleyball's kind of a hassle. But football, basketball, and hockey—those are a lot of fun." Matt didn't look much like Bucky. Basically because he was wearing a red sweatshirt and blue jeans and just standing around down on the track. You see, scheduling is too tough to have only one Bucky. So in 1988 there were a record number of five! And in '88 just getting to be one of those five was a chore. Bucky's not just any badger off the street. There are interviews and essays and a selection committee—trying out is like making your way through a presidential primary.

"Mostly they're concerned with kids and stuff. They don't want some guy who's gonna be giving the crowd the bird, although the students," Matt laughed, "would probably love it. We go to thousands and thousands of elementary schools and old folks' homes. There are at least two things a week. Just the other day, I went to a surprise birthday party at the hospital for some sixty-year-old patient. They call you up, tell you where to go. You show up, pat bald people on the head for a little while. You do a lot of this. . . ." Matt gave me a thumbs-up. About twenty feet away, Bucky was doing the same to a little blond-haired girl. Mom was taking a picture. "But that gets a little tricky," Matt chuckled. "Bucky doesn't have a thumb.

"All of it's fun. Going to the schools, riding in the *Bucky Wagon*'s a blast." He glanced over at Bucky again. This time a little boy was perched on the fence. And Dad was taking the picture. "But I'll tell you, what's really cool is the kids. I was doing this thing last spring . . . here in the stadium. I sat down over there in the bleachers." Matt pointed over to where the band members sat. Usually, anyhow. They were out entertaining. "There weren't many people around. But within fifteen seconds there were twenty kids sitting on my lap knocking on my head, hanging all over me. It's just amazing. They really love Bucky."

"Is it tough?" I wondered. "You know, being Bucky when you're down by forty points."

Matt looked up at the scoreboard and laughed. "You mean forty-eight? No way. That's one thing about Wisconsin. This is a crazy place. Look at 'em." I turned and leaned against the fence. "We're getting killed, it's a shitty day. And they find their own little fun."

The student section had grown since half time. Cups, after they got

rounded up and somebody shouted "Fire," flew back and forth between O and P, and from across the field looked like swarms of gnats
hovering over the students. A wave started in the student section and
headed counterclockwise toward the press box. A normal-speed wave,
it carried around the horseshoe, through the alumni, past the press
box, and back around to the students. When it reached the start, it
zoomed into hyperspeed. Kids jumped up and down, and the supersonic wave buzzed back in a flash. Then, slow-mo speed, the wave
dragged around Camp Randall like a tape recorder running on dying
batteries. When the students got bored they just sent one clockwise—
rolling back into the first one. Waves crashed.

"The craziest thing," Matt laughed, "is that the alumni do it too."
Why not? I figured; once Madison's in your blood, it probably never
leaves you.

"One thing I didn't tell you about," he went on, "is all the fringe
benefits that go along with being Bucky. . . ."

The *Bucky Wagon* sirens screamed and the lights flashed. Cup fights
halted. Toilet paper rolls peppered the end zone. The band cranked out
"On, Wisconsin" and Bucky ran around in circles signaling number
one. The Badgers scored. The extra point was good. Another eruption.
Score: Michigan, 48; Wisconsin, 7.

Bucky ran over and high-fived Matt. He patted the top of my head
and then ran off. Cheerleaders jumped up and down and hugged the
Big Badger. "Yeah, lots of fringies," Matt yelled. "I'll tell you, you get
to know the cheerleaders really well." We looked over at the Badger
babes, busy cranking out a touchdown cheer. "Bucky rides in the same
van with 'em. He takes all the road trips with 'em. He practices and
parties with 'em." I glanced over again. "But one catch . . . sorry
. . . you got to be a full-time student."

One Badger TD later and the gun finally popped. The massacre was
history: 62–14. Anywhere else in the world the stadium would've been
empty, traffic jams already clogging up the neighborhoods, beer garden
taps back in full swing. Not at Camp Randall! On the press box side
of the field, a few folks were trickling toward the exits from the big
upper deck. But only a few. As for the student section, it was bulging.
Packed from the field way up to top row where the skinny kid had
chucked the tennis shoe from, students were socking in for their
favorite part of the day. Battered Badger football players dragged

themselves off to the locker room. Fans clapped. The band assembled in the end zone. Fans clapped louder. On the scoreboard, under QUAR-TER, a 4 disappeared and a 5 popped on; 62 and 14 stayed up, probably as reminders that nobody really cared. The main feature was about to begin! Mad City's finest moment . . . Camp Randall's Fifth Quarter.

A big red brass rectangle marched cleanly, and stern-faced, to a snare drum beat onto the field. The rectangle halted and faced the press box. Mike Leckrone hopped up on his ladder and looked down at his band. Horns pointed at attention up to their director. He raised his arms. *Tweet-tweet-tweet.* The band broke into Michigan's "Hail to the Victors." No big deal, I figured; it seemed like most postgame band shows—right? Well, sort of. Wisconsin had just been creamed, battered up and down the field. I half expected Michigan's fight song to be greeted with massive booing, for Wolverine fans to run for cover from a cup fight barrage. But I forgot "Victors" is a great clap-along. Why not? Badger fans joined Wolverine fans, clapping along to the Michigan fight song. They finished it off with a big round of applause.

*Tweet-tweet-tweet.* The rectangle about-faced to the student section. The students roared. Three more tweets and the band about-faced back toward the press box. Students groaned, and at the same time spun around. Almost all of 'em in O and P, from the first row to the top, stood with backs to the band. Three more tweets, and the band whipped back around to the students. Students, looking back over their shoulders, whipped around to the band with a roar. Five or six times, the two groups turned face to face, then back to back. Not a single note was played, no dances, no songs, the only tune from a little steel whistle. But each time the roar got louder, and the spin quicker. Michigan fans at the other side of the field, Michigan fans who had never been to Camp Randall before, just stood there, looked up at the scoreboard, squinted at the 62 and the 14, and scratched their heads.

Finally, *tweet-tweet-tweet* and the band, at attention, backs to the student section which was facing the press box, cranked out "On, Wisconsin." Camp Randall thundered. Everybody, folks in the upper-deck rafters, folks lingering around way down in the far end zone, students in O and P and L and K, clapped along. The students, though, clapping and singing their school fight song, were doing it while looking over their shoulders, with their backs to the band. When it ended—thunder—the student section rocked. They knew the rest of the day was theirs.

*Tweet-tweet-tweet.* The band spun to the students. Students spun to the band. Directors climbed down from their ladders, sprinted up the band lanes to the student side of the field. Ladders, a band member on each end, hurried along behind. Students cheered. Thousands screamed. They waved their arms over their head, and bowed up and down to the Wisconsin band—and the party really rolled.

Traditional and kind of misty-eyed, it started slowly with "Varsity," the alma mater. Like most, Wisconsin's is kind of slow and great for swaying to. Thousands of folks locked arms: former cup fighters buried the plastic hatchet, fans in the upper deck under the press box, down in the end zone, and I even think out of the corner of my eye I caught a few nervous Wolverine fans locking arms—everybody swayed. And sang! Only in Mad City would students know all the words to their alma mater. A slow soft swaying, sing-along, the tune rose softly out of the stadium up toward the heavens—and then, wham! All hell broke loose. The neat, stern band rectangle at attention out on the field broke formation and spun into all sorts of crazy shapes. Drums circled cymbals, horns circled Bucky, cheerleaders circled trombones, trumpeters even played sliding along the carpet on their backs. Band members who weren't playing polkaed. Band members who *were* playing polkaed. Fans in the stands, old folks in the upper deck, kids in the end zone seats polkaed. "Tequila," beer-hall sing-alongs, happy-go-lucky crazy tunes—Camp Randall turned into an "organized" nut house.

"Bud, we want Bud!"

"We want the Bud song!" In between tunes, students yelled for it. They screamed and chanted for it. Like Leckrone had said, they begged for it, and he made them beg for it!

"BUD! BUD! BUD!" They begged till another song popped, then they shut up and danced and clapped and sang along. They shark-clapped and they chicken-danced; they jumped up and down to the *2001* theme when the band jumped up and down and played the *2001* theme. Ten minutes, twenty minutes, a half hour, the place got crazier and crazier. It got louder and louder. I looked around and nobody, not a soul, was thinking about Wisconsin's rushing yardage for the day. Nobody cared if the Badgers were the absolute worst team on earth. O didn't even care if P said they sucked. Everybody was happy and waiting. Waiting for one thing. The final fling! The crowd favorite. And when it hit—just a few notes at the end of a chicken dance, those few *da do do do* notes that make you reach for a Bud—Camp Randall lost it. The second verse kicked in . . . "When you say Bud . . . *da do do do.*" The stands thundered. Clapping got louder and louder and louder, each verse . . . till it hit the ending . . . and all together the whole place shook . . . "WHEN YOU SAY WISCONSIN . . . YOU'VE SAID IT ALL!"

Two and three times the Bud song rolled. Louder each time. Then back to the chicken dance and more beggin' for Bud. And just when things were about as crazy as they could get, just when you thought people would start tossing themselves over the top of the stadium, the band stopped and played the alma mater. Students stopped—they swayed and sang along. After two verses, the Bud song fired up one last time. All the way through—clapping and singing and dancing. And with the scoreboard lighting up a big 5 with 62 and 14 underneath, with Wisconsin standing at a miserable 0–4, under a gray drizzly sky, Camp Randall beamed a great big smile. Everybody, Badgers young and old, cheerleaders and fans, band and Bucky Badger, and Michigan folks down in the corner, everybody let loose one last time and Mad City erupted . . .

". . . WHEN YOU SAY WISCONSIN . . . YOU'VE SAID IT ALL!"

# 4
# UNIVERSITY OF MICHIGAN
## THE WOLVERINES

| University of Michigan Ann Arbor, MI | Michigan Stadium |
|---|---|
| Best Breakfast | Angelo's |
| Best Bar | Fraser's Pub |
| Best Burger | Crazy Jim's Blimpy Burgers |
| Best of... | |

**The Best in Big Ten Country**

| FIGHT SONG |
|---|
| 1. Michigan |
| 2. Wisconsin |
| 3. Ohio State |
| 4. Michigan State |
| 5. Iowa |

"**O**h, he was just fabulous! He caught that kickoff on the five-yard line and took off up the left sideline, right towards us, and by the time he hit the fifty they were all behind him."

Herb Wagner's eyes lit up. He smiled and shook his head. "Red Grange. Oh, he was just fabulous!"

The year was 1924. Herb Wagner was twenty-six years old. He and his wife, Lillias, had road-tripped from Ann Arbor to Champaign, Illinois, in Herb's Model T Ford. Wide open it cruised at a cool thirty-eight miles per hour. They and another couple had left at 3:30 on Friday afternoon. They drove all through the night and reached town just in time to see the game. And although Michigan got hammered 39–14, Herb saw one of the greatest college football players of all time play maybe his greatest game ever. It was a day to remember. And a moment that popped into Herb's head whenever somebody asked him, "Who's the greatest football player you've ever seen?"

Herb is ninety-one years old. He has lot of college football memories. And a whole lot of University of Michigan football memories—461 games' worth going into Saturday's Michigan–Michigan State game.

I was lucky. I just sat back and listened. Al Renfrew, a friend of Herb's and ticket manager for the university, had told me about him. I'd asked if he knew anybody that represented the best in a Wolverine fan. Somebody a little bit special, who wouldn't mind talking to me. Herb Wagner, he said, was my man. So after I picked up my brother, Drew, at the bus station, we drove to the old guy's house, and there we spent almost two hours on Friday night, in a cozy living room, talking with Herb. About his life. And about Michigan football. The two went so well together.

"I came here in 1916 as a freshman. I didn't know anything about anything then." The old guy leaned back in his easy chair. He spoke surely and slowly. "Had never been to Ann Arbor. I just knew this is where I wanted to be." And where he wanted to stay too. After serving a year in the navy during the Great War, he came back to school and graduated in 1921. The next day he went to work for the university as an accountant. Forty-five years later, he retired. And all along the way he'd been a Wolverine football faithful.

"I can tell you how many games I've been to, 'cause I know the ones I've missed. Let's see, I missed two in 1918." That's when he was in the navy. "I missed one in 1944. I was in Chicago on business. In fact they were playing while I was on the train coming home. In 1968 I missed the Minnesota and Michigan State games. And in 1984 I missed the Ohio State game—the last game of the year. I've missed six home games since 1916." Which means that Herb Wagner has seen a Michigan team play football in Ann Arbor 421 times. Add another 40 road games, including all but one with the Spartans up in East Lansing, and you've got 461 games. Saturday would be 462.

Herb knows some magical moments. Like that day in 1924 when the Galloping Ghost hit the sidelines in Champaign. And some funny ones too. In 1925, the season after Red Grange streaked Michigan, Herb's "very good friend" the great Michigan coach Fielding Yost talked about the rematch—a game in which Grange hadn't scored, and Michigan had won 3–0. Herb chuckled thinking back about it. "Fielding said, 'You know, in that game the redhead didn't gain enough ground to bury himself.'" All the memories flowed so effortlessly. He remembered scores, and standings, and moments. He remembered Saturday afternoons like they'd happened last week. Pretty good for a guy who'd been around for almost a century. But then again, when you're talking from the heart, memories come easy.

Herb lives with his wife, Lillias, in Ann Arbor. She's a few years younger and a Michigan grad too. Herb told us, "Oh yes, she's a good fan. She seldom misses." At the door, Lillias revealed that she really went to the games for the sunshine. As for Herb, he just loves college football. And when I asked him why, he paused, he thought, and then he beamed. "It's a wonderful outlet for enthusiasm and it builds a good rapport among the student body. It also picks people up and gives 'em something to think about."

So we did a little thinking. The best Michigan team of all time? "That's a tough question." I guess it wasn't really fair to pin him down. I mean he'd seen seventy-two different ones. Even so, he had a couple of favorites. "The 1925 Michigan team was extraordinary. We had a terrific team. Bennie Oosterbaan was just a sophomore at the time." He told us all about the Bennie-to-Bennie (Friedman-to-Oosterbaan) passing combo, and described how Bennie O would catch the ball. "He made some of the most miraculous catches I've ever seen. You know how a basketball player tips the ball up in the air?" Herb looked at us and slowly reached his two arms up into the air as if he were tipping a basketball. We nodded. "Well, Bennie would be in the end zone with two men hanging on him and tip the ball up in the air and grab it and score a touchdown. Oh, Bennie was a great player.

"The '48 Rose Bowl team was terrific too." And Herb's third great Michigan team: Bo Schembechler's first year, 1969. That was the Michigan team, according to Herb, that won the most significant single game out of all of his 461. "Four different things were on the line that day," Herb noted of the afternoon in '69 when the Wolverines beat Ohio State 24–12. Slowly, steadily Herb went down the list. "First of all, the Big Ten championship. Second, the NCAA championship was at stake for Ohio State. Third was the Buckeye twenty-five-game winning streak. And fourth, the Rose Bowl was on the line. And when it was all over—we never expected to win that one—I remember sitting up in the stands and wondering what was going on down there. We really couldn't believe what was going on!"

Herb thought back to a game even crazier than Bo's big win. The game had taken place in 1923 at Camp Randall at the end of another Wagner road trip. Herb and Lillias, in a Studebaker this time, drove up to Madison with some friends. A hard-fought 3–0 Wisconsin lead turned into near riot on a second-quarter punt return. "Tod Rockwell, our quarterback and a very good runner, was waiting for the punt to come down. Well, the ball came down and hit him in the chest. Then it bounced sideways toward the sidelines and he ran over to his left and picked it up." You could tell from the excitement in Herb's eyes, and the anticipation in his voice, that Rockwell was about go on a mad dash. "Well, in those days the rules said you weren't down until you were all the way down. Rockwell picked it up in front of the Wisconsin sideline. Three or four times he was knocked off his feet. The Wisconsin players thought he was down. And the Wisconsin fans thought he was down too. But Rockwell got up and kept running. When he got to the fifty-yard line, a Wisconsin player running alongside him just gave up. Rockwell went into the end zone, put the ball down, and the referee signaled . . ." Herb paused and with a little more emphasis, kind of like he was in the booth announcing, said, *"Touchdown!*

"The Wisconsin crowd just went berserk. A couple fellows sitting in front of us turned around and wanted to fight. People were booing and throwing things on the field. That Wisconsin crowd . . ." Herb raised his voice about as high as a ninety-year-old guy can. *"Oh, they were just crazy!*

"At half time our band was on the field playing the alma mater." Herb explained that in those days all the fans from both sides got up and took off their hats for either school's alma mater. "Well, Wisconsin fans didn't stand up. And their band came right out onto the field playing 'On, Wisconsin,' which was of course just a mortal sin." He shook his head. "I think they apologized later."

Things got worse in the second half. "The referee's name was Robert Eckersaul. And all the fans were yelling, 'Get Eckersaul! Get Eckersaul!' Oh, and the women. The women were crazy. One little spark probably would've incited one of the biggest football riots of all time. My friend said that if it hadn't been for Prohibition, 'taverns would've been flowing red with blood.' "

The Rockwell dash was the last score of the day. Michigan won 6–3. In Madison, though, folks saw it a little differently. Herb took a breather from all the excitement and went on. "According to Wisconsin, the final score was Eckersaul, six; Wisconsin, three; Michigan, zero. They had it flashed all over campus and in the newspapers. When the game was over, the whole Wisconsin team circled around the officials to protect them. The Wisconsin coach had to take Eckersaul by the arm and escort him to a taxicab so the fans didn't get him. We walked out of that stadium, the Michigan group walked out of that stadium, and we didn't open our mouths at all. I think if we had opened our mouths, well . . . *Oh, they were just rabid!*"

As for Michigan State on Saturday, Herb's only wish: "A clean game. A fair game with no disputed decisions." It wasn't important, really, who won. I guess when you've seen all the Michigan–Michigan State games but one since 1916, it's not so much the outcome that matters. Just that the referee didn't end up lynched. Actually, one thing about the game did bother Herb. "I wish the rivalry was a little bit friendlier. I've always said this. I've said it time and time again. They're both fine institutions and there's room in this state for both of 'em."

After the Eckersaul stories, the Bennie-to-Bennie stories, after reminiscences about the Galloping Ghost cruising down that left sideline in Champaign, and finally after hearing just about all there was to hear about Wolverine football, we got up and Herb walked us to the door. The night was crisp. All three of us stood in the doorway. Herb was cold. He rubbed his arms to stay warm. But he had a few more stories he wanted to tell. He told us about some friends of his who'd been good Wolverine fans. One had started going to the football games in 1901. He'd seen the Wolves play for seventy-five straight years. He'd died in '76. Herb told us about another friend who'd passed away. A Michigan fan who had been to three hundred straight games—home and away.

Herb thought about his friends, he shook our hands, he wished us luck, and he thought a little more about Michigan football. "I've seen four hundred sixty-two games counting tomorrow. That's seventy-three years." He smiled. "I'd really like to make it seventy-five."

Ann Arbor has never been my Shangri-La. It's a place I've always put just about on a par with the nastier sections of New York City. A place I figured if I was real bad in this life, I'd somehow get reincarnated to in the next. It's a town I try real hard never to think about. In fact, about the only time I ever do is in the middle of some predawn nightmare. I've been that way for the past twelve years, ever since I

dedicated myself to green and white. Drew's a State grad too, and feels
pretty much the same as I do. Actually, aside from the "Magic years,"
when Kelser and Magic Johnson did a little Michigan-pounding, the
thought of Ann Arbor has probably kept a lot of Spartan fans awake
at night.

Four days softened me. One night softened Drew. As we drove away
from Herb's place and talked about how wonderful he was, Drew
turned to me. "You know, Michigan's like girls when you're in grade
school. You try to hate 'em. But sooner or later, whether you want to
or not, you just start liking 'em."

It was a weird way to put it, but Drew was right. Actually, I was kind
of relieved. Until it hit him too, I thought maybe I was getting sick or
something. All week long I'd been getting soft on Michigan. Ann Arbor,
the university, even the football program—as much as I wanted to
keep hating them, I just couldn't. I actually (gulp) kind of liked the
place. It grows on you. The town's filled with quaint, cozy little spots.
And so many of them are maize and blue and steeped in Michigan
football tradition. I'd visited with some really nice people who on
Saturday afternoons actually wore "Go Blue" shirts and booed the
Spartans. It was something I hadn't ever dreamed of. Something I
never ever wanted to admit. To be in Ann Arbor, Michigan, and actually
enjoying myself.

There are a lot of reasons the place wins you over. Not just a college
run of bars and taverns and pinball joints, Ann Arbor is bookshops and
restaurants and old buildings, molded into a small-city setting. Big
block M flags hang from downtown lampposts. The Michigan Theatre
still runs its 1950s marquee out front. College kids bustle everywhere.
It's a quaint place that weaves itself into the heart of campus.

The campus too is neat. A mix, classic in its architecture but young
in thought, it's still one of the country's most liberal schools. You see,
there's an air about the University of Michigan, one that in the sixties
used to run throughout all college campuses. It's a refreshing optimistic feeling, a "one person really can make a difference" attitude that
catches the U. It flourishes throughout town, but seems to radiate from
a quad at the center of campus called the Diag. The Diag's where kids
congregate, where Preacher Mike spends almost every day preaching
to anyone about anything, and where student-built wooden huts serve
as a reminder of South African apartheid oppression. Students meet at
the Diag. They talk. They lobby. They set up petition drives. They

issue student statements, a lot of them political. They even fill the wooden bulletin boards with announcements about something other than Greek rush dates: "Stop World Oppression," "End World Hunger," "Save the Environment Before It's Too Late." Ideals that used to occupy the minds of college students in a more liberal time still do in a more liberal place. In Ann Arbor, Michigan. At heart—still a throwback to the sixties.

Take that 1960s attitude and set it in a place that still looks like it's the 1860s—and you have the university.

The place is buried in red brick and ivy, and it does so many things the old-fashioned way. Like the way it sells football tickets. For the past fifteen seasons the Wolverines have led the country in attendance. For the past eighty-one games, going into Saturday, they'd seated over 100,000. How do you sell tickets at a place like that? With the help of technology? In a new plush office building with the most sophisticated computer on the market? With terminal linkups all over the civilized world? Try by hand. Yes, 101,700 seats, every game, sized up, shuffled, ordered, and stuffed by hand.

The ticket office sits on State Street, five or six blocks down from the hub of campus, next door to ancient Yost hockey arena. It's a tiny two-story red-brick building; ivy oozes over the front and reaches all the way up to the roof. The vines are so thick that one set of upstairs windows is just a wisp of glass buried in green. Alongside the red brick and ivy is a thirty-foot cast-iron gate, the old Ferry Field gate. Ferry Field was the old football field, the one from the days before TV and artificial turf. It's the one that Fielding Yost's boys played on. The field's gone but its archway remains. A sign stands between gate and doorway. Nothing fancy, just maize letters on a blue background, it says, "Ticket Office."

Inside is a miniature Wolverine Football Hall of Fame. The lobby is tiny and mostly wooden. Three small windows at the back look like wager windows at the racetrack. Behind those windows is where the 101,700 tickets get sorted, and where if you're lucky you might be able to grab one in the back row of the end zone for a Golden Gopher game. Glass cases line the lobby walls. Inside hang traces of the Big Ten's richest tradition. There are newspaper articles: January 1, 1948— "Michigan trounces USC 49 to 0." There's a painting of the Little Brown Jug with the 1903 game ball alongside. The real Jug, I figured, was probably stuffed away somewhere in Bo's office. Team photos capture some great images. The 1896 team, one of Fielding Yost's "Point a Minute" squads in 1904, and the 1947 Wolverines—the guys who trounced USC 49–0. A thick wool turtleneck sweater hangs in the case. Dark blue with a big block M on the chest, it matches the players' sweaters in the 1896 photograph.

In front of the cases, taking up a good chunk of the lobby, sits an old oak cafeteria table. Eight chairs tuck in underneath it. The table is actually kind of worn, and in about the same condition as when it was dragged out of the basement at the Student Union a few years back. The legs are painted blue. In the center of the tabletop is an engraving, a big blue M overlaid by the cut of a football. The grooved outline of the football is yellow. Engraved numerals on each side of it—19 on the left and 48 on the right—are yellow too. They identify one of Michigan's greatest teams. Inside the football, radiating out like the spokes of a wheel, are the 1948 season's final scores: "UM 13, MSU 7; UM 54, Indiana 0; UM 13, Ohio State 3." All nine games—victories. It doesn't say on the table, but it did in newspapers around the country back then, that the 1948 Michigan football team also won the national championship.

The table, by itself, is classic, but its best part is the scribbling that covers it. Names of students, some players, some not, are engraved all over the table haphazardly, in different handwritings, like tar names on a concrete pier. There's "Hoot," "Perk '51E,'" "DMB" under a carved-out goalpost, and "Charles A. Wilkenson Lit '51" inside a carved-out square. It's the 1948 version of a university tradition that goes back to 1904, when the Student Union first became an institution. Each year students engraved their names into an old oak table. The final football record, a source of collegiate enthusiasm, was recorded in the middle. The 1904 tabletop, with Coach Yost's team scores in the center, still hangs on the wall in the Union. The '48 version sits inside an ivy-covered building. A building that stands alongside the old Ferry Field gates where tickets still get doled out the old-fashioned way.

Football tickets, however, are available by other methods. Even on sellouts! And if you don't mind the price and dealing with unofficial University of Michigan ticket agents, just visit Ann Arbor's version of the New York Stock Exchange.

"One of my law professors said it's the last true place for capitalism." Joel was talking about where University Avenue runs into State Street, on the sidewalk in front of the Student Union. "That it's truly a buy-and-sell atmosphere. No constrictions. No restraints. Economics at its finest!"

Joel's the "daddy" of the State Street brokers. He's a graduate of the University of Detroit, and intends to be an athletes' agent down the road. But for the past ten years he's been a University of Michigan ticket broker. I asked if that meant he scalped tickets. He handed me a business card and told me, "I *sell* tickets.

"Ann Arbor's a cool place. It's pretty liberal. Kind of like Amsterdam. They let you smoke pot, they let you . . . they let you sell tickets. Charge you ten bucks and give you a license."

I ran into Joel for the first time on Thursday noon. But I saw him all week long—whenever I cruised the Union during primo ticket-selling hours (eleven to five). The Union sidewalk is where people dump extra tickets for the right price, and where if you want one for Saturday's game, you can always get one, also for the right price. The dumpers, depending on their experience, hang around and haggle with the brokers. If they just want to get rid of a pair, they pull the car up, park, hustle over, and make the sale. Since Joel was "on the clock," I got the Ann Arbor ticket-selling lowdown between sales.

"Who's your stiffest competition?" I meant besides the university.

"There's actually three big guys that sell up here." Just hanging around for ten minutes told me Joel was one of the big three. "One has gone to a juggling festival this weekend. The other guy's out of tickets. That's why he's not here. And then you got a bunch of little guys around too."

I looked around at the "little guys." Five or six black kids worked a corner. They didn't have business cards or Joel's ten years' experience; in fact they looked young enough to still be in high school. A haggard-looking white guy in a Wolverine hat and coat and blue jeans sat on the concrete wall in front of the Union. He looked like he was worth about a pair. Other "little guys" moved in and out, but didn't stay long. Two dudes—Willy, a tall stringy black guy, and Joe—seemed to be middle-of-the-roaders. Not little guys, but not among the big three. Each day I saw Joel selling, I saw Willy and Joe selling too.

"What's the biggest game you ever did?" I was familiar with some pretty good Michigan–Ohio State ticket-scalping stories. I had a friend who'd paid ninety-five dollars once just to sit in the Michigan end zone.

"Two years ago, Michigan–Michigan State tickets were going for a hundred to a hundred twenty-five dollars apiece. That's about the most I can think of them going for." He excused himself and hustled over to the corner. Some guy was dumping tickets. A minute or two later Joel was back, two tickets in hand. "Got the pair for a hundred thirty dollars." He stuck them with the other dozen. "Already got buyers at a hundred apiece.

"Where were we? . . . Oh, yeah, the best day. Michigan State's good, the Ohio State game's good too. But I can remember a game back in '80 or '82 against Purdue. And even though they were only going for fifty or sixty bucks apiece, I can remember crowds of people begging for tickets." He stopped, eyed a group on the corner, and went back to his story. "Those were back in the days of deregulation on TV. Teams could only be on two or three times a year. Purdue had Mark Herrman. That was a big game for us."

It's not all gravy, though. True—it's a living till the agenting business gets rolling. True—it's a great way for Joel to meet the athletes he might later represent. True—he turns a pretty sweet profit. But the State game Saturday was gonna be a tough one. "Nobody's got any tickets. Usually by now guys have handfuls of tickets. And everybody's selling." One of the reasons for lack of supply was the UM-MSU rivalry. Word was that everybody who had a ticket was going to the game. Another problem was the new student ticket booklets. "They almost took the student tickets off the market." Students, he told me, got their tickets at half price and faculty at three-quarters price. "It used to be everybody'd come out here and buy student tickets. It was a really big market. Great profit, plenty of tickets. Then Don Canham decided he didn't want the sales going on, so he put the tickets in books." Joel showed me one containing all four remaining Wolverine home games. "In order to get into the stadium on a student ticket, now you have to have the book. They rip the ticket out at the gate. It's kind of hurt sal . . ."

*Beep! Beep! Beep!*

Joel reached for his belt and turned off a little black beeper. "Excuse me—it's the office." He hurried over to a telephone booth a couple of feet away, stepped inside, and dialed a number. I checked out some of the other guys. Willy and Joe were just hanging out.

"I've been doing games here for the last seven years. But this one, this is a tough one. Ain't no tickets anywhere." Joel wasn't the only one having trouble finding tickets. So was Joe. "But on good games, man, it's great! Hey, Ohio State you can make a thousand bucks."

Willy, the tall stringy black guy, started laughing. "Man, you had to eat four hundred dollars one year on the Ohio State game." Willy turned to me. "You gotta go with the flow. Can't work yourself into the ground. Can't sell 'em for a thousand dollars apiece. Can't sell 'em for nothing if you ain't got 'em" He looked at Joe and laughed. "But if you work it right you can do all right."

Joel hustled back from the phone booth. "Four more buyers. Just can't dig up any tickets." Willy and Joe turned their palms up and shook their heads. "Nope, no tickets."

Ann Arbor is a little like Sheriff Andy Taylor's hometown, Mayberry, North Carolina, at least in the barbershop department. In Mayberry, Floyd's was always the best place for the guys to discuss Barney's latest mess. Well, Ann Arbor has itself a Floyd's or two. Coach Four Barbershop sits on the corner of State and Hill streets, a few blocks from the ivy-covered ticket office. Four doors away, sits the State Street Barbershop. They are both old-fashioned, come-in-sit-down-for-a-clip-and-a-shave places. Both are draped with maize and blue. And the stories floating about, well, they're something every true blue Wolverine fan should drop by and hear.

Coach Four is the older of the two. It's been around since the thirties. Jerry's owned it, as he puts it, "for the past seventeen seasons"—not years, seasons! The other place is run by Bill, a guy who twelve seasons ago worked for Jerry. He cut for a couple of weeks, branched off, and four stores away entered the Ann Arbor haircutting competition.

"Sure, we're alike," Jerry said, when I mentioned that it was kind of strange, two barbershops just a few doors away from each other, just a few blocks from Michigan Stadium in the middle of a college campus. "We're about as alike as K mart and Hudson's."

Actually the two shops are alike, but each owner would wear Ohio State Buckeye underwear the rest of his life before he'd ever admit it. Then again, like the ticket exchange they provide Ann Arbor with an example of the free-enterprise system in its finest form. Both shops have more team photos and jerseys and Wolverine stuff on the walls than any tavern in town. Both get every kind of customer, from old fans and former announcers (Bob Ufer used to stop by Bill's on Fridays before the big games), to football coaches and football players, to normal everyday college kids. Both guys are self-proclaimed "Uppers," which means they grew up in Michigan's Upper Peninsula. Both tell a pretty good story. And most of the good ones are about Michigan football.

"He's my buddy!" Bill, the State Street shop barber, was talking about the number 1 jerseys hanging above his mirrors. Bill's about thirty-five. He has a red beard and red hair, and looks like he's never been to a hairstylist in his life. "He's my buddy. Anthony stops in whenever he's in town."

Two number 1 jerseys hung on the wall above Bill. One was white with a blue number 1 on the back. The other was maroon, an old Michigan Panther jersey, with a white number 1 on the back and "Carter" on the shoulders. They were sandwiched between a string of other jerseys, mostly blue ones with maize numbers and maize letters. Harbaugh and Leach, Morris and Grant, and a couple of other not-so-famous versions.

"Anthony said as soon as he gets an extra Viking jersey, he's bringing it by."

A kid in the barber chair turned around to Bill. "OK, I need the sides shaved. Almost like a Mohawk. But not really. I just want it shaved a quarter of an inch on the sides, then on the top, and back about this tall."

"Kind of like a modified Mohawk?" Bill asked as he tied a dark blue apron around the kid. The apron almost hung to the floor. A big block maize M in the middle of it covered the kid's chest.

"Yeah, that's right. A modified Mohawk." The kid leaned back, relaxed, and watched the TV hanging in the corner. Geraldo was on to something sleazy. Interviewing a transvestite, about switching back, I think. The sound was loud enough for everyone to hear.

"How often you use that thing?" I pointed to the blue apron.

"Oh, this." Bill started in on the modified Mohawk. "Usually just Fridays and Saturdays. But on the big games—Michigan State and Ohio State—we pull it out all week long."

I gazed around the place. Unbelievable! It was a Michigan fan's dream. Signed basketballs, signed footballs, a goalie facemask, and a hockey stock. There was 1980s winged Michigan football helmet, and one even more classic—an old leather prefacemask model. Team photos, football and basketball mostly, but also an occasional hockey or baseball team mixed in. The place was just covered in Wolverine.

But what made it so neat was that everything else could've been pulled from Floyd's. The swivel barber chairs looked like they were a good thirty years old and the seats for waiting customers twice that. Bottles of all sorts of different-colored tonics crammed the shelves. Shaving cups had shaving-cream brushes sticking out of them. A few family shots even grabbed open inches of shelf space. In fact there probably weren't two square feet inside the place that didn't have something covering them up.

Like all good barbers, Bill cuts hair and talks equally well, and at the same time. Which worked out great for me. I got an answer to every wall-photo question I asked. And a few extras too. "We have two customers who won gold medals this fall, Jim Abbott and Greg Barton. Barton's the kayak kid. And Jimmy, he was just in last Saturday. He's a great kid. Saw him pitch a couple times last spring." Bill shook his head. "The kid has a hell of an arm. Mark my words, he's gonna make the bigs."

"How 'bout the football games? Go to any of them?" That was like asking Bo if he ever wore blue.

"Every one! Game days we're open till eleven A.M. I usually get over there by noon."

"Thanks." The kid in the chair hopped out. He turned to me. "Nobody back home in Holly can cut hair like this." The finished product kind of reminded me of Michigan's football helmet. And I wondered aloud if the barber had ever cut a block M into anybody's hair. It seemed like a collegiate thing to do.

"You know, a couple years ago I cut the football helmet in Vitale's hair." He gave the kid his change and thanked him for stopping by. "The All-American center. Know him?" I nodded that I'd heard of him. "Well, I cut the helmet kind of like this." He outlined it on the top of his head. "Did a great job too. He went down to the football building a little early. He had a meeting that afternoon. Bo saw him first, and said, 'You come to the meeting like that and don't plan on playing football here the rest of the year.'" Bill laughed. "Bo don't like that kind of crap. I'll tell you, ole Vitale was back here in a flash. Begged me to shave it off. So I did." Bill shook his head. "I worked my butt off on that helmet."

"I call it my hobby." Jerry, the seventeen-season vet, revealed his haircutting philosophy. Once Geraldo had finished his interview over at Bill's I'd moseyed the four doors down to Coach Four. "Hey, if you can pay the bills, keep the wolves off your back, don't treat it real serious, and have fun, that's what it's all about."

Jerry popped a Labatt's for me. He was working on one himself. So was an older guy who was getting a trim—beer in one hand, a magazine in the other, with an eye on Geraldo, who was into another sleazy interview. It was almost quitting time at Coach Four.

"That's what life's all about, eh? After they put you in the ground and kick the gravel over you, you're gone. Doesn't matter how serious you were or how much money you got. When you're gone, you're gone." He put down the scissors and took a swig. "You can't send it ahead. You can't take it with you."

Jerry's place is nearly as maize and blue as Bill's—just a little less basketball, a little more hockey, and a lot of football. The basics, though, are about the same. A bench for customers. Piles of things to read. A couple of swivel chairs for cutting. A TV hanging on the wall in the corner. Jerry's specialties, however, are not jerseys. They're photos. And a couple are classics.

The date is January 1, 1979. The place, Pasadena, California—the Rose Bowl. The scene's a familiar one for most Michigan fans, and probably the source of plenty of maize-and-blue nightmares. The Wolverines, in white, backs to the wall, are entrenched in a memorable goal line stand. USC is running a play into the middle of the Michigan line. Number 12, Charles White, in Trojan maroon, is airborne. He's hovering somewhere over the one-foot line. He's about to tumble into the end zone. A line judge is about to signal a touchdown and give Southern Cal a lead it'll never relinquish. The problem is, the ball's lying on the ground back at the two. It's the phantom touchdown. The one that never was. The one that won the '79 Rose Bowl. Why is the horror show trapped in a cheap gold frame and tacked on Jerry's wall? Well, this particular photo provides a couple of extras that *Sports Illustrated* never did. First off, it's taken from somewhere up in the stands, on the press box side, I think. It looks right over Mr. White's shoulder pads and into the end zone. Not only do you get a great view of the non-touchdown, but you also get a great look at somebody else's view. Standing on the end line, not more than twelve yards from the play, hands on knees, staring straight at the Trojan and the loose football, is the back judge. Somebody's taken a black felt marker and circled the official's head. A line runs from the circle to the side of the photo, and at the end of the line a legitimate question is posed: "Is this man blind?" The guy asking the question has signed it: "Bo Schembechler."

Another classic hangs next to the door. It's a portrait of a man in one of those 1970s checked sports coats. He's doing something he doesn't do much on TV—smiling. Across the bottom of the happy photo is another message, this one about haircuts instead of football. It reads: "To Jerry, the worst barber in Ann Arbor—'Go Blue'—Bo."

Jerry is Bo's barber and has been ever since Bo came to Ann Arbor in 1969. "I even cut Bo's littlest guy's hair. I gave him his first haircut. I gave him his prom haircut. I just gave him a haircut for school. He left for Miami of Ohio."

I was still caught by the Bo photo. The one where he ranked Jerry last in town in the haircutting department. I wondered how he'd gotten Bo to take that blue hat off long enough to cut his hair. Hell, the picture was the first time I'd ever seen Bo's head.

Jerry went on. "Yeah, ole Bo, he'll come in about every six, eight weeks. I'll trim it up. It'll start looking like crap. But he'll go another month before he comes back. He's loyal, though. There's only been one time in twenty years he's gone someplace else. And that was out at the Rose Bowl."

Jerry told me the story that Bo had told him about that one time. Whenever it was Bo talking, Jerry used a cranky kind of voice. The way Bo talks. "Bo was out on the West Coast and needed a haircut before the Rose Bowl. So he asked the UCLA coach where to go. Coach told him to go to this certain salon that he went to. He says, 'Well' "—Jerry started talking cranky—" 'I went in and there were all these sissies cuttin' hair. I said, to hell with this, I'm not going here. So I walked back outside, got in my car, drove on down the boulevard. It was getting a little darker and a little darker. I saw a rickety barber pole on the side of the building. I got out of my car and went inside. There were these three Mexican barbers, tattoos up and down their arms, and I said, "Can you cut my hair?" And one said, "No problem." I said, "High and tight all the way around." Well, he finished. I got out of the chair and said, "How much?" "Three-fifty," he said. I gave him four bucks. I figured what the hell. I'd let him keep the fifty cents.' "

Jerry took a swig. "That's Bo all right."

# MICHIGAN STATE AT MICHIGAN
*Michigan Stadium,*
*Ann Arbor, Michigan*

| Standings | Big Ten | | | All Games | | |
|---|---|---|---|---|---|---|
| October 8, 1988 | W | L | T | W | L | T |
| INDIANA | 1 | 0 | — | 3 | 0 | 1 |
| ILLINOIS | 1 | 0 | — | 2 | 2 | — |
| MICHIGAN | 1 | 0 | — | 2 | 2 | — |
| PURDUE | 1 | 0 | — | 2 | 2 | — |
| IOWA | 0 | 0 | 1 | 2 | 2 | 1 |
| MICHIGAN STATE | 0 | 0 | 1 | 0 | 3 | 1 |
| OHIO STATE | 0 | 1 | — | 2 | 2 | — |
| MINNESOTA | 0 | 1 | — | 2 | 2 | — |
| NORTHWESTERN | 0 | 1 | — | 0 | 4 | — |
| WISCONSIN | 0 | 1 | — | 0 | 4 | — |

**Other Big Ten Games:**

NORTHWESTERN AT MINNESOTA

OHIO STATE AT INDIANA

PURDUE AT ILLINOIS

WISCONSIN AT IOWA

The University of Michigan football program has always reminded me of the Romans—big and tough and pounding on the little guys. The Michigan State football program has always reminded me of the Christians—not so big or tough and always getting pounded by the Romans. You see, I didn't turn Spartan till after Duffy Daugherty left. About all I know is Bo. And since he came around in '69, it's been pretty much

"M Go Blue." In nineteen Bo seasons Michigan has won fifteen times and Michigan State only four. So how do I survive come Michigan week? Easy—I think back to only two games. The first, 1978—Eddie Smith and Kirk Gibson and State, 24; Michigan, 15. And more recently, 1987 in East Lansing. A Big Ten championship, a Rose Bowl win, and best of all, State, 17; Michigan, 11. Careerwise, as far as I'm concerned, we're up 2–zip. The fifteen losses? They don't exist, in mind or in conversation. I honestly don't even remember them. And since my two teller-machine secret-code bank-card numbers are 2415 and 1711, the wins pop up daily. Consequently, each season I'm optimistic. Each year, regardless of the spread, by game time I'm convinced we'll win. Some years more than others, in '88 less than most. The Romans were rolling. The Christians—well, it looked like feed-us-to-the-lions time.

It just didn't make any sense! The defending Rose Bowl champs, my home team, the season of *Big Ten Country,* and the '88 Spartans couldn't cross a goal line. One TD against the always-tough Scarlet Knights of Rutgers, none against Notre Dame. A big seventeen combined points against Florida State and Iowa. In four weeks, State had swirled to three losses, one tie, and three TDs. The D was still lethal, still just hammered on teams, but a loss to Michigan would make it coffin nail time. And the season was barely a month old. Michigan, on the other hand, just a kick or two away from 4–0 and a number one ranking, was about to explode. The Wolverines almost beat Notre Dame. They should've beaten Miami. And they were coming off a Badger massacre. Plus, they had that '87 loss at East Lansing to avenge. Add all that to a stadium filled with about a billion Michigan fans, and a band cranking out an endless round of "Hail to the Victors," and things didn't look so good. But being the ever confident Christian that I am, I ignored the obvious. Drew and I rehashed old stories, the two big wins, Saturday morning on our way to Angelo's for breakfast.

Angelo's is the greatest breakfast place in the Big Ten. Your classic brick-front one-room hole-in-the-wall, it sits on the corner of Catherine and Glen across the street from the university medical center. Game day from 8:30 on, it's packed. Folks curl around the block in an hour-long wait. All just to eat toast, hash browns, bacon, and eggs that happen to be the best on earth. The folks that run the place are great. Their fresh-baked raisin bread is world renowned. And each table gets its own Heinz ketchup bottle—for the whole breakfast!

We'd gotten up early. The place was bustling. Customers hustled for tables; waitresses hustled for customers. But no hour-long waits yet.

We grabbed a counter seat next to the cash register. Since we were the first Spartans to arrive and since almost everybody in the place was in maize and blue, our State green glowed.

"Go, green!" A waitress scurried by. She wasn't ours, but had noticed our colors. She was a State fan.

"Go, white!" I popped back. I guess by now it's a reflex.

"I don't like football." A lady sitting next to me at the counter, a regular, answered my "You going to the game?" question. "Too violent. But I come here every Saturday morning. Watch 'em come in. All dressed in blue and yellow. They have a lot of fun." She took a sip of coffee. She smiled. "I go to all the basketball games."

Drew had spun around on his stool and was talking with another green-and-whiter who'd dropped in. Booths and counters and everything else at Angelo's are pretty close together. It's kind of like eating in the dining room back home. "Mandarich is finally back." Drew was talking about the All-American mountain who played tackle for State. The NCAA had bumped him three games for some stupid rules violation. Still, it'd given us an out. Our lousy start we attributed to no left tackle. "Defense looks good. If McAllister doesn't screw up we got a chance." McAllister was the State quarterback. He'd been screwing up a lot of late. Odds were he'd continue the string against Michigan.

"Maybe we'll pull a '78," the green-and-whiter suggested. Good man, I thought. He thinks like a Christian.

"Twenty-four to fifteen," I interrupted.

"Smith to Gibson." We all three nodded our heads.

"What can I get you?" A heavyset Greek lady was working the register and the counter.

"Get the eggs Benedict." The Spartan waitress cruised by again, this time with a trayful of breakfasts. "You'll like it!"

"Can't question a Spartan. Eggs Benedict and coffee, please."

"You got it. And you, sir?" The Greek lady turned to Drew. He was going for the light breakfast. Planned on loading up at the tailgates.

"I'll have some Frosted Flakes."

The Greek lady looked at him. She smiled a great big smile and growled . . . "Grrreaaat!"

Mrs. Angelo, that's what they call her. Well, that, and some folks call her Mom. She's a character. She and Angelo opened the place in 1956. He'd just arrived from the old country. She'd lived in Ann Arbor all her life. They got married and built their lives around the restaurant. In the old days both of them worked all hours, he on the grill, she waiting tables. They served everything—breakfast, lunch, dinner, and then some. Now it's just breakfast and lunch. And the place only stays open till four o'clock instead of eight. Angelo's retired. His son Steve, who grew up on the grill, runs the show. And as Dad did for twenty-five years, he arrives before dawn to bake the bread. Mom still helps out on game days, runs the register, and visits with folks. And growls like Tony the Tiger.

"Always this crowded?" I wondered.

"Game days and Sunday mornings are the big days. But yeah, there are usually a few folks here." Mrs. Angelo smiled.

Drew looked around. "How come, I wonder?"

The answer was in front of us. The cereal was cereal, but the eggs Benedict was gorgeous! Fresh Angelo's bread, Canadian bacon as thick as a good-sized stack of flapjacks, and a couple of upside-down eggs you couldn't even see, they were swimming in so much hollandaise sauce.

"Enjoy, boys."

Breakfast eaten, confidence rising, we headed up toward campus. I figured I might as well take Drew around and show him that you could loathe maize and blue but still like Ann Arbor. First stop, the ticket brokers at the the "New York Stock Exchange."

"I'm clean, man. Gotta reload." Willy was out. Tickets were still tough to get ahold of. For most guys anyhow. Not for Joel—he had a fistful and was already wheeling and dealing.

All the brokers that I'd seen during the week were there. Stringy Willy and Joe, a couple of black kids, and some of the other "little guys." Without tickets, though, they didn't have a whole lot of leverage. Capitalism in its truest form was taking a beating . . . at least from the brokers' point of view.

"About noon I'll head down to the stadium. They'll be plenty down there." Willy didn't seem too stressed by it all. He was pretty good at playing it cool, considering the circumstances. In fact most the fellas were just kind of hanging out and playing it cool.

All but the State Street "ticket daddy." Joel bustled up and down the walk, like a Wall Street businessman at rush hour. He worked his green roll of bills like a First National Bank teller, and cemented himself at the top as one of State Street's "big three." He stopped and said hi.

Stayed long enough to show us a future investment, a pair of Indiana-Michigan tickets.

"I picked 'em up this morning." A half-dozen State tickets joined the Indiana pair. "State tickets are up to a hundred dollars for the sidelines, seventy-five in the end . . ."

"Who's got tickets?" A couple of guys dressed for Saturday college football hit the exchange. An "Excuse me" and Joel was back on the prowl.

State Street, the campus main drag that links the stock exchange with the barbershops, and further down a right turn to the football stadium, is the Michigan "Game Day Ave." Frats and school buildings up by the Union give way to convenience stores, breakfast places, and finally the old, old athletic buildings as you close in on the stadium. About ten, when we cruised, the people stream was just a trickle. Blue, yellow, and a little bright green dotted the sidewalk. Two hours later it'd be a thick flow of maize and blue.

We dropped in on the two barbershops. Jerry had just got back from coaching his kid's hockey game. He was inside getting ready for a ten o'clock appointment, but he wasn't too busy to tell Drew the Bo haircut story. And not too busy to toss a couple of jokes in on the side or to wish us luck on the way out.

Four doors down, leaning against State Street Barbershop window, also waiting for a ten o'clock customer, Bill was sipping a beer and watching the crowds thicken.

"This is great, isn't it?" Bill was prepared. Had on a blue sweatshirt with a little football helmet on the lapel. It said "Michigan" above it and "Football" below it. A big block M smacked his blue ballcap.

"It'll get thicker and thicker. Right up till game time. Then it turns into a ghost town." He took a swig. "The empties, toilet paper rolls, confetti—it'll look like they ran a parade through here." He laughed. "And that's before we beat ya!"

"We'll see." Drew defended the green.

"Hey, Bo—let's not forget last year." I was trying hard not to.

Bill laughed, took a break from his lean, and led us inside. One more mini-tour of the Michigan jersey gallery. A few more stories. And a photograph, one I'd missed the day before.

"Oh, that's my highlight. Sorry, I must not've showed you yesterday. Yeah, we had two three-time All-Americans in the place at the same time." The photo showed Bill smiling, with a full red beard, between his "buddy" Anthony Carter and Herb's all-time favorite, Bennie Oosterbaun.

"Pretty nice, eh?"

The door swung open. A college kid, out of breath, burst inside. "Hey, Bill, sorry I'm late. Still got time?"

"No problem." The kid hopped up in the chair. Bill sat down his beer and pulled out the blue apron with the block M in the middle. The "big game" apron. He shook it and tied it around the kid.

"Mohawk?"

"Not today, thanks—just a trim."

A couple of doors down from the State Street barbershop, a little closer to the stadium, sits Mo's Sporting Goods. The little store. The big Mo's is uptown. Mo's is the best souvenir store in the Big Ten. Best, not because of its color choice. Maize and blue cram the place. Not because of the stuff it sells either. T-shirts and key chains, sweatshirts and bumper stickers, aside from the logos, are pretty much the same everywhere. It's not even the sixty-year-old pecan-wood custommade cabinets that hold all the stuff that make Mo's such a classy place. No, Mo's is best 'cause of what it doesn't sell. It's the only true blue, totally loyal, "we-refuse-to-carry-anything-but-the-hometown-stuff" store in the world. Nobody else does that. Every college in the country has a place where you can get just about anything with "your guys' " logo on it. And each store is buried in school colors. But they've all got one thing, at least, from someplace else. Not Mo's. Not even a dribble. No Michigan State. No Illinois. No Ohio State. Nothing, unless of course you count the "Happiness Is Crushed Buckeye Nuts" bumper stickers.

We peered inside the window, were barraged by maize and blue, decided to pass it up, and continued down the walk. All along the way we'd been totaling up just what had to happen if the Spartans were going to win. Aside from a little intervention on God's part, we came up with the basics. No McAllister interceptions, no Spartan fumbles, a good kicking game, and the officiating had to be good. Most important though, André Rison had to break a long one. Rison was State's '88 version of Gibson. In fact, he'd already broken almost all of Gibson's receiving records. Well, all but touchdown catches. Like I said, green shirts weren't getting into the end zone much in '88. But today, we figured, was gonna be Rison's day. We just knew it. And if it was, we knew the Christians—er, the Spartans—had a chance. Victory, we'd convinced ourselves, was possible! And with that, we crossed Hoover Avenue into University of Michigan tailgate land.

It just doesn't get any better than University of Michigan tailgate land. Five square blocks of hatchback popping, pulling out the card tables and the cookers and ice chests, big blue flags with that maize block M, and "Hail to the Victors" fight songs. Each section is set off by a building or a baseball field or a string of trees, so that it's in its own little world. It's like roaming through separate towns of tailgaters. Grassy spots next door to Yost Arena, the ancient hockey stadium, are the first to go. And they go early. It wasn't even eleven o'clock and coals were already glowing. Back behind the railroad tracks that cut the square in half, lots were filling up too. People piled out on the grass, fired up the cookers, and talked Michigan football. Across Stadium Boulevard, just south of the Michigan Stadium, stretches the university golf course. Behind a chain-link fence that keeps slices from shattering windshields, more food, more fun. Vans and motor homes and all sorts of assorted cars drive right up and in and line the grass. Folks grill brats under pines and maples. It's gotta be the best single place in the world to pop a hatch. And if you're a Wolverine, probably the closest thing to heaven. Back across the street, next door to Chrisler basketball arena, more parking lots swallow up the stadium. This time concrete ones with yellow lines. The big football bowl sits up above the cars. Michigan's hardest-core tailgaters sock in below the bowl, eat and drink, and reminisce about all those Wolverine victories.

Once we hit the main lots, Drew and I split up. He had a couple of buddies he wanted to look up. I needed to find more Spartan fans who remembered 1978. I figured the more Eddie Smith stories I heard, the better chance history would have to repeat itself. We decided to meet back at our ticket gate. First, though, I tossed Drew my mini–tape recorder. He really wanted to dig up an interview, maybe find somebody who used to watch State-Michigan games back when it was the Spartans who'd done the pounding. Me, I just roamed and concentrated. No fumbles, no interceptions, get Rison the ball, and we'll be all right.

A giant carnival—that's the Chrisler lots. A giant carnival on opening day if you catch them with Michigan State in town. The colors and sounds and the smells—they just explode. Big blue flags saturate the place. On Saturday, a few green ones mixed in. A couple of Winnebagos even flew the two together, side by side, with the Stars and Stripes sandwiched in between. Brats and burgers and chili smells smoked together and floated about. Thousands of folks were laughing and talking, toasting the game, toasting the series, and just toasting the sunny day. I sifted through and sampled the sights. I bumped into Wolverine fans who had speakers blaring "Hail to the Victors." I bumped into State fans who had speakers blaring "The Spartan Fight Song." I bumped into a Michigan State family that wasn't too happy about a particular situation.

"It's no problem. It's no problem." It wasn't a problem for Mr. Davis, the father of Travis Davis, State's All–Big Ten junior lineman. It was a big one, though, for his wife, Travis's mom.

"Look at this." Mrs. Davis turned to page 150 of the Michigan–vs.– Michigan State program. She pointed to one of the little black-and-white photos under "Meet the Spartans," a photo that looked like it'd been taken in a five-for-a-dollar supermarket booth. "This isn't Travis . . . this is, I don't know who this is."

"It's no problem. It's no problem, don't worry about it." Dads don't worry about supermarket photos on the back pages of Saturday programs. Moms do. Sisters, on the other hand, get to wear their brothers' Rose Bowl jerseys, if they played in one. Gwen Davis modeled her big brother's green jersey—a white number 75 on the back, with red roses on the shoulders.

"What do you think, Mrs. Davis?" I tried to get her mind off the program screw-up. "We gonna win today?"

She smiled. "Positive thinking. It'll take positive thinking."

"We're thinking positive," Gwen popped up.

"Positive thinking." Mrs. Davis busted out laughing. "And the good Lord willing."

Another of the Davis clan strolled up, one who hadn't seen the program. Mrs. Davis flipped through the pages. "Look at this, they got Travis . . ."

"It's no problem. It's no problem."

The closer it got to game time, the bigger the crowds got, and the more festive the occasion became. Both bands added to it. The Spartans assembled at a gap in the Winnebagos, back by the fence that marked the end of the lot and edge of the railroad tracks. I was roaming

up near the stadium when they cranked it up. Scrunched against tailgaters, the green-and-white band paraded up the drive. *Boom, boom,
boom*—snare drums and cymbals kept time, while stern-faced kids led
by the flags and the twirlers marched past all the tailgaters. "Go, State,
Go!" "Go, State, Go!"—the chanting marchers kept time with the
drumbeat. At almost the same time from the other side of the lots,
fresh from Revelli Hall, the Wolverine band hit the lots. Marchers
chanted to a pounding drumbeat. *Ba ba ba boom boom boom.* "Go,
Michigan . . . beat the Spartans!" "Go, Michigan . . . beat the Spartans!"
"Go, Michigan . . . beat the Spartans!" The Wolverine band paraded
on toward the stadium. Behind them like a gush of water, filling the
void, maize-and-blue fans bore in on the gates. It looked like a billion
people pushing toward the place.

"Bob, over here!" It was Drew. He caught me at our gate. The gate
broke a big Michigan Stadium chain-link fence, and was bottlenecked
with all sorts of people.

"You won't believe it. I interviewed Mark Nichols." Nichols was
bad! A Roman when it came to hitting, now an alum like us, Nichols
had been State's meanest defensive lineman in '87. He was Drew's
favorite Spartan and probably the main reason nobody could run on
State last year. "It's great! You gotta hear it!"

We were scrunched into a mass of bodies. Elbows and legs and
stomachs all one. The ooze almost stood still. Drew fumbled for the
start and pushed the play button.

"Mark Nichols . . ." It was Drew's voice. "I just wondered what you
thought of the Michigan–Michigan State rivalry."

"The Michigan game . . ."

"That's Nichols. Is he great or what!" Drew was pumped.

"It means a lot. It's one of the great rivalries in the country. And
to me it means a lot 'cause . . . well, 'cause I hate Michigan." Yeah!
Drew and I high-fived. Nichols went on. "It's more than a game. It's
kind of a war, a type of thing that comes from within, that nobody can
explain unless you been through it. When the Michigan game rolls
around, nothing else in the world matters."

Drew continued, "Do you remember your best hit at State? One that
sticks out in your mind?"

Nichols laughed. "Yeah, last year in the Michigan game. I forget who
it was. One of their tackles was pile-judging." We figured "pile-judging" was football player lingo for standing around with your thumbs in

your butt. "I had about a twenty-five-yard sprint. He was just standing there, wasn't looking. A blindsider. I hammered him."

Yeah! The ultimate Roman hit, a blindsider, dished out for a change by a guy in a green-and-white uni. The war was on! There was no doubt about it. We knew, with the Nichols legacy intact, State was gonna roll!

From the outside Michigan Stadium isn't much. An asphalt drive bordered by Domino's Pizza stands circles it. It lets you breathe again after being sardined at the gates. You can't see in. The stadium's only a story or two high. It actually goes down instead of up and makes you wonder just where in the hell everybody sits. But once you hit that ramp, once you go under and back up and into the sunlight again, and are barraged by all the color and sound of Saturday college football, you just shudder. It's like walking into a city. A city full of Michigan fans. And you realize real quickly where they came up with the term "home field advantage."

Michigan Stadium is not as crazy as Camp Randall, or even as loud as a good day in Spartan Stadium. Later on on my trip I'd find out that both Iowa's Kinnick and Ohio Stadium rocked its socks off. But the Wolverine lair intimidates. Its size alone blows you away! Over a hundred thousand bodies for the past fourteen seasons, the past eighty-one games. Acres and acres and acres of maize on a sunny day. Acres and acres and acres of blue on a cold one. It just bursts with color, and everywhere but one little block in the end zone it's Michigan colors. This Saturday, State's end zone green just kind of melted away among the 106,208 fans, the second-biggest crowd ever to see a college football game.

The Michigan crowd isn't a constant eruption. It's more like a lumbering giant. Fans watch and they wait and entertain themselves in the process. "GOOOOOO" rises in a long, loud chant from the far end zone. It drifts like rumbling thunder across the green carpet. A "BLUE" roar answers. "GO"—BLUE!" "GO"—BLUE!" The two slowly thunder back and forth, while down below Bo battles for field position. Thousands of students pull out their car keys and shake them on key plays. Marshmallow fights, the Big Ten's new student section in-thing, kills the between-TD time. But when the football team gets rolling, when Bo's soldiers cross the goal line, that's when the place explodes. ABC cameras shake. Toilet paper rolls fly. And that fight song fires up. Each "Hail, Hail to Michigan" is met with a "HAIL,

HAIL" roar from the crowd and fists thrust into the air. It's usually about that time you give up on the game plan and go back to praying for a little intervention from God.

State didn't wilt, though. They hung tough for the first half. Both teams sized each other up. Both teams ran the ball. Just what Perles needed. Something close to 0–0 so we had a chance, so that Rison could make the difference. Michigan opened up a 10–0 lead, and left the field for the bands to duke out half time.

"What do you think?" We were still in it. Drew was optimisitic.

"Yeah, but we're not moving. No offense. We need a break." I thought back to the '87 game at East Lansing. "One of those seven interceptions would sure be nice now." With one exit per section, and ninety rows of folks cramming it from above and below, half time at Michigan Stadium is not bathroom time. Unless you want to stand on steps for twenty minutes.

"Rison, we gotta get the ball to Rison." Drew was right. He hadn't touched it in the first half. Somehow he had to in the second.

Well, he didn't! And a game that had stayed close for two quarters swirled to Spartan disaster in the third. Michigan's first pass of the second half was picked off and returned to the Wolverine four-yard line. The green-and-white end zone section erupted! Finally a break! But three dives into a brick wall later and we settled for three. State kicked off. The green D stiffened. Michigan punted. A Spartan broke through and smothered the kick; a white shirt grabbed it in the end zone. Touchdown! The green-and-white end zone section erupted again! Wait—no touchdown. A penalty—off side on the green-and-white team. We got zero. Seven plays later, a fake Michigan punt— Mike Gillete, the Wolverine kicker, dashed past three Spartans and over a ref on his way to the far end zone. "Hail to the Victors" and screaming, celebrating Wolverines shook Michigan Stadium. The scoreboard lit up at 17–3. And just like that, the party's over. The rest of the way was Michigan flexing muscle, running the ball, and pounding on State. Even the green-and-white left offensive tackle, Tony Mandarich, the 316-pound mountain, had to be helped off the field. A sad day in Spartanville. For Michigan just another day at the office. For Bo, 16 out of 20, and a step on the road to Pasadena. For me and Drew, and the other green-and-whiters there, the rest of the game was slow torture. Michigan's fight song played over and over; the "GO"— "BLUE!" thundered back and forth. The popgun sounded and Michigan fans celebrated, but not as jubilantly as State fans had in '87. The goalposts survived, probably because football victories in Ann Arbor are old hat. The Romans are used to beating the Christians.

When it was all over, when the scoreboard read MICHIGAN, 17; MICHIGAN STATE, 3—after the Spartans had slid to 0–4–1 and the Wolverines had reasserted their state of Michigan domination—Drew and I sat there. In the end zone, 'bout forty rows up. We waited till the place cleared out. We waited till the bands way, way down on the field, in a different part of the world, had played their postgame show. And left. We waited till the kids picking up pop cans and beer bottles for the ten-cent return had dragged their bags past and cleaned up all the empties. We waited till forty or so cops, all of 'em lined up abreast, had made a final swing from one goal line to the other and herded the remaining kids off the field. We waited till we were about the only two left in the place. We sat and watched and thought about what came next.

_ "You know," Drew said, "that was some win last year up at East Lansing, wasn't it? Seven interceptions."

"Yeah, it was." I squinted across to the far end of the field, to the end zone opposite the one we'd sat in. The one the Michigan punter had faked his kick and sprinted to in the third quarter. The one that, when he crossed it, had been filled with rolls of flying toilet paper. The "GO" part of the thundering "GO"—"BLUE!"

"See, over there. About where that kid's standing." I pointed across to a lone kid dragging a bag full of empties. Scavenging the last of the ten-centers. I pointed to spot a long, long way away. "That's right about where we sat in '78."

Drew nodded. "Uh-huh."

"And down there." I pointed to a cop trailing the field sweep. I was feeling better. I had my Christian optimism back intact. "Down there, that's where Gibson made the catch I was telling you about. Man, he went up . . ."

# 5
# UNIVERSITY OF IOWA
## THE HAWKEYES

| University of Iowa Iowa City, IA. | Kinnick Stadium |
|---|---|
| Best Breakfast | Bruegger's Bagel Bakery |
| Best Bar | ...follow the beer band |
| Best Burger | Hamburg Inn #2 |
| Best of... | |

**The Best in Big Ten Country**

SCHOOL COLOR LOYALTY
(Game day - who wears the most)

1. Iowa
2. Illinois
3. Ohio State
4. Michigan State
5. Michigan

I finally found it—the very friendliest place on the face of the earth! Iowa City, Iowa. A town in the state that Professor Harold Hill conned into a seventy-six-trombone boys' band, without knowing even a single note! A town in a state that has the best version of a pro football team—none. And where its own football team, the Iowa Hawkeyes, wear on their helmets a tribute to the American farmer. A friendly place, a place filled with good people, people who when they ask you, "How's it going?" honestly hope you'll answer, "Great!" That's Iowa City, and the University of Iowa, at the end of Iowa Avenue, along the rolling banks of the Iowa River. Sounds kind of cornball, doesn't it? Every place should be so cornball.

I should've guessed—Iowa City wasn't just any normal Midwest town on my drive in. About fifteen miles outside the city limits, cruising along on Interstate 80, I passed a silver corn silo with a big gold square painted on it. GO, HAWKS in bold black letters screamed from the square to passing cars. All right, I figured, so folks are loyal. Or maybe I should've noticed that things were just a little off when I reached town and pulled up to a stop sign, in front of a crosswalk. The lady standing there waiting to cross, before she crossed, nodded, waved, and thanked me for stopping. OK, so they're polite too. Or maybe I should've gotten the hint that Iowa City was not your run-of-the-mill college town at the corner gas station. The guy at the inside register, a guy who spent forty hours each week answering stupid questions, wasn't bothered when I asked mine. He said, "Hello," gave me my directions, took my traveler's check . . . and didn't even ask for ID. A trusting place too? The final straw, the moment I realized that this Iowa City hospitality was just regular everyday Iowa City stuff, came during my four-minute stay inside a Hawks Spirit Shop. Four minutes at a place that survived on the sale of Hawkeye T-shirts. Four minutes, just enough time to turn a one-dollar bill into phone change. And I didn't even browse. But as I left to find a pay phone, the girl behind at the register called to me, "Thanks for stopping."

I gave up, turned around, and answered, "You're welcome."

Iowa rubs off on you. It rubs off on the people who visit the college for four years. And although it's mostly made up of Iowans, the university brings in a lot of students from a lot of other places. When a college of thirty thousand students is located in a town of forty-five thousand people, there must be some imports. Chicago high-school students learn manners and how to be Hawkeyes at the same time. New Yorkers ought to get in-state tuition rates and be required to attend—just to learn how to smile. Regardless of where they come from, people who leave Iowa City—maybe four years later, maybe five, or as in my case just a couple of days—if nothing else, leave with a little better handle on the words "please" and "thank you."

I ran into my first Hawkeye transplant, just a kid, a junior majoring in education, working in a Hallmark card shop. No other students were anywhere around. Midterm week at the University of Iowa, kids study. Townsfolk weren't cramming the place either.

The Hallmark junior was from Chicago. "Most of my friends went to Champaign," she said. "They give me a lot of crap for going to school here. Whenever I'm home, they ask if I'm still gonna be a farmer.

"But I don't care. It's nice, really nice here. You'll see."

People aren't all that's neighborly in Iowa City. So are the buildings and the homes, even the campus. Tucked into a pleasant little valley off I-80, Iowa City breaks a bit with all the corn that frames it. Quaint neighborhoods fill in the cracks all about town. Big Victorian homes sit back amid oaks and maples and big grassy front yards. Pretty homes. Tidy homes. Nice places—places that don't pop to mind when you think of student housing. And they bump into the campus all over the place. Up above the river, on the west side, the Iowa band and neighborhood soccer teams share the same practice field. Just a grass field at the end of a bunch of quiet, uncurbed streets. Five o'clock drilling of the Iowa fight song joins families sitting round the supper table. It brings a touch of quaintness to the supper table and to band practice. Big old Greek houses, the frat and sorority kind, pop up in the middle of otherwise normal-looking Iowan houses. And always there seems to be an art center or some other school building someplace you wouldn't expect it. But someplace that it seems to fit.

The university campus is nice too. And friendly. A rolling, kind of sleepy campus, it's not what you'd call gorgeous. Rather, it looks and feels lived in. A place where you don't need a car to be cool, where a good bicycle will do. And a place where there really isn't much to worry about, except maybe getting to class on time. Catching it in the middle of October didn't hurt either. Reds and yellows were peaking. Brick walkways winding below the west-side dorms and footbridges over the river provided nice, quiet picture-postcard strolls. A breath of fresh air, the Iowa campus looks like a good place to kick back and concentrate on college life, before hitting the real world.

Up above the river, across Clinton Street from downtown, the Pentacrest best catches that college flavor. Made up of five big old stately buildings, the Pentacrest serves as the heart of the university. At its center sits the original state capitol, built in 1842. Topped by a golden dome, with white columns, the old capitol stares down Iowa Avenue. And while it used to greet legislators, now that it's refurbished, just tour groups drop by. The other four buildings house classrooms and, like the legs of a table to the golden-domed centerpiece, anchor the old capitol. Trees and shrubs and old-fashioned lampposts dot the grass and walks in front. Together, the five serve as the student hub. It's where from noon to one, each day that the sun's out, Iowa City political statements are made. It's where, if you want to sell anything for any cause, you get your best response. The Pentacrest, a place where nobody minds if you walk on the grass, is to the campus what sunglasses are to Hayden Fry.

Finally there's the megapolis—downtown Iowa City. All four or five square blocks of it. Across Clinton Street from the Pentacrest, downtown exists for the university. But it's not just a college town. In fact, it looks like something you might find somewhere off any Iowa highway—with just a touch of college thrown in. Three-storied red-brick buildings dominate the downtown area. The same buildings, maybe with different signs out front, that have dominated downtown Iowa City for decades. Pizza Hut and Burger King blend in quietly with the homemade-ice-cream parlors. Bars, a lot of 'em just holes-in-the-wall, get a good mix of townsfolk and students. A couple of old movie theaters still feature the old marquees. And a beautiful little red-brick plaza marks the city center.

Under the shadow of the Holiday Inn, hidden from the Pentacrest by the Clinton Street shops, the pedestrians-only plaza takes the place of streets. Young trees, growing up out of tidy squares of dirt and wood chips, dot it. Wooden park benches provide places to sit and rest. A fountain tosses water in the air, and then lets it trickle down its side. Throughout the day, the red brick teems with activity. Kids walking to class, or stopping and sitting it out, depending on the weather. At night, particularly on the weekends, the place is a hub of excitement. Lines from the Fieldhouse and Vito's and other college bars intertwine. Hot-dog and brat carts and temporary taco stands kill the late-night munchies, and add a pleasant aroma to the place. A tiny Midwest town, zapped with some college life, easing out along a pleasant red-brick plaza. It's a nice place, just a really nice place.

One last feature lights up Iowa City. In fact, all of Iowa, really. And that's the Hawkeyes. Hawkeye football in the fall, but also Hawkeye wrestling and Hawkeye basketball in the winter, and probably every other Hawk sport every other sport season as well. And the townsfolk don't hide their affection. The Tigerhawk, that gold hawk head on the football helmet, blankets Iowa City. It's everywhere! Bookstores and bar windows off the plaza almost all have at least one painted across the glass somewhere. Restaurants usually feature something, on the wall or on the menu, that's Hawkeye-ish. Outside of town, things like the GO, HAWKS silo constantly pop up. A grain and feed storage facility, at another highway exit, gets an annual gold-and-black paint job. Cars even get into the act. Almost every other Iowa City bumper sticker features Iowa City's favorite saying, "It's Great to Be a Hawkeye."

In return for the support, Iowa grads don't just disappear. They keep coming back and contributing to the school and to the community. For instance, City High School ran into a roadblock two years ago. Its Little Hawks football team, nicknamed for Iowa University's team, wanted the Tigerhawk decal for its helmets, but suffered from the typical public-school problem—no money. Pro football player Joel Hilgenberg, an ex–City High/University of Iowa star, stepped in and forked out for the decals. Now the Little Hawk helmets of City High match the "Big Hawk" helmets of the University of Iowa.

Farmers around Iowa City, particularly the last couple of years, have been hurting big time. Ex-athletes haven't forgotten them, either. Guys you'd never think were Hawkeye hoop stars, guys like Downtown Freddie Brown and the Jazz's Bobby Hansen, have come to the rescue. The last two summers they've put on a fundraiser basketball game featuring old Hawks vs. other old Hawks. Proceeds went to something called the Farm Scholarship Fund. Because of it, three farm kids a year, kids who couldn't normally afford to go to college, now can. Hayden Fry's football team backs the farming community too. A couple of years ago the Tigerhawk got a partner on the U of I football helmet. A simple gold circle, right between the gold stripe and gold hawk. Inside the circle are the block letters ANF (America Needs Farmers), a tribute to Iowan farmers. All of this, the ANF, the Farm Scholarship Fund, even the Little Hawk football helmets, creates almost a family bond between the university and the community.

There are a lot of reasons why Iowa University and Iowans get along so well. The I-Club, though, might be the main link. The idea of an I-Club is nothing new; all Big Ten schools have something similar. The Spartans have their S-Club, Ohio State their O-Club, and Wisconsin a big red W-Club. The clubs recruit alums, and their big bucks, in exchange for bumper stickers and alumni pins, invitations to golf outings, and fifty-yard-line seats. Proceeds go to help the school's sports programs. Well, Iowa's, in addition to all that, captures the sincerity of a high-school booster program.

First off, you don't have to be an alum to be an I-Club member, just give twenty-five dollars and love the Hawks. Consequently, most of the club support comes from "just plain people" around the state. Another reason the setup is so successful is the number of clubs. Over fifty stretch across the country—Los Angeles, Chicago, Phoenix, Cincinnati, Denver—I-Clubs pop up everywhere. But the most important ingredient of the organization's success is the people involved. Mark Jennings organizes it. All fourteen Iowa head coaches pitch in, and they all work their tail off. Split into teams of seven, with Hayden Fry and Tom Davis as the headliners, each spring they comb the state of Iowa. Each seven-coach team covers fifteen towns, giving speeches and eating dinner and talking with Iowa fans about the University of Iowa. In Carroll, Iowa, 250 miles from the university, five hundred people turn out to listen to Hayden Fry talk about the Hawks. Not bad for a town of ten thousand people. And Belle Plaine can usually be counted on to deliver three hundred or four hundred. That's almost a tenth of city's population!

The bond's amazing! Amazing that a big-time college athletic program would show up in a place as tiny as Belle Plaine. Amazing that the town would close down and turn out full force for the show. But then again in Iowa . . . maybe not so amazing.

For home football games, Fridays are one of the primo I-Club get-together times. I was lucky—I got an invite! Actually anybody in the world who wants to can go, but Mark Jennings thought I might have a good time.

"It starts at six-thirty," he told me. "With Michigan this week, there'll be close to five hundred folks. So you'd better get there early!" Strange, even early seemed kind of late, a Friday night dinner, with a big game the next day. "That's six-thirty A.M.!" Mark corrected me. I got my answer without even asking.

A.M. in itself sets off I-Clubs from the O-Clubs and M-Clubs and W-Clubs around the college football world. A lot of alumni clubs have some kind of gathering for the home games, but not a lot have it at dawn. Usually it's someplace in town where a handful of rich people, thousand-dollar-a-year donors, come in for a noon luncheon. Usually a Hilton or a Sheraton, underneath fancy chandeliers, accompanied by mixed drinks, chicken cordon bleu, and a tossed salad. Iowa's Friday morning bash was outside town, just off the highway, at a tired-looking place called the Highliner Restaurant.

At 6:10 A.M. when I stumbled up, the line already bulged through the Highliner's double glass doors and out into the dark parking lot. I stepped in behind Rosemary Lyons. Rosemary looked like my mom, except for the fact that my mom doesn't own a gold sweater or anything with a Tigerhawk on it. Rosemary's gold sweater had a Tigerhawk on the lapel sandwiched between "Iowa" above it and "Hawkeyes" underneath. Rosemary was in line by herself; her friend, who she told me had been a Hawkeye football fan for twenty-five years, was inside saving seats.

"My husband came a couple years ago," Rosemary noted. "Back when we had that 'real great-looking' cheerleader. Said he wanted to see her up close. That's the only way I could get him here."

The "real great-looking" cheerleader had graduated. So had Rosemary's husband . . . from the Friday morning I-Club, anyhow. He was still a big Hawkeye fan, just not at six in the morning. "He thinks I'm nuts," she added. "But I still drag him here once a season. Usually Homecoming, in case the 'real great-looking' cheerleader comes back."

For Rosemary and for her seat-saving friend Pat, the Friday morning I-Club is a six-times-a-season event. A necessary stopoff before the eight-to-five shift at the university hospital. For them and the other three or four or five hundred that pack the place, eating breakfast and listening to Hayden Fry talk Hawk football isn't only a loyalty test, it's fun too!

"Pat says the social season here in Iowa starts in the fall." Looking around at the hundreds cramming the place, I'd say she was right.

By the time we hit the pay line in front of the buffet, Rosemary and I were talking all about Hawkeye football. She told me about the I-Club, that she'd been coming to these Friday morning gatherings for last five or six years, and to Hawk games since '74. She said Pat had been coming a lot longer. We talked about the Michigan game too. And the Hawks' chances on Saturday. From the buffet table, with a cram-it-on-your-plate sausage, potatoes, eggs, and bacon breakfast (no quiche at the I-Club), I could make out the sights and sounds from the big dining room ahead. It sounded like a half-time show—a jam-packed half-time show.

Luckily, Rosemary's friend had saved an extra seat. The round tables, ten seats apiece, were all pretty well packed. Latecomers just squeezed in wherever there was room, which meant that not everybody at each table knew one another. But since it was an Iowa get-together, by the end of breakfast most everybody did. My table was filled with women. All dressed in something gold or least something with a Hawk pin sticking to it. In fact, almost everybody there was dressed in something that matched the Hawks. And a lot of the fans inside were women, mostly mothers and grandmothers, some with their husbands, some without. All week long they kept popping up, and not just at the predawn breakfast either. Walking in the shops, and Saturday around the tailgates and at the game, Iowa women "love their Hawks." It's actually a refreshing change of pace, and a great way to learn about football. Women possess a loyalty that men don't! A loyalty that transfers nicely over to college football. If the guy's a bum, be he player or coach, moms normally find a good side to him. Or feel sorry for him, that he's not better. Well, our table was full of loyalty. Conversations carried the tone of a mom talking about her kid on the high-school football team. The boys usually got mentioned by first name, and Hayden, definitely not Hayden Fry, coached the Hawks. No better place to listen to Hawktalk. Even a season that had so far been a so-so one sounded pretty good!

Around the place folks woke up, worked on breakfast, and discussed the big Saturday game. Herky the Hawk, a kid with Hawk football pants, jersey, and shoulder pads, and a huge plastic Hawk head, flitted through the crowd. Up in the corner, at the front of the room, the brass section of the Hawkeye marching band blared out the Iowa fight song. Cheerleaders, unfortunately minus that "real great-looking" one that lured Rosemary's husband, lined the speakers' tables in front. They smiled and jumped and shook their pom-poms. Even the Iowa twirler did her thing. She spun and danced and twirled about in front of the room. And talk about precision. She'd toss her baton twelve feet up, just high enough to graze the ceiling, turn a cartwheel, and catch it. All without bumping into a single table. An Iowa Hawkeye football breakfast celebration, and I'd completely forgotten the *Today* show was still an hour from starting!

The speakers' table brimmed with Iowa dignitaries. A big old gold banner filled with block IOWA letters was tacked on the wall behind it. A bright yellow block I about a foot or two tall, made out of yellow carnations, perched at the end of the table. A couple of big-time alums—an ex-governor ("the best this state's ever had," according to Rosemary) and a priest dressed in, you guessed it, a black Hawkeye sweater with a gold collar—rounded out the table. Only the center seat was empty.

"Here he comes! Here he comes!" shouted the brass band's drum major.

And as the weekly master of ceremonies, resurrector of the Iowa football program and one of the world's smoothest speakers, strolled in, the Iowa band blasted out another rendition of the Iowa fight song. The crowd pushed away from their coffees, stood, and clapped. Hayden Fry, complete with sun glasses, nodded his thanks. I-Club Friday morning was complete.

And let the festivities begin!

The priest in the Hawkeye collar took care of the benediction, and ended it with "Lord, give the Hawks strength tomorrow." Then came the weekly raffle . . . for all sorts of Hawkeye stuff. Gold Hawkeye jackets and black Hawkeye jackets. Gold Hawkeye shirts and black Hawkeye shirts. A voice from the microphone at the podium asked for all persons please to check their ticket stubs. The voice would call the winning ticket's first three numbers. The band in unison would ask, "Yes?" The voice would call the last three numbers. And the band in unison, if no band member won, would issue a groan. The happy winner, dressed in a Hawk sweater, would jump up and hustle to the speakers' table to accept another Hawk sweater, while everybody, band included, clapped. The biggest cheer came when Herky, then minus his plastic head so he could put away some potatoes and eggs, won the big yellow carnation I at the speakers' table.

"I've never won a thing here," Rosemary sighed, and was seconded by a couple of other dedicated ladies.

Speeches followed. The best ex-governor of the state talked for a while, and then introduced the best Hawk football coach ever. And each speech was filled with Hawkeye jokes, and Hayden jokes, and roast-everybody-at-the-table type jokes. The crowd got into it. We laughed when something was funny and clapped when something was important.

After Hayden tossed a few return cracks at the ex-governor, he got down to business. And when he does that, wherever it be, you're in for a treat! Hayden Fry is one of college football's finest speakers. I'd caught his act in Seattle at a Coach of the Year Clinic a couple of years earlier. Coach of the Year Clinic is where junior-high and high-school football coaches get to listen to the big-timers tell how they made the big time. Most of the speeches are filled with X's and O's. What's the best offense and what's the best defense? How do you really block the sprint draw? Not Hayden's. He never once mentioned a play or a strategy. Or even a particular game. He talked about life. About motivation and about people. When he was finished, I'd decided if I was ever reincarnated as a college football player, I'd be at Iowa in a heatbeat!

Part of being a good speaker and a good coach is being a good sandbagger. And being a six-and-a-half-point underdog to the tough Michigan team, Hayden was at his sandbagging best.

"This is the best Michigan team I've ever played against," a Hayden specialty, was met with a drawn-out groan from Rosemary, Pat, and all the other loyal Hawks. Then for about fifteen minutes, the Iowa coach went down the Michigan starting lineup position by position, like he was pushing each for the Heisman. Still he ended with a "We'll give it our best." Rosemary, I'm sure, felt at least a little better.

But before Hayden thanked all the loyal folks for showing up, he said he had a story to tell. "I want to share with you something that happened to me," he said, "perhaps the most inspirational thing I've ever witnessed in my life." Folks who'd intently listened to the Michigan Heisman balloting got more intent. They enjoyed Hayden's stories.

This one was about a funeral from which he and some of his assistant coaches had just returned, the funeral of the father of three of Hayden's players, all of whom had worn the number 41 black and gold of Iowa. One of them, Mark Stoops, still played at Iowa. Another, Mike Stoops, still coached there. The third, Bobby Stoops, had gone to two Rose Bowls with Iowa. Hayden talked about the man, Mark's and Mike's and Bobby's father, Coach Stoops, who'd died the week before. He told the story of how he'd died—on the sidelines of a Youngstown High School football game. He told how, even though Coach Stoops was hurting, he'd refused to leave the game. How he'd coached his team till the final whistle of their overtime victory. How he'd called the game's last defensive play, then walked to the end of the bench and collapsed into a coma. He also told us of Coach Stoops's life. It was the story of a man who never missed a game for twelve years while his sons participated in the Hawkeye program. A man who every fall coached his Youngstown team on Friday, loaded the family into the car, and drove through the night to get to Iowa City. He told us how early Sunday morning after the Iowa game, he'd load everybody up again and make it back in time to grade the high-school films. He talked with great respect about a man dedicated to his team and to his family.

"The funeral," Hayden said to a very quiet I-Club, "was the most beautiful funeral I've ever seen. Thirteen priests and all the nuns were present. . . ." People had lined up outside in rainy 40-degree weather to attend. "It really was beautiful."

Even so, the Iowa coach solemnly revealed, after the ceremony, something was wrong. Mrs. Stoops wasn't satisfied. Hayden told us why: "As honorary pallbearers, we had the opportunity to be present when Mrs. Stoops told us something just didn't seem right. Not until we'd walked in with an Iowa jersey, black and gold, a number forty-one on it. The number that each of her kids had worn. . . ." The number that Coach and Mrs. Stoops had religiously followed for twelve years across the Midwest. Hayden handed that jersey to Mrs. Stoops.

"Ladies and gentleman," he continued, "she had her children prop Coach Stoops up and put that jersey on him. Right there. Bobby Stoops took his Rose Bowl ring off, he had two . . . and he put one on Coach Stoops' finger. And that's the way that gentleman was buried."

Hayden paused and reflected for a moment. "The family was so happy, so delighted that they knew that their father was at peace. That he was comfortable. Mrs. Stoops told her husband, 'Now you'll always be warm. . . .' " He paused again. "Afterwards she had a smile on her face. She told us, 'Now everything's all right!' "

We all took a long deep breath. Hayden finished up. "I told you this because I wanted you to know there are a lot of people out there that love Iowa football." And he stepped away from the microphone. The quiet crowd, still envisioning that number 41 jersey being pulled over Coach Stoops, stood. Everybody clapped. The band broke into one last rendition of the fight song. Recovered, the loyal I-Clubbers said their goodbyes and headed off to work, a Hawkeye jersey and a coach in a casket on their minds for a long time to come. Hayden Fry stayed and shook hands. He was the last one out the door.

If the Friday morning celebration ended eerily, Friday night's was gonna be a blowout. And I had another Iowa invite. This time to the Pentacrest for the weekly home game march of the Hawkeye Marching Beer Band. "It's a trip! You gotta come!" I was told earlier in the week up at one of the band practices. So at 9:00 P.M. I was on the Pentacrest sidewalk, while advancing pieces of the Iowa Marching Beer Band rolled in.

Kids with horns and drums and saxes, crammed the sidewalk. Others were on the way, most in twos or threes, some by themselves.

Each got a "How's it going?" from somebody already standing around and waiting. The music was totally unorganized; a dozen recitals of tunes bounced about, none of them more than a few stanzas. A little Dixieland, a trombone warm-up of the Iowa fight song, freshman scales renditions, and drums knocking out some modern-day rock-and-roll beat. A Friday night campus stream of cars whooshed by. They passed in bunches, according to the light change. Occasionally one would honk or somebody would yell out the window. Most were answered by a *da da da dat da da*—*charge* salute.

"You made it! Great!" Erin, a junior trumpeter, dressed in your basic blue jeans with the now-stylish rip in the knee, plus a big gray Iowa sweatshirt, saw me.

"You really gonna go beer-banding with us?" another trumpeter, a friend of Erin's, asked. My "As long as I get free beer" answer was met with a chorus from two trumpeters: "No problem."

While the girls described the setup, that beer band was not official Iowa University band policy, that they did it on their own six times a season, that it'd been going on "forever," Tony walked up. He was carrying a big box.

Tony's a crew-cut, marine-looking guy, and conductor of the Hawk-eye Marching Beer Band. A regular trombonist on Saturday after-noons, besides conductor Tony was also beer band's secretary-treasurer and T-shirt orderer. And the order was in, hot off the press. Beer banders gathered around.

"Cool"—a voice popped out of the group.

"Awesome."

"Tony, they look great!"

The official beer band uniform—a white T-shirt with all sorts of beer band symbols—passed with flying colors. On the front, "Party Naked" was crossed out and in its place was "March Naked." A beer stein sat next to the naked march, and "Chug 'n' Go—HMB Beer Band" below that. The back said "1988 World Tour" at the top, then listed in order the ten stops for the night.

"You want one?!" Tony looked my way. Besides being a beer band director, Tony was a salesman. Beer band, like any other band, needed funds, if nothing else than to pay for T-shirts. The cost was only eight dollars, and the cause was good. So I donated, and with my official shirt became an honorary 1988 beer band member.

Tony kept selling. He spread around more shirts for more bucks, till half the group was uniformed and beer band was itching to get going. "Let's go," he yelled. The forty or so kids that'd shown assembled at the curb. Tony took his place at the front. He blew his whistle three times, and the Hawkeye Marching Beer Band blasted out their first of what would be close to fifty-three renditions of the Iowa fight song. On the last note, we all crossed Clinton Street, at the same time starting up "In Heaven There Is No Beer." We were off on the world's greatest Friday night barhopping (at least if you like the Iowa fight song, it was the best) there ever was!

Joe's Place on Iowa Avenue—in any other town on earth just another corner bar, but in Iowa City, on Friday night before the Michigan game, Joe's had the honor of being beer band stop number one.

"Remember," Tony commanded at the doorway, "this may be beer band but it's Iowa's beer band, and it's gotta be good!" Cheers answered him.

And at 9:10 P.M., pumped for the tour, the band flooded Joe's. Song number one at stop number one brought the house down. The beer band, consisting of mostly horns, a handful of drums, three kazoos, and a couple of clarinets, so crammed that trombone rods couldn't find an open space to shove to, shook Joe's with the Iowa fight song. Patrons joined in if they knew the words, and the bar sounded like a happy Christmas Eve sing-along, just with a different theme.

At each bar the Iowa fight song led without a breath to "In Heaven There Is No Beer," the band's fight song. The beer song always included a short break in middle. While some of the band kept time, the rest locked arms and polkaed and sang. Each "beer song" also ended in a beer band eruption of cheers.

"That's our favorite," Erin yelled. "But Bump won't let us do it at the game." Erin was referring to Bump Elliot, the Iowa athletic director, who'd probably never caught the Friday night beer band in action, and who'd probably never hung out at Joe's or Mickey's or even Tuck's Place.

Meanwhile, Joe's got the rest of the song list. Tony, standing on a table, flashed hand signals for selections. A time-out T meant "Tequila." An index finger up for 1, or I depending on how you looked at it, kicked off the Iowa fight song. An upside-down three-fingered M called for the Michigan fight song—if not the cleanest, then certainly the most imaginative tune of the night. Give or take a line, it's the same song every college kid at every college that's ever played the Wolves has joined in on. No musical accompaniment, aside from the three kazoos, is even needed. Thirty-six beer band voices rolled off a "Hail to the Victors" rendition filled with all sorts of rhyming, nasty, and degrading verses. Bar patrons loved it! The final verse, a "Hail, hail to Michigan, the cesspool of the East," was always met with hooting and hollering and wild applause.

With the last of five songs, whatever the fifth happened to be, beer band chanted, "BAND WANTS BEER! BAND WANTS BEER!" Bartenders at each stop obliged. Joe's already had the plastic cups out and the free beer flowing by the time the first chant was rolling. Ten minutes of gulping and revealing to all the interested patrons what the actual words to the Michigan song were and it was time to hit the road. Tony got back on the table . . . three sharp whistle blasts, one last long loud band-filled chant—"ONE, TWO, THREE . . . THANKS, JOE'S!"—and beer band marched to the exit. Off to Mickey's—stop number two.

Each stop along the way was greeted with cheers, the band's as well as the packed house's. Each stop along the way had a song the customers wanted replayed. Some yelled out, " 'TEQUILA'! WE WANT 'TEQUILA'!" For others it was the Iowa fight song. Most fans yelled for the revised version of "Hail to the Victors." At each stop, or on the way to each, other little bits of beer band trivia, like the reason for the presence of three kazooers, surfaced.

"We're in the flag corps," a freshman kazoo player revealed, on the way to stop number three. "Flags don't fit in the door." Good point. They didn't.

"So these are our instruments!" And she reeled off a stanza of "Tequila."

To reach stop four, beer band detoured across Iowa Avenue and marched through a corner of campus. The route ran the sidewalk, between Seashore and Van Allen halls. Drumbeats marked the cadence and echoed between the tall buildings. Beer banders yelled letters in unison: "I-O-W-A, IOWA! IOWA! IOWA!" Cheers followed chants, then started over again. Cars on Iowa Avenue stopped and honked. People at the corners stopped and cheered. Roaming cops even cracked smiles.

Stop number four, Tuck's Place, is the sentimental favorite. It's the band hangout, because as an excited flutist yelled out on the way, "Tuck's awesome. He has our picture on the wall."

Tuck's is another Iowa City hole-in-the-wall. With a twist. It has a long skinny bar that's usually bellied up to by a host of old folks. Beer band burst in. From the sidewalk outside, at the band's tail end, I could hear an eruption of cheers.

"Where ya been?" somebody at one of the booths yelled out.

A horn in the back countered with *da da da dat da—charge.*

No standing and playing out with the patrons at Tuck's. The kids, as many as could, crammed in behind the long skinny counter—shoulder to shoulder to shoulder, all the horns tilted up and facing out to the cheering crowd. Those that couldn't fit behind the bar sandwiched folks bellied up to it. Tony, who'd found a chair to stand on, flashed the 1 to signal the fight song, raised his hands up like a conductor's, and beer band rolled. "Iowa," the beer song, "Hail to the Victors," and "Tequila." Patrons toasted each song, sang along when they knew the words, and provided pretty wild applause when each ended.

"One more time on the beer song." A plump, old, gray-haired guy wanted to hear the beer band theme again. It was Tuck! The band cheered, and played it again. Even louder. Tuck's wife, meanwhile, turned on the taps. Cups full of Pabst circulated.

Before Tuck got his "ONE, TWO, THREE . . . THANKS, TUCK" salute, a presentation was made.

"Quiet, everybody," Tony yelled.

A couple of voices echoed Tony's "Quiet."

"To beer band's favorite bar. And beer band's favorite bartender—Tuck. Your very own beer band T-shirt." The place erupted.

"Tuck's awesome," a voice yelled out. Some of the kids hit the beer song one more time—a tribute to a great bar. Tony gave the awesome bartender his own brand-new "March Naked" beer band shirt. Tuck pulled it on. Flash bulbs popped. And beer band headed outside, off to inspire the rest of campus.

After a Quick Stop grocery store serenade, and a roll back through Seashore and Van Allen halls, by the time we got back to Iowa Avenue a second time, Friday night campus crowds had thickened. Streets were hopping with roaming kids and alums. Some were looking for a place to stop and have a brew. Others browsed shop windows. Most though, were just having a pleasant stroll on a warm October night. The echoing, I-O-W-A–ing beer band shattered the warm October quiet. Beer band hit the red-brick plaza, destination: the Sports Corner.

The Sports Corner is the halfway point, and a good place to catch a second wind. Beer band had been rolling for almost an hour. Some of the lips that had blown out barroom medleys five times already took a break. Inside, Sports Corner shook with brass and cheers.

"This is the greatest," Todd, a big junior horn player, revealed. He was sitting and leaning against the window. Most of all, he was resting. "Last year I didn't go out for band. I blew it. This year I did, and it's the best time I've ever had. Especially this." He pointed his horn toward the inside noise.

Another less sentimental member, late, ran past us, through the door into the Sports Corner. "It's a cheap way to get drunk."

"That too," Todd noted. "But I've got to rest. I've got to pace myself. I'm wiped. Last week I came out here and gave it all I had. Played all night long. And I couldn't even get through the Saturday half-time show, my lips were so tired."

Erin, meanwhile, was just beginning to roll.

"She's crazy." The freshman kazoo player filled me in on Erin. "She'll play anything." Down on the corner a group of alums were clapping along to the Iowa fight song. Erin, probably one of band's best trumpeters, stood in the middle and blasted away.

"Last week she got *three bucks,*" the freshman shrieked, "for 'My Funny Valentine.' *Three bucks!!!* Over there across the street." The freshman pointed to Mickey's. "People in that room above the bar threw it down to the sidewalk. *Three bucks* for 'My Funny Valentine'! She's crazy!"

Erin bounced up. "Sixty cents for the Notre Dame fight song. That's it! I can't believe it, a lousy sixty cents. It's all they'd give me." She stopped and lit up. "So I took it." Inside, the beer song got a second go-round.

A beer band fan, just a normal Iowa City lady out and about, joined us on the sidewalk outside the Sports Corner—Erin, the freshman kazoo flag corps marcher, Todd the big junior, and me.

"My daughter loved that beer song," the lady piped up, like she'd been with us all night long. She was short and plump. The kids gathered around and looked down at her.

"When she was in junior high, she heard you kids playing that beer song. And she said to me, 'Mom I want to go to Iowa.' "

"Did she?! Did she?!" Everybody wanted to know.

The plump lady sighed a sigh that only mothers sigh. And only when they talk about their kids. "She was valedictorian of the class. She got a thirty-two on her ACT. And Iowa, in all of its infinite wisdom, wouldn't give her any money." Mom stopped, probably silently hexing Iowa. "So she went to Western Illinois."

"OH, NO," the four of us groaned.

Mom went on, "And every day she asks the Western Illinois band director why can't they play the beer song." Groans turned to cheers. The kazoo joined Erin with a beer song rendition, on the house! Todd, the big junior, still pacing himself, rested.

Behind us, filing out of the Sports Corner, beer band trucked on. "Pregame at the fountain," Tony yelled.

"What the hell for?" a voice from the rear shot back.

Tony sometimes gets that kind of response. Sometimes the soldiers think Tony, a volunteer drill sergeant with no MPs to back him up, is on a power trip. But usually they listen to him. He conducts. They follow. He keeps things under control. Even as the empty beer cups accumulate, the band members stay cool. All night long. They play their tunes. They chant their "BAND WANTS BEER!" They chant their "ONE, TWO, THREE . . . THANKS." They make sure that Iowa Marching Beer Band is the best marching beer band in the NCAA . . . without any violations. And they keep it sharp. Especially on show, at the fountain.

The fountain is Iowa City's hot spot. At the center of the red-brick plaza, in the shadow of the Holiday Inn, it's the place where everybody who's out walking on a pleasant Friday night ends up at least three times. It's just a block from the Sports Corner. Just a block from about a hundred Iowa City bars. The band trucked over in twos and threes, some serenading folks along the way. At the fountain they reassembled. Horns up, beer band came to attention on the red-brick steps facing the water. Tony climbed up the fountain. Standing on the water's edge, about twelve feet up, he pointed a 1 and raised his hands. Crowds of people, alums and high-school kids, college kids too, slowed down and gathered for the show.

*Tweet tweet tweet.* Beer band rolled. This time, though, since it was in public, and not in front of beer-guzzling Wolverine haters, Michigan's filthy fight song was omitted. No problem—public support was great! A group of high-school girls clapped and danced along to "Tequila." The Iowa fight song got alums joining in. When the beer song rolled, more than just the beer band polkaed. And when they finished, everybody standing around the fountain, especially the band, cheered for the band . . . and it was on to the finale.

And what a finale! The jam-packed Fieldhouse, beer band's stop number ten, is Iowa City's favorite Friday night hangout. It's beer band's second favorite . . . after Tuck's.

Normally squeezing in the Fieldhouse door, especially at eleven o'clock on a Friday night, calls for a two-buck cover and at least a thirty-minute wait in line. Not for the Iowa Marching Beer Band! The dance floor was waiting. Straight through the front door, past the bouncers, the band assembled at the back-end lower level. Everybody cleared the way. Cheers thundered as the marchers hit the lower level. Beer banders, all present and accounted for, crammed the floor. A mirror behind them reflected their backs, and all the clapping patrons squeezed off to the side. It looked like a billion people crowded together. Tony found a makeshift conductor's barstool, set it up, and jumped on top. Trombones and trumpets and flutes pointed up toward him. Some rested on the head of the kid in front . . . but they all fit. Tony blew his whistle. The kids hit the cycle one last time. The Fieldhouse erupted. After one repeat of "Hail to the Victors," the barroom deejay turned up the rock and roll, and the trumpeters with their trumpets, the trombonists with their trombones, even the kazooers with their kazoos just started dancing, swarmed by the mob crammed onto the dance floor.

And the beer band stars of Iowa City, Tuck's favorite band, Erin the marching street musician, Tony the conductor-marine, and Todd the big junior once again became normal college kids on the dance floor. Harmless—except for the slide of an occasional boogieing trombone. All I could think was: My god, what would happen if Iowa's beer band got together with the University of Wisconsin Marching Band, someday, somewhere, for somebody's Fifth Quarter? Music would never be the same again . . . maybe the world, either!

# MICHIGAN AT IOWA

*Kinnick Stadium,*
*Iowa City, Iowa*

| Standings | Big Ten | | | All Games | | |
|---|---|---|---|---|---|---|
| October 15, 1988 | W | L | T | W | L | T |
| INDIANA | 2 | 0 | — | 4 | 0 | 1 |
| ILLINOIS | 2 | 0 | — | 3 | 2 | — |
| MICHIGAN | 2 | 0 | — | 3 | 2 | — |
| IOWA | 1 | 0 | 1 | 3 | 2 | 1 |
| PURDUE | 1 | 1 | — | 2 | 3 | — |
| MINNESOTA | 0 | 1 | 1 | 2 | 2 | 1 |
| MICHIGAN STATE | 0 | 1 | 1 | 0 | 4 | 1 |
| NORTHWESTERN | 0 | 1 | 1 | 0 | 4 | 1 |
| OHIO STATE | 0 | 2 | — | 2 | 3 | — |
| WISCONSIN | 0 | 2 | — | 0 | 5 | — |

**Other Big Ten Games:**

ILLINOIS AT WISCONSIN

MINNESOTA AT INDIANA

NORTHWESTERN AT MICHIGAN STATE

PURDUE AT OHIO STATE

The forecast called for 70 degrees and sunshine. Another full house, Kinnick Stadium's fiftieth straight. Bo was in! Iowa City was pumped; the I-Club and beer band had done their job well. A rivalry that had swung on a single kick two of the last three seasons, in '88 would provide the victor an inside track to Pasadena. This would be college football at its very best. And I couldn't wait!

First, though, I had to shake off Friday's beer band run . . . not quite as versed at barhopping as I had been in college—and we'd hit ten of 'em! But with a couple of cups of coffee under my belt, by nine o'clock I was out of the Roof, and headed out of Cedar Falls to Iowa City through acres and acres and acres of corn-covered farmland. What a day! What a drive! Yellow and red treetops peaked in a beautiful bright blue sky, the October sunshine shone full force, and all sorts of Hawk-talk was already filling the radio waves. My only regret was that I couldn't have made it a few hours later. With two major roads feeding Iowa City, and the way Iowans cover themselves and their cars with that bright gold and black, the game day flow must have looked like a swarm of happy giant bumblebees en route to a dandelion factory.

No bumblebee lines for me. With a 2:30 TV start I beat the swarm and by 10:00 was bageled, cream-cheesed, and cidered in downtown Iowa City. After searching through a few shops and digging up an all-cotton, black IOWA T-shirt with a gold Tigerhawk on the chest, I was dressed too, and strolling through campus while it began waking up for college football.

A campus game-day wake-up call is always refreshing. Usually a buzz of excitement during the week, with kids on their way to class, bikes and cars and joggers out and about, the campus lulls on the weekend. On a football Saturday morning, it's a lull before the storm. Or in Iowa's case, like the peaceful eye of a hurricane. Walking down tree-lined paths, kicking through the mounds of fallen leaves, crossing over the Iowa River, just taking in the sights and the smells on the way to the stadium, I saw Iowa in her best dress. And visited with the few folks out and watching her wake up too. Four and a half hours before kickoff, you can spot the football fans. If they're out, if they're covered in school colors and walking campus, they're the life-and-deathers, the ones who can't sleep Friday nights before Michigan games. They're the ones that, come kickoff, are as psyched as the guys on the field. And the ones that light up when you ask, "Well, can the Hawks take 'em today?"

While campus takes a while to awaken, the stadium gets moving at the crack of dawn. Tailgaters start filing into the parking lots. The real hard-core ones, motor-homers from someplace far off in the corn, folks who spend their Friday night in the stadium shadow, just wake up, roll outside, and toss some bacon into the skillet. And the band stops by for its 8:00 A.M. morning practice session. The Iowa fight song drifts from Kinnick, across the street, and through the stirring parking lots.

Kinnick fits the Iowa campus, and the town and the townspeople. It's a tiny stadium, at least in Big Ten terms; it seats only sixty-seven thousand. It's kind of homey too. Big archways cut the simple red-brick shell and open up to the inside. Unlike Ohio Stadium or Camp Randall at Wisconsin, or even Spartan Stadium, the Iowan blends into its Iowan neighborhood. There, even if you're looking for it, the stadium doesn't really make much of an announcement. Inside it's just as cozy. Through the brick archways and under the seats, where the hot-dog and soda stands pop up, the concourse is narrow, and on game day Hawk fans cluster together. Skinny walkways up into the stands force fans filing up and in to stop and wait, as much as they walk. Even the seating is simple. No roof or upper deck—both sides consist of seventy-nine rows of bleacher seats up from the field, and about half that in the end zones. Four separate sections drop right down along the turf's edge, and pile fans on top of the action. The way Iowans drench themselves in black and gold, with all those seats crammed right on top of the field it makes a Saturday afternoon crowd of sixty-seven thousand look more like a million! And sound like twice that when the Hawks score!

Melrose Avenue, just a block from Kinnick, is a pregame platter of activity, and the first place that catches a Saturday morning Hawkeye buzz. A skinny two-laner, it runs out past Finkbine golf course and all the way to the highway. The bumblebee parades from all over the state use it to reach Kinnick. Cars, all black-and-gold Hawkeyed up, in from Des Moines and Cedar Falls and the Quad Cities, honk their horns and crank the stereo, and just get psyched for the Hawks. Pure Iowa City, Melrose doesn't bother with any fancy extras—no curbs, no passing lane, no computerized "Don't Walk" signs—but just the same, it's game day's Broadway. And it's crammed from 11 A.M. on. As on Breeze Terrace alongside Camp Randall up in Madison, old weathered houses skirt Melrose. Their front lawns get turned into Saturday afternoon rentals of all sorts, for cars, for souvenir stands, and for brat tents, and of course for tailgating.

"How many can you get back there?" I asked an old lady dressed in a Hawk sweatshirt. She was sitting in a lawn chair in front of one of the Melrose homes. The sign in front of her said "Parking," but it was lying on the lawn, barely visible, as if everybody already knew.

"Oh, we'll squeeze in seventy before the day's done." That, at seven dollars a crack, I figured, would stuff a few mattresses. "It'll be all filled up by game time!" Melrose was starting to hum. Lines from the

Finkbine end and lines from the Iowa City end were turning the skinny street into a moving parking lot. Which was great for the Melrose side street lots, like the one that the lady in the Hawks shirt guarded.

"Come on, let me show you."

We wandered back. Her sister took over collections. Already a slow flow was rolling up the dirt drive, through a gap in the fence, back to a deep, nearly block-long lot. Lots next door, huge flat grassy lots, stretched way back too. Trees and small fences ran in line, and separated the Smiths' from the Joneses' from the Browns'. Tailgates were out and cranking, parallel-parking style!

"It'll all be filled by two o'clock." She pointed to the rear. "And this"—she motioned to the primo space roped off up alongside the garage—"is for Cedar Rapids. Reservations, you know, cost an extra dollar. But they've been coming for about five years now. Always pull in 'bout an hour before game time." She stopped and reminded me, "Yessir, good people from Cedar Rapids."

Back out front, two cops, and left turns onto Hawkins Street, kept the slow flow slower. Stadium lots started to bulge. Souvenir stands, not nearly the millions that turn out Bucky Badger in every sound, shape, and form imaginable, but quite a few just the same, were up and selling. I waited for a break in the black and gold, crossed the street— into the heart of Hawkeye country. And Saturday afternoon's friendliest Big Ten party.

Iowa's the best place in the world to *roam* tailgates. There are better places, if you've got the cooker and the ice chest, to actually set up. Michigan State and Michigan provide a lot more room, and Illinois tosses in a few pleasant surprises as well. And all three are stretched out like K mart parking lots around the stadium. Iowa's more like, get there early, find what you can find wherever you can find it, and sock in for the show. Besides the hit-or-miss setup, everyone's just so damn friendly. And because of that, my only fall-long Big Ten worry evaporated in all the Iowan smiles. You see, to best explore Big Ten Country I had to play reporter. Well, at least a little. I had to walk up to people I'd never met, say hello, and hope they didn't mind if I asked about "their team." I don't do that kind of thing too well. I figure if they'd have wanted me to stop by, they'd have called and left a message. Plus, I thought they'd all think I was bumming food. At Iowa, though, everywhere I roamed I felt at home. Like I was a long-lost cousin at *my* own family reunion.

I visited my first reunion behind a trailer, across from Carver Hawk-eye Basketball Arena, over in one of the concrete lots. There I munched crackers and sipped beer with the Evanses. I also got a Hawkeye ten-year Hayden Fry update, spiced with a rundown of the most significant wins in Hawkeye history, and an up-to-date review of the '88 season. Jan and Wilma modeled Hawkeye wear—black-and-gold shoes with a Tigerhawk on the side that matched their black-and-gold-striped sweaters. Emmet explained the significance of the bumper stickers on the back of his trailer: "One for each bowl game. Seven in the last seven years. And before Hayden we went through seventeen straight losing seasons. Well, not exactly seventeen," Emmet corrected himself; "there were a couple .500 seasons in there." The Evanses, particularly Emmet, were Hayden fans. They were Hawkeye fans. They were cracker and beer fans too. But not bumblebee fans. For survival's sake, Hayden stories got sidetracked every so often by bumblebee swatting.

On the sidewalk just off the dental building parking lot, I visited with another friendly group—the Lillys. A big wooden cutout of Herky the Hawk stood in front of their party. Decked out in a Hawkeye football uniform, at eight feet tall, the brightly colored Herky, I'm sure, inspired an awful lot of "Where'd you get him?" questions.

"It's actually the basketball Herky," Dr. Lilly, a teacher at the dental college, explained. "I switched him from basketball to football, and put a helmet on him. Cut him out and painted him myself!" The doctor was pretty proud of Herky. And rightly so; he filled the lighthouse role for the Lilly tailgate.

"Herky's been here for about ten years," Von, his wife, added. "Gilbert sets him up in the dental college the week of home games, then moves him out here on Saturday morning."

"Out here" was the doctor's week-long parking spot, which doubled as a Saturday morning backyard barbecue. Von welcomed me in. The Lilly clan, a whole lot of doctors and doctors' wives, sat around talking football. Mostly Wisconsin football. Or more specifically, the Wisconsin band and its Fifth Quarter. The group had been up at Camp Randall the year before. They'd seen and heard the Fifth Quarter. They'd swayed in the upper deck while everybody polkaed. They thought it was one of the greatest exhibitions in the history of college football. I agreed . . . and for my thoughts was offered a little fresh vegetable pizza, and a Fuzzy Navel to wash it down.

Next door to the Evans trailer and the Lillys' Herky the Hawk, Carver Hawkeye Basketball Arena was rolling. Emmet suggested I stop by. "Only time you'll get inside," he said. "During the season you've got to be a Kentucky contortionist to get tickets." This wasn't basketball season just yet—only the official opening day of practice, which, joined to a Michigan football Saturday, turned Carver Hawkeye into a full free house—no Kentucky contortioning needed. Tom Davis's B-ball team scrimmaged up and down the court. Seats, especially courtside ones, were packed. Quiet, skeptical fans, watched, sizing up the season, wondering whether or not to believe *Sporting News*'s Hawks preseason number one pick. It wasn't like this was the first time basketball/football fans had stopped by Carver Hawkeye. Unofficial shirts-and-skins practices, at least the home football Saturday ones, I was told, had been pulling four thousand. Coach Tom Davis, players in uniform, and the official kickoff just doubled it!

Outside of Carver Hawkeye was where I heard it the first time. "OOOO-HEY, pig SOOOEEEY—Razorbacks! Whole hog, half ham, Arkansas, by damn." A few seconds later I heard it again. A high-pitched "OOOO-HEY, pig SOOOEEEY—Razorbacks!" And again it was followed by that same chant—"Whole hog, half ham, Arkansas, by damn." It sounded like a farmer calling in the hogs.

I slid through the popped hatches and between a few cars, turned the corner, and found 'em. Four "southern transplants," a couple from Rogers, Arkansas, and a couple from Mississippi, all decked out in black and gold, surrounded by cookers and ice chests and lawn chairs, were set up on the lawn off Hawkins Drive. The ladies were trying hard not to die laughing, while their husbands hammered out the chant.

"One more time." The Razorback led the non-Razorback. And together the two pretended they were back in Fayetteville: "OOOO-HEY, pig SOOOEEEY—Razorbacks! Whole hog, half ham, Arkansas, by damn."

The McGinnises (Pat and Ron) and Rizzutis (Wendy and Mike) were a pair of hard-core college-football tailgater families. They'd tailgated all over the country. In fact, the McGinnises had lived all over the country, in nine states. Wherever college football showed, they'd shown. They'd been to Alabama games and Auburn games, and down in Death Valley at LSU. They'd seen the Notre Dame Fighting Irish band hit the field under Jesus and the Golden Dome at South Bend. And they'd watched Southwest Conference championships. They were in Norman when Notre Dame broke the Oklahoma Sooners' forty-seven-game winning streak. Pat said, "We saw people actually crying in the stands!" But for the past fifteen years, they'd been Hawks! Iowa City every Saturday afternoon, and on the road in Minneapolis and Madison, and even once off to Hawaii.

The Rizzutis' Iowa migration was only fourteen years old. But they were just as Hawkeyed. "I took her out of the hills of Arkansas and dragged her up here to Benttendorf, Iowa." Mike still had that southern twang. They all did, actually. But Mike's was the twangiest.

The ladies kind of took their husbands in stride. Let 'em roll on 'bout Razorback football, sing songs, and tell jokes, and filled me in on college football lore.

"I can't explain it," Wendy said to me. "We'd just love to have our friends from Arkansas come up and see a Big Ten football game." She stopped and thought for a moment. "But I can't tell you why."

"I know what you mean," Pat agreed. "We're the same way. I'll be on the phone talking to a friend, I'll invite them up to an Iowa football game. I'll get all excited talking about it. But if they ask me why . . . I just don't have an answer. 'Cept maybe that people are so friendly."

"And they say they can get that in Arkansas."

"Well, what's the difference—I mean between the Big Ten and southern football?" I was curious. I'd never met a Razorback, let alone a Razorback football fan, before. "You guys look like you've adapted well." Everything they were wearing, everything they had stuff stored in, was shaded black and gold.

Ron figured it, "Here it's friendly rivalries. It surely isn't down south. Southeast Conference—Auburn, Alabama, Georgia—rivalries are hard core. We've got Michigan people parking next to us. Hell, down there they'd get killed."

Pat picked up where her husband left off. "They really are nastier down there. The rivalries . . . not the people! Alabama, Auburn, LSU—it's just not nice. I mean, we love Alabama football, but I've seen people break windows in their own house when Alabama lost. You'd never see that here!" She shook her head. "We have a couple friends. They're married. One went to school at Mississippi; one went to Alabama. When the two teams play, they have to watch the game in separate rooms in the house. And they're sixty years old!"

"In the Big Ten people just have a good time!" Wendy backed her up. "Another thing . . . women know their football a lot better up here. In Alabama, seventy-five percent of 'em don't know who's playing."

"That's right. They get dressed up, put on their heels; they just go because it's the social thing to do."

"Maybe it's the weather." Ron hit his most serious statement of the day. "People sit through all kinds of shit up here. Snow, ice, rain, they'll sit through anything for Iowa football."

"Like I always say, there's just two seasons in Iowa—fall and crummy." Wendy looked up at the blue sky and laughed. "Thank goodness today it's fall."

"But then tomorrow it could be crummy!"

It was like sitting in on College Football Fans 101. A lecture discussion series on college football fans all over the country, appropriately taught with a beer and a brat, by folks who had seen it all.

"Here they come! Hey, big M," Ron yelled to a waving M flag, and the group below it, that he'd been messing with. Since they worked in pairs, Mike got 'em too. "Hey, big M—here comes your team!" The Razorbacks' tailgate spot, the curb lawn on the Hawkins Street turn, the main road to Kinnick, on game day was closed off to everything but team buses and important university vehicles.

"Michigan always comes in Iowa buses, Iowa in charters." Wendy had seen them plenty of times before, and wasn't as excited as the fellas about the buses.

Three busloads of Wolverines, three big Hawk buses motored past. In bus number one, in the front-seat passenger side—God, it'll be stamped in my head forever—Bo! A silhouette, stone-jawed, staring straight ahead. He sat there like a rock, probably grinding his teeth, and seething that every other year he had to take his Wolves down into the middle of some cornfields and play in a place where his team couldn't hear the quarterback's signals.

"That's them. Every year they take the same route. Same buses. Same Bo."

Wendy clicked on the portable tube. Big Ten Game of the Week— Illinois (Illini fans, according to the ladies, were the only Big Ten fans who weren't friendly) and Wisconsin. The brats were brown, so they bunned a couple, and we sat back and pulled for the Badgers. We talked a little more football. And a little more football fans. We talked about Hayden's speech at the I-Club the previous morning. They were four of the hundreds that had awakened before dawn, just to get a seat. Like everybody else who heard it, the Razorbacks too had that image of the casket and the ring and jersey in their heads.

Mike invited me back next fall. Ron pulled out an Iowa pocket schedule. "OK—October 7, Michigan State, we'll be expecting you."

Mike raised a beer. "We'll wave to Mr. Perles."

"Maybe next fall you can teach me that Razorback chant."

"Yessir, my man, we will do that!" And I headed off to Kinnick. Behind me, "OOOO-HEY, pig SOOOEEEY . . ."

By the time I'd squeezed inside the big brick place, after cruising back through the stadium lots, and just plain shoving through the hordes of black and gold, other Saturday game scores were swirling. Blaring PA announcements and transistor radio updates filtered through the crowd and, depending on whom fans were pulling for, got answered with group boos or cheers. Notre Dame was on to an early pounding of Miami—to rounds of Iowan applause. Michigan State was finally winning a game—even if it was against Northwestern. More nails got hammered into the Wisconsin coffin—the Illini version, this time. And Ohio State officially broke with the Woody Hayes era by rolling over dead to Purdue.

Meanwhile, Kinnick buzzed. Colors and sights and sounds. For the Hawks, this was it! Michigan. On the road up in Ann Arbor the past two seasons—it was payback time! The sky shone blue. The warm sun kept kids in shorts and T-shirts. The whole place screamed black and gold, and was jam-packed full. Down at midfield on a center-stage platform, Herky the Hawk—fists in the air—danced around like Rocky Balboa on the steps in Philly. Cheerleaders shook their booties and waved pom-poms to the Iowa fight song. Two huge I flags ran circles around Herk. The band rolled. Fans rocked. The whole thing looked and sounded like some tribal ritual. Kinnick had ignited. When Hayden and those black-and-gold jerseys hit a human tunnel for the sidelines, it exploded. And from Chuck Hartlieb's shotgun-shredding first-quarter drive through the Michigan defense, the crowd didn't take a breath all game.

Row 64 on the ten-yard line, in the middle of the Hawkeye student section, my "seat" had to be the best in the house. And I caught it all . . . without ever hitting my butt. Nobody did! From ground level all the way up to row 79, each and every snap, each and every commercial and TV time-out was watched and cheered by students standing on the bleachers. "LET'S GO, HAWKS! . . . LET'S GO, HAWKS!" A slow loud tribal beat rumbled out of the stadium's four corners and erupted in the student section. In the middle of the end zone, crammed into a lengthwise rectangle, the band played and played and played till their lips fell off. When the Hawks scored to make it 7–zip, they even got their beer song. All game long, Kinnick shook!

Mostly, though, the standing student section shook. Cheers roared and died for almost anything. "LET'S GO, HAWKS!" was common language. The wave rolled on a tidal basis—at least through the end zone. Time and time again, the kids would start one, only to have alums across the field squelch it. Not even a trickle passed the end-zoners.

"Once they did it," a guy sitting next to me yelled, mad at the alumni, angry that they never joined in and rolled the wave through. "One goddamn time! When we beat Michigan twelve to ten. They make too much money to get off their asses!" But the kids didn't give up. A Hawk TD, the second of the day, and a first-half 17–3 lead, another beer song in the end zone, more let's-go-Hawking, another wave try, and this time folks across the field got "off their asses." The wave swept Kinnick. One time! One time all day, one time in three years. But enough for the happy student section—which roared its approval.

The game was an Iowa-Michigan classic. A bone-crunching down-to-the-wire struggle. Best of all, Bo was in rare form. He hates going to Iowa and can't stand the Iowa fans. Every year he makes it clear in the papers after the game. This time afterward he called them "unsophisticated." Probably 'cause they wouldn't let his QB hear the snap count. Second quarter, they cost him a flag. The crowd, a hundred decibels louder than a jet plane taking off, backed Steve Taylor, the Wolverine QB, off the ball. The forty-five-second clock ran out. An official tossed a yellow flag—"delay of game, Michigan." Bo lost it. He charged up and down the sidelines and out onto the field; he ranted around, screamed in the face of the white-capped referee, stomped the way only Bo can stomp. The crowd got louder. When the ref tossed another yellow flag and it plunked to earth at Bo's feet—"unsportsmanlike conduct on the Michigan coach"—Kinnick lost it.

When the flags and the smoke had cleared, after the screaming Iowans had stopped play three times 'cause it was just too damned loud to hear anything, after the Hawks had lost a time-out because of all that noise, after four and a half quarters of screaming, cheering, singing, standing in the noisiest place I'd ever been in my life, I'd seen a 17–17 thriller with a whirlwind finish. A Michigan fumble on the Iowa one with 1:20 to play, the Hawks shotgunning for field goal position and eventually running out of time-outs, finally a popped gun and the exit! Bo leaving to stream of boos, the officials to a flood of them. And Hayden and his boys, who'd blown an early fourteen-point lead but hung on at the end, left to a standing ovation. Seemed a hell of a lot better than kissing sis to me.

Still, it was a tie, and ties are strange. You never figure on them before the game, and you never plan the standings expecting a tie to be thrown in. If you win, you know where you stand; if you lose, you know where you stand. But a tie screws everything up. And even though the game had been terrific, the standings, particularly since it was the Hawks' second tie, were a mess—probably. But then again, not for sure. It was something to be straightened out back at the tailgates, or the bars, or the frat houses. So while darkness crept into Kinnick, tailgaters filed back to the parking lots. Some did their standings evaluations on the way home. Slow lines of cars in the dark rehashed the game. The hard-core fans, the ones who never slept well on Friday nights before a Michigan game, reopened the taps and the coolers, some recranked their cookers, and did their rehashing while the crowd thinned. Hartlieb's passing show, Hayden's play calling, the time-outs and the time-out penalties, along with one more tie in the standings, got a good Iowa tailgate review.

And at the end, after talking a little football in the dark, in the parking lot, with some of the folks that'd hung around, I headed back toward my car. Back toward the river, to Iowa City. Along the way, on Melrose Avenue, the first place to buzz and the last to pack up, I discovered a lady who probably didn't know a thing about football. A lady who didn't know Chuck Hartlieb from Chuck Long, or Hayden Fry from Bo Schembechler. A lady who probably hadn't contemplated what another tie would do to Iowa's Rose Bowl chances. But a lady who'd been hanging around Melrose since 10 A.M.

Anna Murphy, stood behind a table in front of a big black hanging quilt. It was dark, pushing 10 P.M. All the other souvenir stands and brat tents, even tailgaters, had packed up. She was winding up her day's work.

"Hello. Would you like to contribute to our Kelsey Deacon raffle?" The lady kind of caught me by surprise. I was mesmerized by the quilt. A huge black square twice the height of Anna Murphy. The thing was covered with Hawkeye symbols. All black stitching in small gold squares. The centerpiece traced the outline of the state of Iowa. And all about it, Herkys dressed up for Iowa bowl games. Herky and roses commemorated two Hayden Fry Rose Bowls. Herky in an Uncle Sam hat marked the All-American Bowl. Herky with a gator for the Gator Bowl, and Herky inside a peach for the Peach Bowl. Other little outlines, like a symbolic swing of Iowa's four seasons, caught the edges, but Herky was the main man!

"Sure," I answered, still trying to figure each of the little symbols. "Who's Kelsey Deacon?"

Anna lit up and told me a story about a little blond four-year-old Iowa City girl. Kelsey had been born with a spinal disorder, a club foot, and worst of all a deformed heart. "Twice they told her mom and dad that she wouldn't live." But nobody gave up hope. Mom and Dad kept praying, and Anna Murphy kept plugging away, some days twenty hours, on the quilt. Anna smiled. "She's going to be OK. Her foot's all right now. And her dad told me just the other day, after the second operation, 'My little girl's pink, not blue anymore!'"

Kelsey was hanging in there. She was home! Life for her would probably always be a little precarious. But she'd beaten the odds. And after two major operations, constant medical attention, several trips to the Mayo Clinic, and after some of this country's finest surgeons had predicted no chance for her, Kelsey was a normal little girl. Just a year away from kindergarten.

But her dad, who ran an Iowa City auto parts store, was buried in medical bills. Iowa City had come to the rescue. A *Press Citizen* newspaper article on the table told how. Coin canisters sat on Deli Mart counters around town and collected Kelsey Deacon donations. The Moose Lodge scheduled a benefit dance for the little girl. Fall fundraisers popped up all over town. And a 104-by-114-foot 100 percent cotton quilt, hand stitched on "an old frame owned by a couple of Amish women," was Anna Murphy's contribution. It'd taken seven hundred hours and some sore fingers to stitch, but a glass jar on the table was stuffed with one-dollar raffle tickets. The metal cash box overflowed with dollar bills.

"We hope to raise four thousand dollars." Anna looked down at the box and beamed. "People have been so good." Anna was proud of Iowa City. She recalled a disabled Vietnam vet who'd stopped by when she and the quilt were set up at the mall. He'd come up in his motorized wheelchair with a small black satchel sitting on his lap. But he was paralyzed and he couldn't pick out the money.

"He asked me to pull out two dollars and put Kelsey's name on the tickets. I felt so bad for him. But so happy too that he'd thought of Kelsey." The vet must've thought a lot about Kelsey. "Two days later," she said, "he brought back his own seven-year-old girl. He told me, 'Cindy wants to help out Kelsey.' " And the little girl, with her dad sitting alongside, gave a dollar of her own money. "She wrote Kelsey's name on the ticket."

Even punk rockers, "kids with weird hair" Anna called them, got involved. "Some would walk up to me out at the mall. They were really kind of scary looking." Anna laughed, recalling the kids. "But they must've known what the quilt was for. They never said much. They'd just walk up and drop a five-dollar bill on the table, and tell me, 'Put five Kelseys in,' then walk away.

"Everybody's been so good! The whole town's been pulling for her. You know, Kelsey's going to do the drawing. It's Thanksgiving at the Moose Lodge." Anna paused and looked at her quilt. "I think it'd be so neat if she pulled her own name. Kelsey's such a special little girl."

That's Iowa for you. Folks looking out for folks. A big black Hawk-eye quilt. Iowa City punk rockers dropping five for a "special little girl." Boys' bands in River City. The Hawkeyes in Kinnick. LET'S GO, HAWKS on corn silos. I-Clubs everywhere. Six-thirty A.M. Friday morning breakfasts, and beer bands on Friday night. Like they say in Iowa City, "Love them Hawks." You just gotta!

# 6

# UNIVERSITY OF ILLINOIS
## THE FIGHTING ILLINI

| University of Illinois Champaign-Urbana, IL | Memorial Stadium |
|---|---|
| Best Breakfast | Aunt Sonya's |
| Best Bar | Chin's Wok-n-Roll |
| Best Burger | Murphy's Pub |
| Best of... | |

**The Best in Big Ten Country**

### TAILGATING

1. Michigan
2. Illinois
3. Michigan State
4. Iowa
5. Ohio State

Champaign and Urbana, Illinois, are sister cities. Unfortunately, though, neither one is much of a looker. In fact the two are so plain and so similar, nobody is exactly sure where Champaign ends and Urbana begins. Ask U of I students about it and they just nod. "The two kind of come together over there. And over there. Oh, and over there too." Anyway, somewhere in between the over theres sits the University of Illinois. And aside from a big beautiful quad smack-dab in its center, the campus, like the two towns, is also pretty plain. It's not overgrown with ivy, like the two Big Tenners in Michigan. It's no Wisconsin or Indiana or Northwestern when it comes to elegance. And Minneapolis is much more of a cultural night-life spot than Champaign. More than Urbana, even. But the school does have tradition, tons of it. My little tour through the campus was like one giant tradition exploration. By the time I was through, I'd found everything from an Indian chief school symbol, to a good-luck charm in the guise of a shiny nose on a statue, to a football field erected to honor those who'd died in the Great War.

Actually, I was lucky. I probably wouldn't have made all my neat little collegiate discoveries if I hadn't been provided a lot of neat little leads first. I struck gold at my first campus stop, the Student Union information booth.

Normally campus information booths are manned by work-study students. The kids put in their fifteen hours a week, get their financial aid, and do their humanities readings all at the same time. If you ask them where something is, they smile, say hi, and toss you a cheapo campus map. If you ask for more, they shake their heads, claim ignorant freshman status, and direct you to the best happy-hour special in town. Not so at Illinois! I ran into three kids who knew more about their school than the Graduate Library Archives Department did, and all three were just bubbling with eagerness to tell me about it.

"Illinois was the very first school to have a homecoming," Walt, a sophomore, who'd spent the previous summer giving campus tours to visiting alums, revealed. "Let's see, it began back in 1910, I believe."

Ann popped in. "Yup, and this Saturday is number seventy-eight! We play Michigan State!"

"We were the very first school to have a mascot!" added Nicki, the third member of the group.

Ann gasped. "The Chief is not a mascot!"

"I mean symbol. I'm sorry." She really was!

Before I left Champaign I would be told *"The Chief is not a mascot"* by at least thirty-three people. Students, alumni, bartenders, cheerleaders, even the Chief himself made that distinction very clear.

Chief Illiniwek is a symbol. The name means "chief of men." Walt told me the campus tour story. "On October thirtieth, 1926, Lester Leutwiler appeared as the first Chief Illiniwek. It was in Philadelphia during the half-time show of a football game between Illinois and the University of Pennsylvania. Leutwiler was a sophomore at the U and was very interested in Indian lore. Well, as the band marched in formation, Leutwiler, who was dressed in an authentic Indian outfit, ran out onto the field and led the band in an Indian dance. At midfield he stopped, and as the band played "Hail, Pennsylvania," he saluted the Penn rooters. The Penn fans went nuts. From the other side of the field, William Penn, impersonated by the University of Illinois drum major, appeared. Together at midfield, the Chief and Mr. Penn smoked a peace pipe. Then, to a standing ovation, the two walked arm and arm from the field. And he's been with us ever since! The Chief, I mean . . . not William Penn."

"There's been twenty-seven Chiefs in all," Nicki redeemed herself. "And five different costumes. And the costumes are handmade somewhere in South Dakota . . . by *real* Indians!"

"She's right. It's a really big deal here. The Chief has to be a U of I student. His dance is an authentic Indian dance. He does it one time each football game, right after the band plays "Hail to the Orange." Then he disappears."

"I think he dances at basketball games too!" Ann added.

"It's really tough to be the Chief. You have to write essays, take a test, and go through an intense interview."

"Chief Illiniwek is *no Bucky Badger*!" Nicki made full restitution.

With Chief Illiniwek aptly covered, the kids rolled on about other university traditions.

"Let's see, there's Lincoln's nose. You've gotta make sure you go and rub Lincoln's nose." The girls brought things up, then Walt provided his short summer-tour overview.

"There's a bust of Lincoln over in the lobby of Lincoln Hall. In 1862 President Lincoln signed a bill that provided a land grant to the state of Illinois, and that land is where the U was built. Tradition says if you rub the statue's nose, you get four years' good luck."

"The Corn Plots. Don't forget the Corn Plots."

"The Morrow Experimental Corn Plots are in the middle of campus, next door to the undergrad library. They've been around forever. The legend is that they built the library underground just so that it wouldn't shade the corn."

"And there's the Eternal Light."

"It's off the Quad too. It's kind of like a mini-monument. It was a gift to the university by the class of 1912. Tradition says if a man and woman kiss under the Eternal Light, then someday they'll be married."

"My mom and dad kissed there." Ann laughed. "Seriously, they really did! Dad says that's why he married Mom. He didn't have a choice after the kiss."

The three went on about the mosts and the firsts and the bests and the worsts. All at Illinois. The University of Illinois, the kids revealed, is the biggest Greek campus on earth. Fifty-four fraternities, twenty-nine sororities. Champaign-Urbana's best burger by unanimous verdict—Murphy's mega-double cheeseburger. "The pickles," Walt said, "make it."

The biggest Greek bar in town: CAMS, or SCAMS as it's called by GDIs (God Damn Independents—people not in frats or sororities). "Everybody goes to CAMS and takes a lap," Ann laughed. "That means they circle the bar and scope out guys and girls."

"And the undergrad library is CAMS without alcohol," added Nicki. "Nobody studies. They just cruise and scope."

CAMS may be Champaign-Urbana's biggest bar, but Chin's Wok-n-Roll is definitely the strangest. It's one of Walt's hangouts. "It's a three-leveled place off the main drag, and it's filled with all sorts of weird, crazy, voodoolike stuff on the walls. It's got Christmas lights on the ceiling and a mounted hammerhead shark behind the bar. Chin's is the only place in town where you can get fifties and sixties music on the jukebox, punk bands live, and Chinese food!" It's probably the only place in the world too.

Finally, Cookie Etc., a tiny sweets shop just a couple of doors down from CAMS, according to the kids, pumped out the town's finest product. "Real live chocolate-chip cookie dough. It's great! Only sixty cents a scoop."

"This is the greatest campus in the Big Ten," Ann boasted.

"She's right!" Walt nodded.

And Nicki offered me a money-back guarantee. "You're gonna love it. I promise!"

So with all my bearings straight; with Bucky Badger and Chief Illiniwek in separate mascot worlds, while the campus geared up for the Spartans and its seventy-eighth Homecoming celebration; with the best burger, beer, and cookie dough hangouts all mapped out and ready for sampling, I took off to explore the University of Illinois.

Out behind the Student Union stretches the Quad. A giant green grassy rectangle broken up by all sorts of sidewalks, it's the heart of the U. And while the campus itself may not be gorgeous, the Quad *is!* Oaks and maples turned orange by the cold crunch of autumn traced the giant rectangle, nearly three city blocks long. Big red-brick rectangular halls sit off the walks and close off the Quad from the rest of the campus. From the rest of the world. At the far end, staring back across the grass at the Union, sits Foellinger Auditorium. Strong stone pillars grace its entrance. Capped with a dome, Foellinger carries the commanding presence of the Jefferson Memorial.

Besides being the U's prettiest place, the Quad's also the most happening place on campus. All week long, all day long, when the clock strikes the hour, the Quad bustles. Kids scurry to class on foot or they fly by on bikes. In springtime the grass gets filled with lily-white bodies trying to turn brown. In the summer it's brown bodies trying to stay that way. The Friday night of my Homecoming visit, the Quad was where the big pep rally was going to take place. And during the week it was where I went searching for my information booth traditions.

A block or so down the Quad from the Union, in the grass alongside one of the big red-brick rectangular halls, is a stone monument. It's small and simple. A limestone bench sits on a tiny stone platform. It curls around in an arc. In the middle of that arc stands a pillar. The pillar's not too tall, maybe eight or ten feet. Branches from a nearby tree reach down and dust its top. Perched atop that pillar is the Eternal Light, the one that Ann's mom and dad kissed underneath. And maybe, like Nickie's dad says, the reason they got married. College campus traditions wield a pretty potent spell.

A little further along the sidewalk, next door to the Eternal Light, is another hall. It's three stories tall, and like almost all of Illinois's school buildings, it's a red-brick rectangle. Nowadays, except for the kids wandering in and out on their way to class, the building's quiet. But back in October of 1911 a festive ceremony occurred on the grass out in front of it. That day all sorts of important people, university and college presidents, scientists and other distinguished scholars, gathered to dedicate the building. Construction had been begun two years earlier in 1909, on the one hundredth anniversary of the birth of Abraham Lincoln. In October of 1911 the job was complete and Lincoln Hall became a part of the University of Illinois, the same university that Abraham Lincoln had initiated with a signature forty-nine years before.

More than just a campus building, Lincoln Hall is also a memorial. Across its facade, between the second and third floors, facing out to the Quad, is a series of murals. Each lifts three-dimensionally out from the wall and each is dated. The murals depict the life and times of our sixteenth president. One, dated 1831, shows a young Abe splitting rails on a farm. Another presents an older Abe confering with Union soldiers. In the 1865 mural, Robert E. Lee and General Grant are shaking hands, thus ending the most bitter war in American history. Encircling the rest of the building, on the same level as the murals, are quotes—from speeches, from written documents, all from the mind of Abraham Lincoln.

The sincerity of the building works its way through the front door. In the lobby sits a worn plaque inscribed with a copy of Lincoln's Gettysburg Address. And just like Walt said, back inside a carved-out arc in the wall is a bronze bust of Abraham Lincoln. It depicts a young man, maybe as an Illinois congressman, before he became president and before the horror of war aged him so. The man's arms are folded across his chest. The statue is simple. It's solemn. It's quiet. No longer bronze-colored, the bust is dark and worn, almost black. All but one spot. All but *the nose!* Abe's nose is bright bronze, and it's as shiny as Rudolph's is on Christmas Eve. A shine that could only have come from some regular "good luck" rubbing.

I popped up and rubbed it a little myself. Not for me, actually. I wished for a Spartan win on Saturday against the Illini. And maybe, just maybe, if Abe was handing out seconds, a bowl bid come January 1.

At the end of the Quad, back behind the auditorium, I found the kids' last "can't miss." The Morrow Corn Plots. And like they said, the plots sit smack-dab in the middle of the campus. A registered National Historic Landmark, begun in 1876, and used for experimentation with corn cultivation, the Morrow Plots are a university mainstay. They're also kind of quaint. Particularly rolled out in the middle of a Big Ten university. And especially in contrast with the tiny one-story building next door. The building, not much bigger than a two-car garage, hardly casts a shadow. It's University of Illinois's undergrad library. It's four stories, but it's four stories *down.* Why down instead of up? Who knows . . . maybe like Walt said, so the campus corn can soak in all of that warm Midwest sunshine.

The University of Illinois is Greek! Nearly as Greek as Athens. The kids at the info booth had told me so, but they needn't have—you see it all over campus. Greek houses line Fourth Street. Kids wear their big fat Greek letters on sweatshirts and ballcaps, on the way to class or while doing laps at CAMS. They also get involved in all sorts of campus activities, and that's good . . . for the school and the kids!

Colleges aren't like they used to be. A lot of the crazy old traditions that used to rule the past have withered away. Stories about Little Brown Jugs and Old Oaken Buckets don't mean as much as they used to. Kids just don't seem to care about that kind of stuff anymore. . . . Why should they? They've got MTV! And VCRs, cars, and supersonic stereos, and too often parents with separate mailing addresses.

At Illinois, though, the Greek system keeps the old traditions afloat, especially on game day over at the football stadium. A big portion of the student-section side of the stadium is broken into fraternity and sorority blocks. Two houses sign up together and spend the season cheering with each other. Another old-time college standby, the card block, while it's disappeared in a lot of places, is alive and well in Champaign. Memorial Stadium's version is called I Block. Eleven hundred kids buy tickets in the block and spend the game turning over little colored cards that paint pictures for the alumni side of the stadium. A lot of I Block is Greek too. A third tradition, Illini Powwow '88, the Homecoming, was organized by the Interfraternity Council. They volunteered; they welcomed back alums; they set up all the events. And while the Spartan–Fighting Illini football game would take care of itself, Friday night was Greek too.

The two Friday night biggies were the Homecoming parade and a pep rally "Powwow" on the Quad. All week long, orange signs and newspaper reminders told people DON'T FORGET. The parade was scheduled for 5:30, just about the time October darkness was creeping in, along with the October cold. The route began down by the stadium, weaved its way up through the fraternity and sororities, slid through town, and ended on the Quad for the pep rally. Champaign-Urbana turned out en masse. Folks dressed in orange lined Green Street, the campus main drag. Moms and dads sat with their little ones on the curb. They watched and they waited. Students showed up in groups. A lot of kids hung around outside the bars with the best Friday happy hours. Frat row, Fourth Street, was packed too as fraternity brothers and sorority sisters lined the sidewalks. Some of the luckier houses with big balconies were crammed with students. All TGIFed up, they hooted and hollered down at the street below.

Nobody was disappointed! The parade was great! It started, appropriately enough, with some fat guy in his orange Illini cowboy hat sitting in a convertible and waving to the crowd. Little kids waved back. Champaign and Urbana high-school bands marched through. Convertibles toted dignitaries, and the important alums who'd gotten special invites. Everyone wore orange. The nineteen floats, almost all Greek, weren't gorgeous, but they had some heart, along with a consistent theme. Fry the Spartans, or, more appropriately, shish kebab them. Each float either stuck a Spartan on a post, turned him on a barbecue spit, or scalped his poor green-and-white head. Regardless of how good or bad or even gruesome they were, cheers rambled down Fourth Street whenever the Greek letters on the float passed the same letters on a house. The Marching Illini paraded through. Cheerleaders stopped and did a few numbers for the streetside crowds and the Illinettes dance team shook their pom-poms. Fifteen kids crammed into the back end of a Chevy pickup held cards, and on cue turned over Illinois symbols—a rather ragged I Block float, it still got a good round of applause. The biggest hand, though, was for a white Corvette convertible and the Champaign County Fair Queen. Well, the cheers were actually for her legs. The second-biggest cheer was for the frat guy who broke from the crowd ran up to the car and kissed the Queen's outstretched hand. It certainly wasn't the Rose Bowl parade, but the march wound through Champaign with the sincerity of a high-school Homecoming parade. And as it passed, after about a half hour, people picked up and went on their way. The happy-hour bars refilled. Little ones headed home with Mom and Dad to hit the sack. And alums and students trucked over to the Quad for the big pep rally Powwow.

The Powwow didn't start till seven o'clock, so lots of people milled inside the Union. They headed down to the cafeteria to get something hot to drink, or they just stood around and talked. The cheerleaders, in bright orange sweaters with a block I and blue skirts, limbered up. They were getting ready for a Powwow stage performance.

"We really are the best!" Karen Curtis, a tiny senior cheerleader from Peoria, Illinois, beamed. "I don't want to sound cocky. But I think we are. We came in fourth in the nationals last year." When I asked then who were the Big Ten's worst cheerleaders, she just laughed, "I can't tell you that!"

Karen was a sweetie.

"This is my last chance for a bowl. Oh, I really hope we go." Performing after the conference finale—it's something Michigan and

Ohio State and USC cheerleaders probably take for granted. Not Karen. So far she was zero for three—but optimistic. "We're doing pretty good! Who knows, if we beat Michigan State tomorrow, and then U of M, we might even make it to Pasadena."

She bubbled on about all the good things at Illinois. "Oh, you have to see the Chief. You really do! He's great! He's not like the other mascots. He doesn't run around and do goofy things. He's not a Herky the Hawk . . ."

"Or a Bucky Badger?" I added.

"Yeah, right." Karen grinned.

Being a cheerleader is not all smiles and parades and Chief PR. The hardest part for Karen? "It's tough if you're getting creamed or you know you're destined to lose and you're out there for the duration. You just keep pumping and jumping around and smiling. You do your own thing and try to have some fun!"

And the payoff? The cheerleader beamed. "Getting people going and knowing you're a part of it! When the student side of the stadium chants, 'Ill,' and the other side answers, 'ini,' when sixty thousand people are screaming, it's incredible!"

While Karen bubbled on about the Fighting Illini's bowl chances, and alums warmed up on cafeteria hot chocolate and did the same, big things were happening outside on the lawn. The Quad was a beehive of people and sound and lights. All nineteen floats pulled in and lined the sidewalks in front of the big brick buildings. Clear across the green almost three blocks from the Union, old Foellinger Auditorium glowed like a Christmas tree. White lights draped down the dome roof and cut the darkness. A big stage out in front gleamed with colored bulbs. Two gigantic video screens sat onstage and displayed the event so folks way in the back could see it all. And on the auditorium steps, rising up like a stairway to heaven, the Marching Illini. They pounded out "Illinois Loyalty." The Quad clapped along and the Powwow took off. First came introductions of the famous alums who rode in the convertibles. Float trophies were awarded. Different groups did different shows. The cheerleaders and the Illinettes did their routines. Then ten guys from a black frat did a rap number that had everybody jazzed up. Even the football team showed up. About a dozen of them took the stage. An offensive lineman stepped to the mike and was overwhelmed by the moment. His voice boomed through the Quad. He was pumped!

"We're gonna show George Perles tomorrow we really are for real!"

He echoed all the way back to the Union. His teammates laughed. Fans clapped. The kid got rolling! "We really appreciate all these beautiful floats and all you people being out here! And we're really gonna go out there and win that game for you tomorrow." He thrust a number 1 into the air. Everybody cheered. The players filed off as the band cranked a fight song.

The football players left, the band kept playing, and still the featured attraction hadn't yet appeared. Each time the stage cleared for a new introduction, chants arose from the crowd: "CHIEF! CHIEF!" Whenever something got a little slow, isolated "CHIEF!" chants broke out. When the band rolled his intro music, and the Powwow sounded like the score for some old John Wayne western, Chief fans took over. "CHIEF! CHIEF! CHIEF!" The yells became louder and louder. Finally, when Chief Illiniwek appeared, the Quad roared its loudest roar of the night.

To "CHIEF" chants, Illiniwek faced the crowd, turned his palms inward, and slowly raised his hands above his head. He looked up to the heavens. Auditorium lights shone down on him. The two big video screens caught a stern, unwavering face covered with warpaint. His red-and-white headdress flowed down over colorful buckskins. His feet were bare. The marching band sounded like a Sioux war party. Fans clapped along to the beat, and Illiniwek bolted across the stage. He ran and kicked, and leaped high in the air. He darted back and forth to the tom-tom beat. An explosion of energy, he electrified the crowd. And when he finished, they roared. Illiniwek folded his arms across his chest, and with a stern face he hailed them. Then disappeared.

While the Powwow celebration trickled down, I slipped around to a side door of the auditorium. I thought maybe I could find the Chief. Off one of the side doors, I did. He was winded, standing in an empty lobby, adjusting his headdress and coming down from his performance. About the time I arrived, an old guy opened another side door.

"I got three Alpha Chis out here. They're fans of yours," the doorman hailed Illiniwek. "They say they have been for years and years and years. They begged me to get you for a picture with them. What do you say?"

The Chief obliged.

Outside you could hear the band rolling through one last fight song. The three ladies were almost giddy, they were so excited. Trudy, the ringleader, a 1957 Alpha Chi, was first to see the Chief.

"Oh, thank you. Thanks so much!"

Illiniwek quietly nodded. With headdress on, he knew his role. And he honored it. If it weren't for the lily-white skin under all the paint, I'd have sworn he was Crazy Horse.

"Thanks so much." The three ladies *really* had waited years and years and years for that moment. They handed me three cameras. "Would you please?" I was honored.

One of the ladies ran up next to the Chief. She smiled. He folded his arms across his chest, stared straight ahead, and never said a word.

"Oh, get a long shot, get a long shot."

"All three of us, please."

"This is going to be my Christmas card!" one of them bubbled.

I must've snapped six or seven pictures, until the old guy standing alongside said, "OK, ladies, that's probably enough."

"Thank you."

"Thank you so much. You don't know what this means to us."

Illiniwek nodded. "You're welcome." And he walked back toward his dressing room. I didn't follow. He was probably about chiefed out for the night.

Trudy was as excited as a little kid on Christmas morning. "The band director has told us all about him. He's such an important tradition here. We were so lucky to catch him!"

One of the girls echoed her sorority sister's good fortune.

I handed the ladies their cameras. The cameras that now contained sacred film, negatives that they'd waited years and years and years to get. Trudy smiled and thanked me.

"He's not just some Bucky Badger, you know!"

Tom & Helen,
A Big Oskee-wow-wow from
'n a real MSU fan from
the Giddy AX! Trudy '57

*October 22, 1988*

# MICHIGAN STATE AT ILLINOIS
## Memorial Stadium, Champaign, Illinois

| Standings October 22, 1988 | Big Ten | | | All Games | | |
|---|---|---|---|---|---|---|
| | W | L | T | W | L | T |
| INDIANA | 3 | 0 | — | 5 | 0 | 1 |
| ILLINOIS | 3 | 0 | — | 4 | 2 | — |
| MICHIGAN | 2 | 0 | 1 | 3 | 2 | 1 |
| IOWA | 1 | 0 | 2 | 3 | 2 | 2 |
| PURDUE | 2 | 1 | — | 3 | 3 | — |
| MICHIGAN STATE | 1 | 1 | 1 | 1 | 4 | 1 |
| MINNESOTA | 0 | 2 | 1 | 2 | 3 | 1 |
| NORTHWESTERN | 0 | 2 | 1 | 0 | 5 | 1 |
| OHIO STATE | 0 | 3 | — | 2 | 4 | — |
| WISCONSIN | 0 | 3 | — | 0 | 6 | — |

**Other Big Ten Games:**

INDIANA AT MICHIGAN

IOWA AT PURDUE

OHIO STATE AT MINNESOTA

WISCONSIN AT NORTHWESTERN

Memorial Stadium was officially dedicated on October 17, 1924. It stands as a monument to all of those Fighting Illini who died in the Great War—the world war that was to end all wars.

Robert C. Zuppke, the winningest coach in Illini football history, was instrumental in helping make Memorial Stadium a reality. Zuppke coached "the orange" from 1913 to 1941. In 1921 he also headed up the Stadium Executive Council. Zuppke applied the same dedication and integrity that brought him such success on the gridiron to his work with Memorial. His goal, and the goal of the many Illini involved, was not just a football stadium, but a very special football stadium. "The Memorial," announced Zuppke, "should be an honor court; and since one hundred and eighty-three Illini were killed in the war, there should be one hundred and eighty-three columns in the honor court. . . . And the stadium towers will be so high that if a searchlight is placed on top, they will illumninate the name of Illinois from the Statue of Liberty to the Golden Gate."

That is the passion with which Memorial Stadium was built, a sincerity that remains with it to this day. Fund drives for the stadium began in April of 1921. In the weeks and months that followed, students and Illinois alumni all over the country pledged their support. In September of 1922, stadium ground was broken. The first football game was played in the stadium a little more than a year later, on November 3, 1923. And finally on Friday, October 17, 1924, Memorial Stadium was officially dedicated.

The stadium today isn't exactly the same one Coach Zuppke spoke of. Budget cuts and shuffled plans took a toll on perfection back in the twenties too. Instead of 183 columns, Memorial features 200. The plans for a huge fountain and the stadium's monumental approaches never materialized, and the towers don't really fire a beam of light from sea to shining sea. But Memorial is a wonderful old place, a solemn tribute to those who died in World War I. And wandering through its hallways makes you feel as though you're walking on hallowed ground.

Memorial towers over the flat Champaign terrain. You can see it from miles away. Two huge red-brick facades, the east and west sides, like sturdy hands cradle college football inside. Big block rectangular towers anchor the stadium's four corners. Along ground level, tiny arched entrances welcome fans. But it is the memorial columns that provide Memorial Stadium with its real presence. Although a little weathered by the decades, from below the columns command attention. They announce a powerful, almost Roman Colosseum–like dominance. Inside and up close, the columns are even more inspiring. They run in two long parallel rows on both the east and west sides. Hallways, one on each side, Coach Zuppke's honor courts, stretch between the rows. Sunlight and wind and rain sneak into the hallways. Standing there, peering out between the thick columns, you look down on the college campus and neighborhoods and farms out beyond. If you quietly slip through the inside row, you disappear into the heart of the old stadium. Strolling the honor court, you get a real feel for the sincerity of Memorial Stadium. You understand its purpose is more than just a place to play football.

A huge stone tablet rests against the wall at the end of the honor court. America's symbol of liberty, a sculpted bald eagle, perches atop the tablet. It guards the words below. "The Memorial Columns are dedicated by the Donors to Illini who lost their lives in the World War." Farther down the tablet, etched into stone, are the names of those young men. Around the stadium the names are repeated, each engraved into a separate column. A date is engraved next to each name. That is the year which the young man graduated from Illinois . . . or the year he would've, had he not died in the trenches "over there."

The honor court is solemn. The stadium facade is awesome. The rest of Memorial is a maze. When you're walking around inside, the structure looks and feels like a tired but friendly old baseball park. Low ceilings squash people together. Fat iron girders just pop up wherever they please. Tiny archways send fans out toward their seats, in single- and double-file strings. And ramps run, inefficiently in different directions, all about the place. In the four towers, the roads to the upper level, the ramps wind around and around and seem to just disappear somewhere high above.

People around Illinois are proud of their stadium. They claim that "Memorial has more seats between the goal lines—seventy-one percent—than any other football stadium in the country." They say that nearly every single seat's a good one. What they don't say is that its finest feature is the voyage it takes to dig one up.

Old Memorial Stadium has been the scene of some wonderful moments. Maybe its greatest was the dedication game on October 18, 1924. That's the day Red Grange ran wild. A couple of weeks earlier, up in Ann Arbor, ninety-one-year-old Herb Wagner had told me all about the game. His Wolverines had been in Champaign for the Fighting Illini's fourteenth Homecoming. Herb, his wife, and a couple of friends had road-tripped down to watch. It was the football game that stuck in Herb's memory as the greatest performance he'd ever seen, the one where Herb said "Red Grange was just fabulous!" Grange accounted for six Illini TDs. He ran for 265 yards and scored four times in the game's first twelve minutes. By the end of the day, "the red-head" had done everything with a football that one man can do. He'd carried the ball twenty-one times, gained a total of 402 yards, and completed six passes for 64 yards. The legendary football coach Amos Alonzo Stagg agreed with Herb about Grange's play that day. Stagg called it "the most single-handed performance ever delivered in a major game." It was a grand way to dedicate a wonderful stadium.

Sixty-four years later, almost to the day, I was in Champaign to watch another football game. The game, Michigan State and Illinois, would no doubt be less spectacular than the one in which Grange had run wild. And the stadium wasn't brand spanking new anymore. But that Homecoming day in 1924 couldn't possibly have been a prettier one. If Mother Nature whittled her best of 1988 down to a single afternoon, this would've been her number one choice. The sky was bright, bright blue, clear across the horizon. Champaign treetops were splashed with reds and yellows. The October air carried a slight chill, just enough for you to bring along a sweater. The Midwest sunshine shone bright, not hot—but nice and warm. After sitting in it, you could take home that fake Florida tan . . . at least on your face. What a gorgeous day for anything. Especially for college football. And all the Illini college football color made it even prettier.

Blue and orange flood Champaign. On game day they're everywhere. People head-to-toe in it. Sweaters and pants and cowboy hats. Flags, big orange ones with blue block I's in the middle, pop up all over. They hang in Champaign shop windows and Urbana shop windows. Attached to little portable plastic flagpoles, they fly from passing cars. They climb steel poles and unfurl over the tailgaters. Sororities and fraternities greet returning alums with a blue block I on an orange field. Orange cars and orange trucks and orange Winnebagos come out of the corn. The whole town is bathed in orange. If Illinois Homecoming ever occurred on Halloween, you could probably detect the ensuing orange color burst from the surface of the moon.

Illini orange burns brightest at the stadium tailgates. And Illinois is fantastic tailgate land. Like the rest of the Big Ten, it features all the basics—vans and cars and motor homes. It's got color and flags and cookers, but Fighting Illini tailgating comes with a couple of extras that give it that special zip.

One of the extras is Old Memorial. Parking lots bank right up against the west side. The memorial columns hover above all the orange below. On the other side of the stadium, cars stretch out across the football practice-field grass. More cookers. More orange. And more hovering memorial columns. The sincerity of the stadium reaches down into the parking lots. It revives old memories. Stories of magical moments carry a crisper ring when told under the watch of the old stadium.

Back on the west side of the stadium sits Fighting Illini Tent Row. It's Memorial's most energetic game day sight. And as Greek Row is to Champaign, and the Quad is to the campus—once you've visited a football game at Illinois, Tent Row is the sight that first pops to mind! The tents, dozens of them, run in two parallel strings, straight out even with the football field's fifty-yard line. Big, brightly colored, county-fair-type tents, they're a burst of color among all the popped hatches. Some are yellow and white, some blue and white or red and white, and there's always orange and blue. Whole communities meet at their tent. They eat and drink and talk Fighting Illini football. They bring the town social on the road to Champaign.

Illini tailgates open up their arms to anyone, even to a visiting Spartan fan. So I roamed, and in my wanderings I visited with all sorts of dedicated "orange." I found Trudy. She'd invited me by for a beer, payment for snapping those Friday night shots of her and the Chief. Underneath a Sigma Chi flag that flew over her van, she reminded me one last time, "You know, the Chief is not a mascot." I drifted past dozens of bright orange vans. I ran into a truck that used to tote Frito-Lay food around Champaign-Urbana until folks turned it into a rolling orange shrine. A rock-and-roll band that was set up across the street in the IM field and an old Dixieland crew, the Medicare Seven, added a little festive music to all the color. And I visited with two very special Illinois fans. Two old guys, one an ex-player turned fan, another a lifelong supporter of the orange; two fellows that "if you looked inside them, you'd probably find a block I engraved on both their hearts."

George Wenthe, an Illini graduate from the class of 1940, is from Effingham, Illinois. He's been coming to see the Fighting Illini for a long, long time. Since 1981 George had been in charge of the Effingham tent. Saturday it was the second from the stadium front door, so close you could hear the pregame band practice. "God Bless America" drifted out from inside the big old stadium.

"I guess you could say I'm a pretty good fan." George is humble.

And on game day covered with orange from the top of his head to the soles of his shoes, with the exception of a pair of blue polyesters. While George mixed me a drink, his buddy Roger Wolf whispered the entire story.

"He won't tell you," Roger said. "This guy loves football. For the past thirty-seven years he's been the voice of Effingham High School football. Friday night he's the public address announcer at the high-school games. On Saturday morning he drives up here to Champaign. And for twelve years, back when the they played at Wrigley, him and his wife, Jeanette, had season tickets to the Bears too. The guy's something else."

Back with a glass of the Effingham drink of the day—a Bloody Mary—George caught Roger rambling. He ribbed his buddy. "Did he tell you he played here?" George chuckled. "Typical lineman. Roger has an eighteen neck and size-three hat. But I guess he did play in the '52 Rose Bowl."

"That long ago doesn't count." Roger laughed. "My kid says that's before helmets and facemasks. But I'll tell you something, I've been there as a player and and I've been there as a spectator, and there's only one way to go and that's as a spectator. No bed check. I'll watch any day."

George reminisced a bit about his Fighting Illini career too—his career as a Fighting Illini fan. "I've missed two games here at Memorial since '46. One of them, I was in Berlin on an Illinois tour. Peter Elliot was the coach then. And I sent him a congratulations cablegram on the victory." George thought back and smiled. "Yessir, Pete and his wife, Joanie, really appreciated getting a cablegram from such a long distance away."

The two friends, player and fan, put their heads together and thought about life on the road pulling for the Illini.

"Wisconsin, they're partying people all right. . . . Ohio State, that's a good place too."

"Good fans. Loud fans. They just shake Ohio Stadium!"

"Ann Arbor." George shook his head. "I refuse to go back to that place. You put a little orange on and they just needle the hell out of you.

"I'll tell you, though," he went on, "Big Ten football is pretty competitive. There were some days when Ohio State and Michigan took the rest of us apart. But . . ."

"But so far this year the 'Big Two' aren't doing it," Roger added.

"I guess we always live for tomorrow," George sighed. "Some years we just had to."

"Some years we've had a lot more fun out in this parking lot than we had in the stadium."

George was optimistic. "This year, though, I've got a good feeling. If we win today, maybe we won't have to live for tomorrow. Maybe we'll get to a bowl this year."

Next door to Tent Row, up against a string of tiny pines, the Minsker family reunion was rolling happily along. Norma, a former Minsker, now a Brown; her husband, Jerry Brown; and Elizabeth, their daughter, were over from Carbondale, Illinois. Norma's brother, Jim Minsker, and his wife, Diane, had just pulled in off the road from Dallas. Their son went to Michigan State. He was due to arrive any minute.

"And no doubt," according to Diane, "he'll be wearing something green!"

The most dedicated of the clan was Bob Minsker, or "Dad" as they all called him.

"You have to talk to Dad," Norma told me. "He's the old diehard alum. Comes up from just outside St. Louis for all the games, has been for the past fifty years. He even played for Zuppke."

Dad—Bob Minsker—was out roaming. He did a lot of Saturday morning tailgate roaming. He'd get to Memorial early and set up with at least one of the family, then roam around and visit old friends. So while we waited for Bob to roam back, his kids told me all about him.

Bob Minsker is seventy-seven years old. He loves the University of Illinois. He loves Memorial Stadium. And he loved Coach Zuppke. Once I met him it wasn't hard to tell why he got to the games three hours early. He wanted to savor the entire day.

"This is a wonderful institution." Bob smiled and quietly opened his Illinois heart to me. "I've never met an alum that doesn't say he owes this university more than he put in. That's the way I've always felt. And the older I get, the more I appreciate it."

Bob could've spent all morning talking about the U of I. It was a sincere love affair. He told me all about the stadium and the columns, and how each Homecoming if you got inside early enough you could listen to the band play taps to honor the war dead. He humbly recalled his playing days, back in 1932 and '33 when he'd gone both ways for Zuppke. He thought back to some of college football's legends whom he was fortunate enough to have known. "Knute Rockne used to come over to Illinois a lot. He and Zuppke were good friends. I got to meet him once. And Red Grange"—Bob smiled—"he's a great guy. A very humble man.

"I knew Red very well," Bob went on. "After he was through playing, we worked together raising money for the university. We used to put on a small presentation. We used the film of that great Michigan-Illinois game in '24, the day Red ran for four touchdowns in the first quarter. Well, we would get a crowd together and show the film. We didn't have sound in those days, so a fella by the name of Bill Rice would narrate. Then Red would get up and talk. After that I'd make a sales pitch." Bob smiled. "After Red talked, my job was easy." His smile trickled into a chuckle. "Those days if somebody gave us twenty-five dollars we thought we were doing great!"

Bob went on about the U. He talked about the stadium, and about Red too. But more than anything or anybody else, Bob spoke admiringly of his old coach. "Bob Zuppke was a great coach. Even more than that, he was a great individual. I think I probably learned more about life from Coach Zuppke than from any other man. We got along real well. Sometimes we'd sit together on the train rides up to the other universities. Once in a while he'd talk philosophically. He was good at that. He had a lot of little sayings." Bob beamed. "One, I think, I'll always remember. He used to say, 'Don't ever give up hope—it might be the most costly fumble of your life.' He really was a wonderful individual.

"He's buried across the street in Rose Cemetery. Just on the other side of the football practice field, even with the fifty-yard line. Coach Eliot is over there too."

Perhaps in his heart Bob lives for "Illini past," but his mind still ponders "Illini present." And future. And the man of the future is new head football coach John Mackovic. "You know," the old halfback went on, "I think this John Mackovic is a lot like Zuppke. He's a real gentleman. You won't see any hot-doggin' out there on that field today. Mackovic's team is here to play football and they're going to be good too. Mark my words. He teaches those kids the right things. He spends time with them. He stresses academics. He teaches them them about life."

Kind of the same way Coach Zuppke taught a young kid named Bob Minsker about life back in the thirties.

* * *

The Marching Illini assembled on Memorial's porch below the columns. Their pregame show rang out across the lots to Trudy's Sigma Chi reunion; it filtered into the Effingham get-together and added a little music to the all the Minskers' fun. And when the marching band was finished, a lot of the roaming crowd that had gathered to listen just followed them inside.

Inside, Memorial Stadium oozed orange. Saturday under that bright blue sky, it crammed into the old stadium's double deck like a grocery store cart overfilled with oranges. A little Spartan green stuck out in the corner of the end zone, but it just kind of melted away into all the Illini.

As for noisemakers, I Block and the band control the stadium tempo. Sorority and fraternity blocks get in their share of cheering, and waving, and partying too. Memorial isn't a game-long rumble. Actually, it's colored louder than it sounds. But when a big barrage of orange-and-blue helium balloons were released upward into the bright blue sky, and the band cranked out "Illinois Loyalty," Memorial Stadium caught some of the Red Grange dedication-game excitement. The place thundered.

The Fighting Illini jumped out to quick 14–0 lead. Their kid quarterback, Jeff George, was hot. And the fans could feel the fever. Like Morse code, I Block flipped cards and sent messages to the other side of the stadium. Alumni cheered back. Karen Curtis bubbled and bounced and the Illini cheerleaders fired up the crowd. *The* chant rolled back and forth across the field. It celebrated the two quick orange scores. "I-L-L," the student side of the stadium yelled out across the football field. "I-N-I," the alumni roared an answer. "I-L-L," "I-N-I." "I-L-L," "I-N-I." The chant got louder and louder, and then when a big play rolled the Illini way, it'd break into applause. The band played its favorite, the *William Tell* Overture, over and over and over. And the Fighting Illini looked for real. But after half time, after the band was through entertaining the orange, and after Illiniwek delighted sixty-seven thousand "CHIEF"-yelling fans, the Spartans finally woke up! They came back to the field and for the first time during the season looked like defending Rose Bowl champs. George still riddled their defense. Thirty-five passes hit their mark. But the green and white were exacting a little payment from the other end of those completions—Illini receivers got hammered. And a Spartan offense that had hibernated for a month and a half ripped off four straight TDs. Finally, Michigan State was playing some football. I figured it'd just taken the Lincoln nose rubbing a little time to catch on.

In the end it wasn't the "I-L-L," "I-N-I" chant that celebrated, but a little sliver of green in the corner of the end zone. "Go, Green!" "Go, White!" "Go, Green!" "Go, White!" the visiting Spartan fans ended up the afternoon yelling back and forth at each other. Their enthusiasm carried the field. State won, 28–21. For Michigan State, a little dignity had been salvaged. For the Illini, it was "back to earth" time. They had a ways to go before their "bowl talking" became reality, especially since Michigan and Indiana still lay in wait.

I finished out the day upstairs on the stadium's east side. I sat there through the final gun. The day was still gorgeous and I wanted to savor all of it. By the end of October each beautiful day has the chance to be the year's last. Mother Nature can turn nasty pretty quickly with November closing in. The band played a postgame show to the few thousand that hung around. I sat there, looked out over the Illinois countryside, caught a few more rays, and relished the victory a little. I stayed until the band left the field and everybody packed up and headed out. Some folks left to tailgate until dark. Others headed back home to Effingham, or to Urbana, or they hit the road to Dallas. A few happy people even took off north for East Lansing.

After a final stroll through the honor court and one down among the tailgaters, as the blue sky drifted to twilight, I walked over to Rose Cemetery. It's where Bob had told me his old coach was buried. Where, he said, if I found the fifty-yard line, I'd find them both. Coach Zuppke and Coach Eliot.

I drifted across Fourth Street. Rose Cemetery, the memorial beneath Memorial, sits just a block from the stadium. It's not a very big or a very elegant cemetery. It's just a quaint and very quiet final resting place. An iron gate opened to a gray gravel path that wove in among the stones. Red and yellow oaks and maples splashed it. Evergreen bushes softened the bright colors with a touch of green. The cemetery was well looked after. It was trimmed and tidied up. Along the fence, overgrown bushes hid the street and the concrete and rushing cars. You couldn't see or hear anything but memorial stones and the rustling maples. A block away, peaking through the trees, loomed those solemn memorial columns.

I searched. A small gray stone not more than a hundred feet from the road caught my eye. Next to it, somebody had stuck a small flag into the ground. The flag, a memorial gift from a friend, was a blue block I on a bright orange field. The stone read "Eliot, Raymond and Margaret." And in the middle, engraved in small letters, was "Mr. Illini." It was Coach Eliot. The stone sat in line with Memorial's fifty-yard line.

Closer to the road only a few feet from "Mr. Illini," nestled into some evergreen bushes, sat another stone. A simple brown marker, it too stood but a few feet tall. The stone said "Zuppke." In front of it lay two smaller stones. One was engraved with "Leona Ray Zuppke—June 21, 1906, to Sept. 25, 1977." The other read "Robert Carl Zuppke—July 2, 1879, to Dec. 22, 1957." And under Robert's were some very simple, but very honest, words. Words I'm sure Bob Minsker would agree with. "He so lived that those whose lives touched his were a little better for having known him."

I stood beside the markers, beside the two coaches, each resting beneath a blanket of yellow maple leaves beside his wife, even with old Memorial Stadium's fifty-yard line. Blue had given way to twilight. Only the rustling leaves of the maples broke the quiet. An orange balloon, one of the millions let loose to celebrate the day, floated down from the sky. It skipped between the markers, kissed the ground, and then blew away. Gone. It disappeared.

A sign, maybe?

Maybe a word from the past, from two old coaches, that everything's all right. Or maybe a gift from the present. An offering to two men who dedicated their lives to the young men of Illinois. Maybe a Homecoming blessing from the solemn structure across the street. A simple, peaceful thank-you. Or just a sign that the two Fighting Illini will never forget . . . nor be forgotten.

# 7
# INDIANA UNIVERSITY
## THE HOOSIERS

| Indiana University Bloomington, IN | Memorial Stadium |
|---|---|
| Best Breakfast | Runcible Spoon |
| Best Bar | Nick's |
| Best Burger | Mustard's |
| Best of... | |

**The Best in Big Ten Country**

## CAMPUS

1. Indiana
2. Michigan State
3. Wisconsin
4. Northwestern
5. Iowa

They're eleventh in the all-time Big Ten football standings, that is if you include the University of Chicago. If you don't—then they're only tenth! They were 0–11 just five seasons ago. They've won two conference championships in eighty-eight tries, and have absolutely no Rose Bowl wins. They've amassed a career 26–34–1 record against the perennially powerful Northwestern Wildcats. And they've made only one solitary January trip to Pasadena—ever. Hoosier football history is a little like that of the Italians in world wars. Not to worry, though!

Times are changing in Bloomington. IU football's good ole days, maybe a little past due, are past due no longer. In fact, all hell's about to break loose! Two years running, the Hoosiers have chalked up more wins than losses. They've had three bowl invites the past three seasons. Fans are showing up in droves. And finally, the program's churning out some team photos they can proudly post in the football offices.

Yes, things are looking up in Hoosier football land! Even so, there's still that other sport down there. And when the world thinks of Indiana football, the first thing that comes to mind, for now anyhow, is Indiana basketball! Well, it's the first thing that comes to my mind!

I was pumped for IU for a lot of reasons. The football game Saturday with Iowa would be a good one, a battle to stay close to Michigan at the top of the heap. Plus, it'd be loud. As long as Hawkeye fans showed, it had to be! The Indiana campus had a great rep; folks all along the way—in Iowa, in Illinois, and up in Madison—had told me it was a beauty. But funny, the thing I was looking forward to most was maybe catching a basketball practice, and The General in action.

Back before Feinstein's *A Season on the Brink* came out, I'd been a part-time Bobby Knight fan. I liked the way he kicked Michigan's butt each year. I liked his attitude toward Kentucky—mine was about the same. Best of all I liked the things he stood for. Studies first and B-ball second—man-to-man defense, self-discipline, and dedication! And that was before the book! After reading it I turned into a full-fledged fan. When I sent Coach Knight an *On the Brink* congratulations letter, and he personally dropped me a "Thanks," I was devoted for life. So much so that his letter's made my over-the-desk, picture-framed "hall of fame," an honor that normally just goes to Michigan State and Frank Sinatra. So even though football was my official reason for trucking down to Bloomington, I was hoping to catch a little basketball too.

Actually, things worked out quite well. The two stadiums, football's Memorial and basketball's Assembly Hall, sit side by side on the north end of campus. And since I was coming down from Indianapolis, the north end was stop number one. I pulled in, got out, and roamed. From the outside neither is much to look at. Memorial, erected in 1960, looks like a gigantic high-school stadium. The press box side is one huge vertical rise, almost straight up! Bleachers hover over the turf, so steep that from the field it looks like if you jumped, you'd sail out over the turf and splat smack-dab at the midfield emblem. Across the way, where the students sit, the stands are about half as high. It makes the stadium look lopsided. For the bands and visitors, a few rows of temporary seats fill the end zones. All in all, it's a rather plain-looking place. Across the parking lot sits basketball heaven—Assembly Hall. Unlike its football partner, Assembly is anything but plain. Huge, white, smooth-surfaced concrete, it's a classic sixties design. Sandwiched inside a mass of concrete parking lots, the stadium looks more like a place to perform psychedelic experiments than a place to catch a clinic in man-to-man defense. But that's where the national championships were won. That's where I headed first.

Assembly flaunts its basketball dominance from every entrance! The tiny west lobby entrance, the one facing Memorial, greets you with five team photos: 1940, 1976, 1981, 1983, and 1987—five NCAA championship teams, all blown up and framed, cover the wall. Tiny stereo speakers hang from the ceiling and crank out Indiana Marching Band fight-song music. The tunes play and play and replay, all day long. They get you into the mood for a trip down Hoosier B-ball memory lane. Then take your pick. Left or right, champion-team-photo-covered walkways usher you to the two main entrances, where you get the real Indiana sports indoctrination—which means basketball, basketball, and, you guessed it, more basketball. At the north entrance, behind the ticket booth—which is pretty much useless unless you're buying ten years in advance—sits the Hoosier Hall of Fame. In everything from field hockey to football, wall portraits count each Indiana Hall of Famer. An engraving below on the rail tells about the star. Actually, it's the one place in Assembly where basketball shares.

The other big lobby, the south one, is solid B-ball. Just a ramp walk away from the basketball offices, it's the place to find the Bobby Knight shrines. Basketball trophy cases line the wall. Big Ten titles, NCAA championships, CBS player-of-the-game scholarship plaques—most of them in the name of Keith Smart or Steve Alford—just trophies piled on top of trophies. And everything not gold, silver, or bronze was trimmed in red and white, or more officially crimson and cream. For a Hoosier B-ball fan, a cruise through the Assembly Hall trophy cases must be like a visit to the Holy Land.

While I was sifting through the icons, tallying up the Alford-vs.-Smart totals, I thought to myself, wouldn't it be great if I could meet the man responsible for all this! It got me thinking. Why not? This is a guy who although he despised the *Brink* had written me a thank-you letter about it. He was the guy who, I'd heard, once bought out a local pizza shop and had a couple of hundred pepperonis dropped off at the overnight B-ball ticket line, just to feed the students. He's a champion of the little guy. Maybe, I thought, he'd see me. I was a little guy.

So I decided to give it a shot. I trucked one level up the ramp from trophy world to an open door that said "IU Basketball Office." I peaked inside, knocked, and walked in. It was like standing in a junior-high-school principal's office, except for all the B-ball stuff. Trophies and newspaper articles on big games, most of them different versions of the 1987 championship win, crammed the room. Almost every available square foot was filled with some basketball memento. *Bob Knight: His Own Man,* a new boring book that just told the good things, was piled in stacks all over the room. A lady on the phone, behind a little desk that was buried in paperwork, peered out from behind some books.

"Just a minute," she said. "I'll be right with you!"

I nodded, looked around, and eased over to the far end of the office, where the trail of Bobby Knight books began. I whistled, like I was just killing a little time and didn't really know what I was doing. I glanced back at the secretary. She couldn't even see me through the paper pile, plus she was still talking. I tiptoed a little closer to the door. Then I thought, wait a second. This wasn't illegal! I wasn't a criminal. All I wanted was a good look inside Knight's office. And the door was open. Why not? I quit feeling guilty, put down my backpack, and stared!

No Bobby Knight, but there were traces of him everywhere. About fifteen Post-its full of phone messages covered the door. Basketball stuff, organized in tornado fashion, was strewn all over the chairs and the table and the floor. There were more trophies and plaques that wouldn't fit in the lobby trophy case; they probably piled up daily. Basketballs—loose ones and others turned into awards—rolled on the floor against the back wall. More good-guy books filled the desk, and even more spilled over onto the carpet. A big framed blowup of the *Bloomington Herald* front page, dating back to that 1987 national championship, leaned against a chair. And on the old oak desk in the middle of the room were all sorts of Knightisms: a "The Buck Stops Here" nameplate; a little carved wooden fisherman dropping his little line over the desk into the pile of books; a group portrait—four faces in the same frame, all profiles, all with fire in their eyes, all gleaming like they were about to pounce on an enemy—three bald eagles and Knight; and around the room other eagles, figurines, and photos, by themselves, without Knight; even an eagle-and-an-oyster parable about life, and why if you wanted to succeed you copied the eagle and not the oyster. The neatest artifact, though, hung on the wall—a plaque that explained what a Hoosier was, according to Knight. I thought about popping a flash of the room, but staring inside was probably rude enough.

"All right now, what can I do for you?" Maryanne, Knight's secretary, had just gotten off the phone.

"Is Mr. Knight in?" I asked professionally, like he was expecting me.

"I'm sorry, not at the moment. Can I help you?"

I figured if I was cool enough I might be able to catch him a little later. Maybe I would mention something about *Big Ten Country,* say that I was an author on an interview. But he hates authors and interviews. So I blubbered on about how great a coach I thought he was and that I just wanted to thank him for sending me that letter two years ago. My cool approach ended with "That was such a neat thing for him to do . . . and he didn't even like the book!"

"Well . . ." Maryanne looked up at me. "That's the kind of person Mr. Knight is. He answers all his mail. People don't realize that. They just see the guy on TV." She wasn't on automatic pilot. She really admired her boss!

"Can I take a message?"

"No, thanks." I thought for a moment. Then said, "Sure. Just tell him a fan stopped by."


It's gotta be tough for the football program. Nothing but success in Assembly, and at Memorial, well . . . Some years, I'm sure, football coaches peered out across the parking lot and Assembly Hall must've looked like Mount Rushmore. Even the walk from B-ball over to the football offices is, in a way, symbolic. It's all downhill! The football offices lie down a two-story stairway, underneath Memorial Stadium.

Built in 1985, at a $2 million cost, the new football facilities are dazzling. A long, graceful hardwood staircase spills down under Memorial into a two-and-a-half-story limestone-finished lobby. Long luxurious hallways, comfy classy offices, a state-of-the-art weight-lifting facility— the setup's enough to turn any eighteen-year-old recruit's head. It's one of the reasons IU football's on the rebound. In fact, the layout's as sharp as any Manhattan IBM office complex. At least at first glance it is. But after you roam a little, after you get over the hardwood and the limestone and the elegance, the old problem comes haunting back. The Hoosiers just don't have any history! No 1960 Duffy Daugherty– type team photos, no Bernie Bierman teams, no Fielding Yosts. No black-and-whites. No scowling players in leather helmets from the prefacemask days over a "We Are the Champions" plaque. Three team shots—that's it! One Big Ten championship from the forties back when half of the good players were still over in Germany. Then 1967's "Brink's Gang" Big Ten champs. And the 1979 Holiday Bowl winners. The 1979 Holiday Bowl? Times have got to be tough.

Which makes this new success all the sweeter! That empty trophy case at the bottom of the stairs is finally starting to plump up a bit. A 1986 All-American Bowl trophy and a 1987 Peach Bowl trophy, though not for victories, at least announce the invitation. Plaques commemorating individual All-Star performances and a couple of autographed footballs have also cut down on available shelf space. The Old Oaken Bucket, the Indiana-Purdue war trophy—a trophy as prized as Floyd of Rosedale or the Little Brown Jug and for a long, long time a Boilermaker fixture—has for the past couple of years visited Indiana. And the chain of bronze block I's and P's, the annual victory update that hooks onto the bucket's handle, well, now it ends with a couple of I's. In fact, the way they have the old bucket sitting in the case, and that fifteen-foot chain looped around and down inside it, the nineteen I's look like they outnumber the forty-two P's ten to one. The Bourbon Barrel too, one half of a big oak whiskey barrel with the Kentucky-Indiana game scores painted on it, looks at home in the Indiana trophy case. Even a tombstone, the Hoosier Graveyard, listing the '87–'88 Memorial Stadium victory burials, looks more appropriate with Golden Gophers and Buckeyes, as opposed to Hoosiers, listed in the RIP column.

Indiana football is finally heading up those stairs! Why? Maybe the law of averages has finally kicked in! You can only lose for so long. Maybe a little magic has drifted over from across the parking lot. Probably the number one reason, though, is the new coach, the man who came to Bloomington five years ago and promptly introduced himself with an 0–11 record. Bill Mallory is a no-nonsense tough guy. An ex–Woody Hayes assistant, two-time Big Ten Coach of the Year, a chip off the old Bo, Mallory's put a little fire into IU football, and a bit of a bulge in that empty trophy case as well! And he's done it with class.

That class showed best up in East Lansing, during the last game of the 1987 season. Indiana and Michigan State faced off for first place. National TV, Big Ten championship, Rose Bowl—everything was on the line. And for the Hoosiers it was a chance to show the world they'd made it back. Three years before, they'd been the Big Ten's worst team, maybe the country's worst; in 1987 if they stopped the Spartans, they were off to Pasadena. But Cinderella wasn't ready yet. Lorenzo ran for a million yards and Michigan State killed them 27–3. East Lansing erupted. Fans danced out on the field. I sat upstairs in the stadium's second deck, dreaming of roses, and watched the goalposts disappear. Underneath, in the Spartan locker room, before the players even had a chance to pop the corks, a visitor dropped by—Coach Mallory. And while the kids sat quietly and listened, the Indiana coach pep-talked 'em. He told them just how important the Rose Bowl was and just what it meant to the Big Ten conference. He told them that that day, that win, was a moment, even more so an opportunity, to be truly savored. He wished them all the January 1 luck in the world and offered his congratulations. This, from a coach at a university that would've killed to go Pasadena, a university that had been to the Rose Bowl exactly once in its whole 103-year history. Coach Mallory swallowed a little pride and showed a ton of class. That class has led the Hoosier football program up the stairs.

While the gigantic twins—Assembly Hall and Memorial Stadium—anchor IU sports fortunes, main-campus introduction duties fall to a tiny church. The Beck Chapel, a stone one-room sanctuary built in 1956, sits alongside the mammoth eight-story Memorial Student Union. Between them, near the rush of a cold creek, lies tiny Dunn Cemetery. A handful of stones, some from as far back as the 1800s, moss filling cracks in names and dates, mark a small square of Indiana history. A blanket of maple leaves, yellows and browns and reds, keeps the stones warm. The cemetery and the chapel and the Union form the heart of the Indiana campus. An absolutely beautiful campus. The prettiest in the Big Ten, and in October it may be the prettiest in the world. After cruising through the basketball and football archives, after looking at the Old Oaken Bucket and basketball trophies, most of the rest of my visit, at least before Saturday's game, I dedicated to exploring the Bloomington campus. What a wonderful chore!

I was lucky. Just by chance I'd scheduled IU for the end of October. Actually, I'd done it for the game. Initially, the Hawkeyes-and-Hoosiers matchup looked like it could be a late-season doozy, one that the bowl scouts would visit en masse. I was right; both teams were still in the Rose Bowl race. But even better than that, the game had brought me to town at just the right time.

Indiana, at least where Bloomington sits, is gorgeous. That's something I hadn't expected. To me, the state of Indiana was always two things. First, like the Indiana school, it was Bobby Knight basketball. Second, it was flat. Flat, boring, and more flat, the pancake state of the Midwest. But south of Indianapolis, Mrs. Butterworth spreads a little sweetness on the pancake. Interstate 37, an offbeat kind of road, swings down through cornfields and stoplights, past tiny towns and roadside farmhouses, an occasional high-school football field, and into rolling hills. As you cut through the farms and the small towns, the horizon rises up around you like foothills to some distant mountain range. Fall colors explode! Roadside cornfields, hammered by a killer summer drought, were finally being put out of their misery. Harvesting had begun. The cleared landscape somehow looked calmer . . . soft again. And to celebrate—October's final flame. A red carpet of color, rolled out from Bloomington, with its throne the Indiana University campus.

Nature has a free rein on campus. Everywhere. Cars are stopped at the entrance, stickered, and directed to parking lots. No noise, no smog, no un-Midasized clunkers cramp the landscape. Quiet concrete walks slip through the woods and open grassy places. Wooden bridges connect them and reach over the Jordan River, which meanders about. And everywhere architecture follows nature's lead. Big old limestone halls blend into the trees—like the halls had been planted, and just grew up alongside them. Recent construction, instead of loudly announcing new, whispers old. Some of it, like the brand-new chemistry building addition, is so carefully built, you have to search out the lines where the old hall ends and the new wing begins. Even the president's house fits. A tidy red-brick Colonial, it sits among the trees, like a forest ranger's lodge at Yellowstone. Out the back window there's nothing but nature—and walks, and footbridges, and students on their way to class.

Behind the Union, alongside where old Seminary College stood and its past still lingers, sits Dunn Woods. Quiet red-brick paths file back into two blocks of underbrush, of towering oaks and maples. Sunlight sneaks through and shadows the trees. It's a shortcut to class, and daylight catches students hurrying through. At dusk, guided by the light from old-fashioned lampposts, boyfriends find girlfriends and stroll hand in hand. And if they kiss inside the old stone well house, tradition says, they'll marry. On Sunday afternoons, young couples walk their little ones through the maple-leaf-covered walkways. The old clock-tower bell chimes the hour. Roaming the woods, you feel the quiet, the birds singing, and the squirrels hustling between trees. The year, even the century, escapes. It just goes away. At least until you come out at the end of a path, or you notice the kid walking by has on a 1987 NCAA championship sweatshirt.

I could've roamed the grounds all week and gone home happy, but by Friday night I had to take a break. I had one last box to check on my "Get to Know IU" agenda, one very important duty left to perform. For my own sanity, I had to find out once and for all what the hell a Hoosier was. So Friday night, for the first time since college, I trucked over to the main library and did a little research!

Now I had my own ideas about Hoosierdom. A couple of years ago I was driving home from work and tuned in to some radio talk show— Paul Harvey or a Paul Harvey clone who picked up on little insignificant things. Anyhow, the guy noted that the state of Indiana was furious. Indiana senators, he said, were organizing retaliation. Lawsuits were imminent. A terrible crime had been committed. The ultimate travesty of justice! *Webster's* dictionary had been revised and updated and the edition containing all the new words had just been released. "Hoosier" was among them. According to the radio guy, Indianans agreed with definition number two in *Webster's:* "Indianan—used as a nickname." It was definition number one that called for a declaration of war. *Webster's* apparently had the gall to define "Hoosier," the Indiana state title, the University of Indiana nickname, a holy sacramental state adjective, as "an awkward, unhandy, or unskilled person . . . an ignorant rustic." The radio guy said there would be hell to pay.

I didn't know. I'd never heard the "ignorant rustic" definition before. And it just didn't make sense to me that a state, particularly one next door to Kentucky, would nickname itself after a bunch of hillbillies. *Webster's,* I concluded, was wrong.

I had heard a couple of stories of my own, though. Once, during a TV B-ball game, the color man attempted to tell the millions at home just what a Hoosier was. He said that back before the U.S. Postal Service challenged rain, sleet, snow, and pitbull terriers to deliver the mail, riverboats carried stuff up and down Indiana rivers. People on the banks, interested in what was coming to port, and not willing to wait till the boats docked, would yell, "Who's your cargo?" "Who's your cargo?" eventually became "Who's your?" which sounded like "Hoosier." It made sense, but it was the first and last time I ever heard the story.

Roaming round IU, I picked up another, even more colorful version. You see, I asked anybody on campus I ran into if they knew what a Hoosier was. Some folks thought I was nuts. Most, however, considered my question with some thought. They'd "hmmm" a little and crinkle their foreheads, and usually come up with a favorite! The most popular choice also went back to pioneer days. Apparently old-time Indiana taverns were hard-core places. A lot of fighting went on there, Hulk Hogan–type fighting; men rolling around on the floor, scratching eyeballs, tearing each other's skin, and once in a while biting off a nose or an ear. Well, the legend goes that after the ruckus, and the participants were banished or re-served, or sometimes buried, the tavern owner would pick up whatever body part happened to have torn off and ask, "Whose ear?" Which caught the Indiana drawl and evolved to "Hoosier." That definition, I figured, was much too racy for the liking of *Webster's.*

To tell you the truth, none of the Hoosiers I talked to was positively sure what a Hoosier was, or where the word came from. Even the "Whose ear?" story, which I heard five or six times, was a little difficult to believe. So by Friday night, after two days of research, I figured it was time to get the official word. Where better than in the Hoosier University library?

"We have a special little file just on that," the girl at the library information desk answered my request. "We get at least four calls a day. More since *Webster's* came out with *their* version!"

She handed me the newspaper-clipping-filled file. I retired to a library table and dug in. First, though, I checked *Webster's,* to see if the dictionary people'd had the gall to send Indiana *their* version. They had! The unabridged seventy-five-pound book, sitting splat on a table in the middle of the room, page 1089, told the blasphemous story.

The Hoosier file told the rest. It repeated the "Whose ear?" story and added a few juicy adjectives. The file had the hillbilly definition too, although it unequivocally stated that the hillbilly version was "unaccepted in Indiana." There was no mention of my basketball commentator's "Who's your cargo?" call. But the file described one close to it. In pioneer days, it said, Indianans answered their doors with a twangy "Who's 'ere?" and "Hoosier" just evolved from it. Another thought derived "Hoosiers" from the Napoleonic wars. A Polish officer who'd served under Little Nap had emigrated to the States and settled in Indiana. The officer told thrilling stories of the exploits of a light cavalry outfit known as the Hussars. Tales of the Hussars got around, and were told and retold. In the process, "Hussars" drifted to "Hoozyars." The article stated that one day in the late 1820s, back in one of those brawling Indiana taverns, a particularly nasty fight took place. The victor, an Indiana man, when asked where he was from, "proudly shouted, 'I'm from Indiana, I am,' and then, recalling the stirring calvary stories, shouted, *'I'm a Hoozyar!'*" It must've been a hell of a moment, because the victory speech caught on!

Finally I hit what looked to be the jackpot. At least it was the story the library liked best. And it dated back to the 1800s too. A contractor named Samuel Hoosier was working on the Ohio Falls Canal at Louisville and was recruiting men to help build it. Since the Ohio River formed a state border, Samuel Hoosier was lucky. He had the choice of pulling work recruits from Indiana or Kentucky. He chose Indiana men because, as legend goes, they were "far superior" workers compared to the Kentucky men. The article didn't mention whether or not the contractor sponsored a city league basketball team at the time. But if he did, and if you asked any Indianans, I'll bet they'd tell you his basketball players were "far superior" too. Anyhow, his workers became known as "Hoosier's men" and later simply Hoosiers.

All the stories worked. And I'll bet all of them, if you looked long enough, found some way to rip Kentucky. But since *Webster's* was obviously off its rocker, and since there really is no official definition—I made up one of my own. It's a doctored version of the one on the plaque in Bobby Knight's office, the one I'd stared at the day before. It seemed to pretty much cover all the Indiana bases. It goes like this:

BOBBY'S:   A Hoosier is a person born or living in Indiana—
industrious, hospitable, down home folk
who enjoys
popcorn, Indian Summers, race cars, basketball . . .

MINE:   . . . and Bill Mallory style IU football.
A person who before he retires to that big basketball arena in the sky,
wants just once, to visit Pasadena!

*October 29, 1988*

# IOWA
# AT INDIANA
*Memorial Stadium,*
*Bloomington, Indiana*

| Standings | Big Ten | | | All Games | | |
|---|---|---|---|---|---|---|
| October 29, 1988 | W | L | T | W | L | T |
| MICHIGAN | 3 | 0 | 1 | 4 | 2 | 1 |
| IOWA | 2 | 0 | 2 | 4 | 2 | 2 |
| INDIANA | 3 | 1 | — | 5 | 1 | 1 |
| ILLINOIS | 3 | 1 | — | 4 | 3 | — |
| MICHIGAN STATE | 2 | 1 | 1 | 2 | 4 | 1 |
| PURDUE | 2 | 2 | — | 3 | 4 | — |
| NORTHWESTERN | 1 | 2 | 1 | 1 | 5 | 1 |
| OHIO STATE | 1 | 3 | — | 3 | 4 | — |
| MINNESOTA | 0 | 3 | 1 | 2 | 4 | 1 |
| WISCONSIN | 0 | 4 | — | 0 | 7 | — |

**Other Big Ten Games:**

ILLINOIS AT MINNESOTA

MICHIGAN AT NORTHWESTERN

OHIO STATE AT MICHIGAN STATE

PURDUE AT WISCONSIN

O K, so I'd spent the past three Saturday pregames in parking lots. Michigan, Iowa, and Illinois fans know what they're doing when it comes to the tailgating! And so what if I'd picked up a few extra pounds along the way. That happens when you live off of bratwurst and Bloody Marys. I figured, though, it was time to get healthy. So for the Iowa-

Indiana game, I decided to try something different. Considering the weather was bright and blue again, and considering I had the world's prettiest campus laid out before me, an energetic walk around town and through the woods, talking "Hoosiers" along the way, seemed just right. Of course, I'd have to squeeze in a stop at Nick's Tavern to tip a couple too.

Bloomington's a wonderful old place! It's a college town. But then again it's not. Kids fill the streets, but don't take them over. Hardware stores and old limestone-fronted pharmacies, bookshops, and even the Indiana Movie Theatre look like if the U disappeared tomorrow, not a thing would change. In fact, it looks like folks have gone about their business the very same way for the past forty years—regardless of trends. A university and a tiny country town blended together, Bloomington provides all the down-home sincerity of southern Indiana, but adds the enthusiasm that only a college can create! It's a perfect place for roaming on a crisp blue Saturday morning. Great too for some window-shopping and visiting with folks. It's also not at all a bad place to "catch a little of that Hoosier spirit"—the football version, for a change.

Little hideaways are a Bloomington specialty. One of 'em is Southern Sporting Goods. Just five blocks from campus, it sits on the city square, across the street from the old limestone courthouse. From the sidewalk, Southern looks pretty normal. All decked out in red and white, just your average, run-of-the-mill Bloomington sporting goods store. But Southern adds something to the balls and hats and shirts and all the other sports items it sells. It adds a soda fountain where morning coffee is brewed and chocolate malts are blended. There, an old oak cash register, straight out of the twenties, rings up drinks, and a dozen wooden stools belly up to the counter.

The fountain is a Hoosier loyalty shrine. Red block letters, THIS IS BIG RED COUNTRY, run across the top of it. Over that hang IU football and IU basketball team shots, the same framed blowups that are on display down at the stadium. Under the sign, next to the Coke machine, an Indiana pennant clock keeps the time—something that nobody in Bloomington seems to worry much about. Red "Catch the Spirit" bumper stickers pepper the fountain mirror, and reveal a new Hoosier football spirit in town. One that's finally worth catching. Just a few feet away from the soda counter, on the other side of the racks of red T-shirts and sweatshirts and IU jackets, a shoe display lines the wall. Nike, Converse, Adidas, all those big-city brands. And there's even a salesperson available to give you a fit. Seem a little simple for a Big Ten university? It's not. It's just Bloomington. Probably the only place in the world where you can order up a cherry soda, sit there and wiggle your toes in some new Air Jordans, and put both on the same tab.

Around the corner, a couple of blocks closer to campus, the Saturday morning farmers' market sets up. I got there around ten o'clock, but it'd already been rolling for three or four hours. Ford and Chevy pickup trucks, mostly old models with homemade wooden railings, had backed in and laid out their October harvest. Fold-out card tables and small wooden benches ran between the truck rows. Big orange Indiana pumpkins sat in piles among bushel baskets of colored Indian corn, and plump orange and yellow gourds. Some folks had the stuff ordered and laid out in grocery store lines. Others just leaned back, sipped a little coffee, and let you sift through the truck bed. Moms and dads walked their kids around and hunted for jack-o'-lanterns. Folks visited, said hello, and raved about the bright blue sky. Like the kids, I sized up pumpkin faces and tried to figure out which would look best with those triangle eyes.

"Big game today." One of the fellas sat down his coffee cup and leaned back against the truck. I must look like a football fan, or maybe just not a legitimate pumpkin buyer.

"Sure is." I nodded. "Looks like do or die."

"Yessir, it is a big one. Still got a shot at the Rose Bowl."

"I don't know—Iowa's pretty tough." After catching the Iowa-Michigan tie, and then seeing what Michigan had done to Indiana, I was kind of wary. Comparative scoring does that to you. I'd already added it five or six times—started with the 17–17 tie, subtracted the 25 points that the Wolverines had hammered onto the Hoosiers, figured in the home field advantage, and still had the Hawks by at least a touchdown.

"Don't you worry. At home, national TV, Mallory'll have 'em ready. They didn't pick him Big Ten Coach of the Year two times in a row for nothing. You interested in a pumpkin?"

I must've been staring.

"Got some good-sized ones over here." He sifted through the bed and realigned the pumpkins. Some of the fallen ones he grabbed by the stem and stood back up. His assortment was a pretty good one—lots of potential jack-o'-lanterns.

"Sorry. No place to put it, plus I'm on my way over to the game." I took another look at the truck bed. "Ya know, though, they're pretty good looking."

"Thanks. Kind of tough this summer. The weather and all. A lot bigger last fall. But . . . I guess they fared better than the corn."

The Hoosier paused and nodded. "You'll see. Mallory will have 'em ready."

On Kirkwood Avenue, between the market and the campus, sits Nick's English Hut. A "Fry the Hawkeyes" sign joined a red IU flag hanging from the overhead facade. All week long people had told me, "Don't miss Nick's." "You gotta get to Nick's, it's where everybody goes!" So, Saturday morning I dropped by.

Nick's is Bloomington's favorite watering hole. It's a treasure chest of university lore, and odd little things all over the walls. Old wooden booths, each with a miniature wall-mounted jukebox and a Heinz ketchup bottle, line the walls. And they're finished off in loyalty style with about twelve coats of red paint. Colored Christmas lights hang from the low ceiling and add a little holiday sparkle to the place. Big fat baseball encyclopedias, a Bill James stat book, and other "Who's Who" major-league baseball facts books are stacked on shelves over the TV and keep baseball season arguments to a minimum. Besides IU football and IU basketball, Nick's is home for local Cub fans. The place just oozes Bloomington charm from every crack in the old wooden walls. It reminded me of Martini's Bar, the place in *It's a Wonderful Life* where Jimmy Stewart dragged Clarence one cold, snowy Christmas Eve. The night Clarence got his wings, and George Bailey found out that he really was the "richest man in town."

Everybody loves Nick's. IU kids love it. They cram the upstairs "attic." National basketball championships and football Saturdays are primo times, but usually each night of the week you'll find midterm celebrations or test-recovery beer gulping in progress. Visiting alums and townspeople love it too, and they usually opt for the downstairs booths. But all ages belly up to the old wooden bar. Particularly if they're in the "Bucket Brigade."

Above the bartenders, between the bar and bar counter, hang a host of little aluminum buckets. On request, the buckets are filled with beer. Each bucket has a number on it. Each number corresponds to somebody's name. And to that lucky name comes one of Bloomington

Indiana's finest privileges—membership in Nick's Bucket Brigade. The initial bucket run of a couple of hundred, set up ten years ago, was limited. Bucket drinking, however, is not! A lot of the Brigade members never leave Bloomington, and Nick's never plans on leaving either, so a good number of buckets will always be kept in circulation. Some, however, do move on . . . temporarily, anyhow. After graduation, if the owner wants to, he can take his bucket with him. But usually both visit and fill up, for old times' sake, at Homecoming. Some buckets are willed away. A kid about to graduate will bring his best buddy down to Nick's, and in an official ceremony transfer bucket ownership. Fortunately, though, Nick's doesn't abide by state law when it comes to wills. If the original owner does return for some reason, both he and his beneficiary get lifelong refills from the same bucket!

Buckets and beers aside, the tavern specialty is what's on its walls. It's like roaming through the Bloomington library archives. There are newspaper articles about people who visited Nick's back in the thirties, and newspaper articles about their kids and grandkids. The stories cover generations of Nick's grads and IU grads. There are Bobby Knight shots, pictures of him back before the standard red sweater, back when he wore that old checked sports coat. And there are autographs from the Mallory football team that stunned Ohio State in '86. Nick's infamous Toilet Bowl Award hangs above one of the archways to the bar. The award, chosen for a celebrity who Nick's patrons decide belongs in the toilet, consists of the smiling winner peering out from inside a very special picture frame—a porcelain toilet seat. On Iowa-Indiana weekend, Michael Spinks still held the honor for his one-round rollover to Tyson. Other portraits of past champions lay hidden beneath Spinks—Jimmy Swaggart, Jim and Tammy Faye, and, of course, at least one Kentuckian—a *Sports Illustrated* cover shot of Wildcat B-ball Coach Joe B. Hall.

Upstairs, a framed *Indianapolis Star* article tells the best Nick's story. It's the story of a very special marriage that took place in the Attic, three years ago. Wilma Ruth Collier's marriage.

Ruthie, as the regulars call her, has been waiting tables at Nick's for a long, long time.

"Forty years next November fourteenth," she says proudly. "I started November fourteenth, 1949." She was twenty-two then. Harry Truman was sitting in the White House, Bobby Knight was nine years old, and "Toyota" wasn't yet a household word—even in Japan.

"It's the only job I've ever had. And the tavern. Well, it's like a second home."

So it seemed only right that Ruthie got married there. She was fifty-nine. It was her second marriage. The groom, Harold, a high-school classmate, was sixty. Dick Barnes, owner of Nick's, gave Ruthie away. And Frank McClosky, Bloomington's ex-mayor, now a United States congressman, performed the ceremony. It was one of the happiest moments at Nick's in a long happy history.

"I really like the customers," Ruthie laughed, when I asked why she keeps working. Ruthie laughs a lot. She's got a lot of spirit; she'd have to, having waited on college kids' tables for almost half a century. "And I guess they like me 'cause, well, they just seem to. I like to cut up with 'em. I can say anything to the customers and they give me a great big answer back! But that's fun. That's what I like. That's me."

Ruthie's no spring chicken anymore. A couple of years ago she shifted over to days, and just this past year she cut that back too. "Pretty soon I'll be drawing Social Security. And I get up each morning at five A.M. to see my husband off. It gets a little tough. So I'm down to Tuesday and Wednesday afternoons—oh, and weekends in a pinch." Ten-thirty to six works out a lot better, though. "I have more time to cut up with the regulars. And I know most generally what they all drink. They'll come in and say, 'Ruthie, are you here already?' And I'll have their drink for them even before they ask."

Still a go-getter, Ruthie spends her off days doing just what you might expect a sixty-two-year-old Nick's waitress to do. She crochets a lot. And, you guessed it, she follows IU basketball!

"My mother and I both are big basketball fans." Ruthie's mom is seventy-seven. She's the night owl and stays up to almost ten o'clock. "When I go to bed, I tell Mom, 'I wanna know how the ball game comes out.'" And if it's not a Tuesday or a Wednesday, and Ruthie doesn't have to be at work, her mom comes over. They crochet and they talk a little IU basketball. It seems just about right from a lady who, when I asked if she planned to keep on at Nick's, answered me, "As long as God's willing."

After a beer, and a little football talk with some Nick's regulars, I skipped out past the line waiting to get in, and headed off for campus. A campus stroll's an IU game day must. It's not like that at every college. At some the stadiums are clear on the other side of town. At others there just might not be enough time, or the weather's lousy, or the parking is bad. Some campuses are the pits, and not worth the visit. And the way TV jacks around kickoff times, you never really know how dark it'll be by the time the game gets going. For whatever reason, not everybody who goes to a college football game spends pregame roaming the campus. But at IU the smells, the colors, pacing down the brick paths that wander through the woods, while the clock tower chimes and the leaves rustle—it's wonderful! I wasn't the only one who thought so.

"This is the main part of campus. These old buildings go back to the 1890s. And they're made of limestone." David Bone was pointing to Kirkwood Hall, one of the U's oldest buildings, and one of its most charming. He was guiding his wife, their friend Laurie, and her daughter Tammy around the campus.

"They try to keep it as natural as possible. I remember back in the fifties, when they decided to add on to the law quad, it took them five years to cut down four trees!" He stopped and looked around the woods. "That's why it's so beautiful!"

David Bone loves IU. He's a graduate from some time back in the fifties, when it took them five years to level the four trees. Both his daughters had already gotten the tour. Both had decided on IU and both had graduated. Now it was a friend of the family's turn.

I drifted up and waited for a pause in the action.

"Hello." I tried not to sound too nosy.

"Hello!" The three adults chorused a greeting. The high-school junior piped up: "Hi."

"I hope you don't mind. I was just listening. And it's my first time in Bloomington." I looked at Dave. "You really know this place, don't you?"

His eyes lit up and I was welcomed into their little conversation. Tammy's mom, an Anderson, Indiana, native, explained why they were visiting.

"To try to help Tammy find a college." She put her arm around her daughter and gave her a little hug.

"And to go to the game." Tammy grinned.

"So then, this is kind of a recruiting trip."

"In a way, I guess." Dave laughed. He was answering me, but looking over at Tammy. "Like I told our daughters, you look around. Look at all of 'em. Don't go to Indiana just because I went there. If you think it's the place for you . . . then go. If it's not, then don't. But whatever you do, look around first!"

"I'm not sure what he'd have done if they didn't choose IU." Dave's wife chuckled.

"Well, it sure is pretty." I had to be honest. "I've been all over the Big Ten this fall, and this and Madison, I think, are the prettiest. Michigan State's nice too. But I graduated from State, so I'm kind of prejudiced there."

"Oh no, Michigan State's very nice!" Wendy, one of the Bones' two IU daughters, had a friend that lived in East Lansing. "Wendy," her mom noted, "spends a lot of time up there in East Lansing. She says it's gorgeous!"

"But I'll bet it's awfully cold in the winter!" Dave even liked IU's weather best.

I thought back to my State winter days. Days when the icy wind would whip through the bare trees, when it got so cold that my mustache would turn to ice and my cheeks would go numb. Days when the sun shone off the snow so brightly that you had to shield your eyes, and the Red Cedar would freeze over. I remembered those twenty-minute walks to class. Piling on the down coat, and the gloves, a big wool scarf, and a stocking cap, and trucking down the river across campus. Then thawing out with a hot cup of coffee at the Union. God, it so was invigorating. You really knew you were alive!

"No," I told them, "I loved it in the winter! Especially when the Red Cedar froze." I explained how, when it finally got cold enough, the river turned into a frozen highway for students.

"The river walk was great!"

Tammy, who'd stood quietly by and listened to the tour, and to me, and to all of the other adults, was fascinated by the thought. "Cool!"

I laughed. "Yeah, it was kinda cool." But I knew by the sound of that "Cool!" what Tammy was thinking.

Dave went on a little more about the campus. He talked about the official university gates over off Kirkwood, the ones at the end of the woods that led out to Nick's. He told me that a fraternity brother of his had given them to the school. We all talked a little IU football, just enough for me to find four more Mallory fans, and be told one more time that it felt good to finally be winning.

I confessed I still had a football game to get to and reminded them they had a tour to finish up. So I said so long. I wished Tammy luck, and hoped she would find her school. I thanked them all for letting me listen in, and I headed to Memorial.

Back behind me, Dave resumed recruiting: "Now, over here . . ."

But I couldn't forget Tammy's "Cool!" I wondered if maybe I'd done the recruiting. I wondered if maybe my "frozen-over Red Cedar" story might've nabbed a future Spartan.

Memorial Stadium is finally buzzing. It's taken a while, but IU football's for real. Mallory's provided the wins, and along with the wins he's drawn Hoosier football fans out of the woodwork. On a bright blue day, with Pasadena still an IU possibility, with ABC trucks cruising around, with Iowa in and the loser out of the title chase, the place was rolling. The Indiana band was going through some pregame numbers next door to Assembly Hall, in the old fieldhouse. Tons of fans, bleachers full of 'em, had drifted over to catch the show. Buses from uptown shuttled folks to the stadium, parking lots were chock-full of cars. People were roaming and talking football. Everything was set for a great college football Saturday. There was only one problem—the Hoosier tailgaters. They still need a little work.

Tailgating, after all, is not something that just happens overnight. Like winning, it's a tradition. It takes lots and lots of learning. That's why the University of Michigan does it best! The team's won, it seems, forever. And because of it, a certain air filters among the Ann Arbor tailgates, an air of perfection that comes only from years of tailgating and years of practice. Years of bringing the wrong foods and switching to the right foods. Years of accumulating all the proper maize-and-blue accessories that make your van snappier than the one that's parked next to you. Years of experimenting till you find just the right music and just the right block M flag. Till you find the correct number of bumper stickers and decide just what bumpers to stick them on. Tailgating is an art form. It's an art form that's learned, and an art form that the Hoosiers haven't quite learned yet.

Their hearts are in the right place. They show up by the bucketful and they drive all the right vehicles. Vans, station wagons, and Winnebagos cram the lots. And with the new-look football program, folks finally have something to talk about. Most Hoosiers, though, tailgate inside. Either in their vans or lounging around their Winnebagos. Even on a bright blue day! Not a lot of IU flags hover over the lots either. And almost no music. It's kind of like folks show up, put in their time, but don't really know what to do.

Inside Memorial it's a whole different story! They may not have the tailgating down yet, but Hoosiers know their red and white. They know how to yell. And they sure as hell know what it's like to win. They learned all that across the lot in Assembly Hall. And boy, does it transfer! Memorial just bursts with red! Bleachers explode with hungry Hoosier crazies. Both sides climb straight up and tower over the field. Alumni sock in under the press box, while a wild, screaming student section takes charge across the way. The band cranks away in the end zone. Cheerleaders bounce up and down on the sidelines. Red! Red! Red! The place was soaking in it. Almost everywhere! All except for the end zone scoreboard, and one little slivered section's worth of bodies way down at the end of the stadium. Both of those were black and gold. A tiny hive of buzzing bumblebees, as pumped as they'd been at Kinnick when Iowa played Michigan. All day long the Hawkeye end zone chanted to the beat of one booming bass drum. Slow and steady, refusing to evaporate in the Hoosier hoopla, like a dream, the chant drifted across the field. *Boom, boom, boom*—"LET'S GO, HAWKS! LET'S GO, HAWKS! LET'S GO, HAWKS!" IU roars would shake the place, and the chant would disappear. I'd strain, I'd listen, and I'd hear it again. "Let's go, Hawks! Let's go, Hawks! Let's go, Hawks!"

All game long Memorial shook! Hoosier fans screamed like it was a Bobby Knight basketball championship on the line, while the Hawks kept hammering away, over and over again, with that slow, steady chant. And I had the world's best ticket—a field pass! Down in the valley of noise with two thundering red sidelines rising straight up above me.

IU came out like gangbusters. Anthony Thompson went crazy. Some lightning to the stadium thunder, he flashed his way around, over, and through the Hawk defense. IU just poured it on! It was 35–3 in the second quarter and screaming Hoosier fans wanted more! "GO, IU! GO, IU!" seemed to get louder and louder with every point. The Hoosier band lit up the place. The student section was almost foaming at the mouth. But down there in that far end zone, down by thirty-two, the Hawks weren't giving up. *Boom, boom, boom* still drifted across the field. And every once in a while Herky and his big plastic head would jump the fence up into the seats and lead the cheers. I thought maybe they were just too far underneath the scoreboard to see what was happening. Or they were watching some other game out behind them on the practice field. Then I remembered—nope, that's Iowa. Ain't no way they're quitting!

* * *

"Did you hear us miss the extra point!" Cadet Judy Mabry yelled to me. She had to yell. The IU band was blasting its half-time show right in front of us. Judy and Cadet Michele Criveau, dressed in full army fatigues, were on ROTC assignment. Positioned at the Hawkeye fan end of the field, their job was to fire the touchdown cannon on every Hoosier score.

"We missed the first extra point. And everybody's telling us about it too!"

"Yeah, already!" Michele helped out.

"It'll be like that all week long till the next game."

"You missed the point. Why'd you miss the point? How come you missed the point?"

I said I hadn't heard them miss the point. All I'd heard was the blasts. The two-foot-long bronze cannon sounded more like a twenty-five-footer when it ka-boomed. The cannon was hot. The Hoosiers were hot! And since it'd been such a wild first half, the ka-booms had piled up. Thirty-five points. Ten ka-booms. Well, nine if you count the miss.

"The hardest part is the extra points. We gotta pour it, stuff it, and get it lit before they score again."

"And we missed the second one!"

"At least we haven't started the field on fire yet. We did that last game!" The girls cracked up, telling me about how during the Minnesota game they'd left a little too much powder on the turf, and it had actually melted the plastic.

"Good fans, huh?" I pointed behind us. The Iowa fans, with the help of Herky, were doing some weird kind of half-time cheer.

"Yeah, they really are! I've been here for every game. Nobody came to the Minnesota game." The band was marching toward us. The closer the marchers got, the louder we yelled. "The Minnesota end was totally IU. And . . . Ohio State had a lot at the start, but when we started beating 'em, they just disappeared. But these guys"—Michele pointed behind us—"these guys really are crazy!"

"Indiana's got good fans too!" Judy was wearing green fatigues, but her heart was crimson and cream!

"You're right!" I yelled. "They're loud as hell!"

A red wave of IU football players broke from the tunnel and stormed out onto the field. The student section shrieked. Alumni jumped up and cheered. The band cranked out a fight song. Memorial thundered.

"What'd you say? I can't hear you!"

"I said they're loud as . . . I said make sure you don't miss any more extra points!"

The Hawks followed the lead of their fans, and in the second half came storming back. Time and again Chuck Hartlieb, the Iowa QB, dropped back. And time and again his strikes found their mark. Pass after pass—first downs, touchdowns, and two-point conversions. "LET'S GO, HAWKS . . . LET'S GO, HAWKS!" The beat stayed steady. Indiana's band, which had blasted for the first-half touchdown celebrations, kept blasting without the TDs. Iowa kept throwing. The score tightened. Sixty passes. Hartlieb threw sixty passes! Forty-four completions for over five hundred yards. A first-half IU blowout screamed into a fourth-quarter shootout. Ten minutes to go and Iowa was down by eight! The two teams turned up the heat for the stretch run and Memorial shook from every corner.

For nearly four hours the two teams battled. Blue skies had drifted into darkness. Warm sunshine had disappeared, the finale lit by the cold glow of stadium lights. Still nobody, not a single soul, had left or given up. All fifty-two thousand were standing and screaming their lungs out until finally, just like that, with seventy-seven seconds left, it ended. One last Iowa gasp, a fourth and long, and Hartlieb was hammered from the back side. "Let's go, Hawks!" fell into a long low groan that drifted across the field. I could hear it even over the Hoosier celebration screams.

Final score: Indiana, 45; Iowa, 34.

It was celebration time in Hoosier land. The clock wound down; students poured over the concrete wall like they were escaping prison. They dropped the seven feet down onto the field and hit the ground running. Droves of them engulfed the field, pushed through the goalpost-guarding cops, and buried the posts. I scurried for cover. In moments both posts were down. The ends of one got picked up by nine or ten guys. They hoisted it up on their shoulders and paraded around the field, like they'd just bagged a wild animal. They kept parading until both post and hunters disappeared up into the aisles and out of the stadium. Screaming and dancing and running around in circles, students carried on like the victory was some wild native mating ritual. ABC cameramen, trying to catch the action, got buried under faces sticking into the cameras. Every time the red light on top of a camera flickered, kids mobbed it. Cops, and the band, and the PA announcer who kept asking for everybody to "PLEASE GET OFF THE FIELD" were helpless, till the posts were history. And the kids, with nothing left to do, and tired of running around on the turf, just decided to leave.

When that had finally happened—when goalposts and cameramen and singing screaming students had finally disappeared, after Hartlieb's passes and Anthony Thompson's touchdown dashes had faded and that "Let's go, Hawks!" echo was just a drumbeat in my head, after the stands had emptied and left behind only toilet paper rolls and gobs of confetti and empty schnapps bottles . . . while the lights cut the blackness and the fall cold took a foothold, while the Indiana band finished up its postgame show, I drifted across the debris-scattered battlefield. Along the way I passed one of the injured goalposts, an upright gone, somewhere out in the parking lot. Or maybe, by then, being sawed into trophy sections or being dragged up to Nick's for worship.

On the way out I passed a cop. A big cop who looked like he'd spent a few nights ordering thirds at Dunkin' Donuts. He was standing around with five or six other cops next to what was left of the goalpost. All of them were listening to the band finish up. The big guy, though, stood out. I stopped at the group.

"Got pretty wild, didn't it?" I noted.

A few nodded; one guy, hands on hips, shook his head. But the big cop, he just laughed. "They got their trophy."

"What's gonna happen if you guys go to the Rose Bowl?"

The big cop laughed again, only louder. "If we go to the Rose Bowl, I might just help tear the thing down!"

# 8

# PURDUE UNIVERSITY
## THE BOILERMAKERS

| | |
|---|---|
| Purdue University West Lafayette, IN | Ross-Ade Stadium |
| Best Breakfast | Triple XXX |
| Best Bar | Harry's Chocolate Shop |
| Best Burger | Schoop's |
| Best of ... | |

**The Best in Big Ten Country**

## BREAKFAST

| | | |
|---|---|---|
| 1. | Angelo's | Michigan |
| 2. | Mickie's | Wisconsin |
| 3. | Triple XXX | Purdue |
| 4. | Runcible Spoon | Indiana |
| 5. | Aunt Sonya's | Illinois |

Football and grass! It's tradition. And it has been since that very first time out back playing catch with Dad. Those pickup games over at the playground, those cold crisp Friday night high-school showdowns, and until Astroturf rolled around, those college football Saturdays under sunshine and blue skies—always played on soft green grass. That's football! That's tradition! That's life! It seems strange that the Big Ten, a conference with such a rich football legacy, plays on plastic. Ancient ivy-covered halls grace sprawling campuses, land grant institutions (most of them founded before the Blue fought the Gray to preserve the Union), and stadiums erected back when people thought the Great War of 1917 was also to be the world's last—all that history and yet nine out of the Big Ten have ripped up the sod and planted plastic. Only Purdue's Ross-Ade Stadium has grass. Only in West Lafayette is the game truly played the way God meant it to be played.

Not only does Ross-Ade feature a grass field, it features the very finest in grass fields. It's PAT—Prescription Athletic Turf—a specialized kind of grass turf that was developed at Purdue in 1971. Since then the system's been updated, improved, and is spreading throughout the stadium world. And maybe, just maybe, with the annual flood of Astro-injuries increasing every season, PAT might finally be the beginning of the worldwide end for plastic grass.

Bo said he hated PAT. Folks around Purdue remember him calling it a "damned sandbox." But that was back in '76 after he'd lost a football game on it. And Bo doesn't take losses any too well. Hayden Fry, on the other hand, loves the stuff, so much so that PAT is coming to Iowa. In 1989 Kinnick's plastic will be ripped up and replaced with grass—the second of the Big Ten to bend to God's will. Other stadiums around the country—among them Denver's Mile High, Miami's Joe Robbie, and Soldier Field in Chicago—have also sided with Hayden. As for the Purdue turf, installed back in '74, and first at any of the biggies, I'd get to see it do what it supposedly did best—drain the rain! My four-day stay in West Lafayette was to be cold and gray and rainy.

Dr. William Daniels, a professor in Purdue's Turf Management Program, developed the PAT system. The idea took root in the fall of 1970 on a West Coast road trip. He was there doing what professors of turf management do best, lecturing on the topic of grass. Along the way he took a little time out to visit the Oakland Coliseum. "They'd just rebuilt their field. It was a very good job. . . . They had their sand and drain pipes underneath the turf. They showed me the drainage setup. They were proud of their field and for good reason. It was one of the finest I'd seen." That was in sunny September. The next time Dr. Daniels saw the Coliseum turf, three months later on TV, it wasn't so sunny. And the field wasn't so pretty. "December twenty-seventh, I was watching Miami play Oakland for the league championship. It had rained all morning. And that beautiful field had turned into a sea of mud. It occurred to me, I bet those drain pipes under the turf are just as empty as they can be. Water surely wasn't seeping down into them.

So the idea came to me how to pull the water into the pipes. Well, how do you do it? You create a vacuum—put a suction on the drain." Nobody had ever considered using the idea with grass before. Purdue patented it. And voilà, the idea of PAT was born.

After Dr. Daniels explained the "light bulb theory" behind PAT, Dan Weisenberger showed me the system in action. As Purdue's turf boss, Dan's job was to make sure Ross-Ade's football field stayed as lush as the university golf course. And while the system might've been Dr. Daniels's brainchild, the stadium grass was Dan's baby. I met him Friday morning at the maintenance offices underneath the stadium—a good day to see PAT do its thing, as a torrent of cold icy rain pelted Ross-Ade. "The easiest way to think of it is as a big bathtub," Dan explained. "They dig down sixteen inches, basically the size of the playing field. Then they line it with plastic. After that they put in drainage tubes. They fill in the hole with fourteen inches of sand, and two inches of top mix—either seed or sod. The idea is that rain seeps through the turf into the sand and finally down into the tubes. Pumps connected to the tubes create a vacuum and literally suck the field dry." And because of the suction, the field doesn't even need a crown. It's flatter than Indiana!

"We've had it since '74." That was two years before Bo condemned it. "We've never played a game in a downpour. But we've had big rains, as much as four inches the night before, and had it ready to go by game time." He smiled and stuck his chest out a little. "It does in six minutes what Mother Nature does in six hours.

"Come on, let me show you." We headed outside, slushed through the cold wet parking lot and across the puddled track that ringed the football field. Empty rain-soaked bleachers stared out across the grass. Dan was dressed for the wet—waterproof yellow from head to toe. Me, I was dressed for under-the-stadium warm-and-dry. So I tiptoed around puddles, and tried to cram all of me under my Michigan State umbrella.

"Don't worry." He noticed I was a little hesitant to leave the wet track for the wet grass. "It's firm." I reached my left foot out onto the grass. Kind of toe-tested it, so I didn't sink five inches into muck. It was actually fairly solid. I shifted my weight and pulled my other foot out to the grass. Solid too! I jumped up and down. No squishes, no squashes. While Dan checked drainage lines, I jogged circles around the end zone. No splashes, no sinking, no big, huge puddles. I bounced across the field. Amazing! The skies had turned on full faucet, pools covered the track, the parking lot was washing away, West Lafayette sewers were about to back up, and the football field was puddleless! Back under the stadium, Dan led me to a dingy little room. Inside it, a pump, looking like some old elementary-school boiler, was pounding away. The pump was connected to the drain pipes out under the field. Water gushed from the sky, to the grass, through the sand, into the pipes, and down the sewer.

"Sucks it bone dry," Dan beamed.

Look out, plastic grass . . . your days are numbered!

It seems kind of ironic that such a beautiful grass football field is surrounded by concrete. But the Purdue campus is mostly just that . . . concrete. Of all the Big Ten campuses, it's probably the least attractive. No IU forest, no Lake Mendota splashing its shore, or quiet meandering sidewalks cutting through the trees. There's really not a lot to it. And it's crammed into a corner of West Lafayette, which is also kind of drab. Gray and flat, West Lafayette sits across the Wabash River from downtown Lafayette. Like a lot of other college towns, it's an intersection of bars, fast-food joints, and college kid places, but it suffers from an identity crisis. There's no wildlike Madison air about town. It's small but not quaint like downtown Ann Arbor or Blooming-ton. While folks certainly are friendly enough, you don't get the feeling you've found friendly heaven—Iowa City, Iowa. West Lafayette's more a twin to Illinois's Champaign-Urbana. A college boomtown, without that refreshing college *boom!*

Like the college town, the college doesn't really buzz. Not like a college can! It's got some great bragging rights and a history filled with all sorts of mosts and firsts. . . . Noplace anywhere has graduated more engineers. It was the takeoff point for Amelia Earhart's famous flight. And only the U.S. Naval Academy has graduated more astronauts. Purdue even contributed to NASA's "one giant leap for mankind." Neil Armstrong, the first man to walk on the moon, was a Boilermaker. So was Eugene Cernan, the last American to do it. With an impressive history of great accomplishments, the school really has its academic act together. But it's tough to find something "just plain ole collegiate" to hang a hat on. And when it comes to football, what could've been a real rich tradition too often got caught in the Big Two (Michigan–Ohio State), Little Eight squeeze.

But things are changing at Purdue . . . physically, anyhow. The campus is in transition. Plans are for a little sprucing-up—new buildings, new halls, and in the center of campus, a new revised Purdue Mall. Still, that's new stuff, and the Big Ten's at its best immersed in the old. In the process of remodeling, the university plans also include ripping down one of the campus's most traditional landmarks. A big red-brick smokestack rises over the campus power plant. It's the lone break in a boring West Lafayette skyline. At night floodlights illuminate it. The red brick glows like a lighthouse beacon. But just for a little while longer. Plans are to level the stack, sell the bricks for a fundraiser, and put up something else. Too bad—it's the Boiler campus's finest pose.

Despite the drab, there are three things that add a bit of that college football sparkle to the place. Purdue is home to a great quarterback legacy, a very special lady dressed in gold, and a bar that's called The Chocolate Shop. All three seal football season in West Lafayette with the Big Ten stamp of approval.

Purdue's the original "cradle of quarterbacks." It sports a legacy that leaves even Miami's Hurricanes in the dust. The "cradle" began back in 1945, with now–assistant athletic director Bob DeMoss calling signals. It's endured for nearly forty seasons. With Len Dawson (1954–1956); Bob Griese, Mike Phipps, Gary Danielson, and Mark Hermann in the sixties and seventies; and Scott Campbell and Jim Everette in the eighties, the school's been a stepping-stone to pro-football quarterbacking greatness. With stellar signal callers at the helm, the Boilermakers have had some exciting moments. Moments that through the years have earned them a reputation as college football's "Spoilermakers." During DeMoss's freshman season, Purdue traveled to Ohio State and buried the number one team in the nation 35–13. In 1950 up in South Bend, a Purdue quarterback named Dale Samuels clipped Notre Dame's winning streak at thirty-nine games. Lenny Dawson, under the tutelage of DeMoss, beat up on the Irish in two out of three seasons. And in 1965, maybe the most famous Boiler upset, Bob Griese hit 19 of 22, as Purdue knocked off another number one Notre Dame team. It's a thing the Boilers have a knack for, pulling off the unexpected. Particularly against Notre Dame. A traditional thorn in the Fighting Irish side, the Boilers have beaten Notre Dame more often than anybody except Southern Cal. Even so, even with all of the quarterbacks and the spoiling, in Purdue's best Big Ten seasons, usually Michigan or Ohio State was unspoilable. And since it took until 1975 for the conference to let anybody go bowl-hopping someplace other than Pasadena, a lot of good Purdue teams celebrated the New Year at home. In the program's one-hundred-year history, the Boilers have played in only five bowl games, and just one time for the roses.

In 1954, one of those seasons in which they upset Notre Dame, a sophomore quarterback took the country by storm. The press nicknamed him the Golden Boy. The kid was Lenny Dawson. That same season, Purdue's marching band director decided to add a counterpart to the Golden Boy for half-time shows. Thus was created the most famous baton-twirling position in the world—Purdue's Golden Girl, the queen of the Purdue All-American Marching Band.

I caught the queen and her court, Thursday afternoon, outside on the soggy IM practice fields. And there I ran into not just a collegiate marching band, but kids with all sorts of specialties. You see, the Purdue All-American Marching Band, maybe the biggest marching band in the world, features more spotlight material than a Broadway musical. There's "Monster, the World's Largest Drum." At ten feet tall it takes four guys just to wheel it around and two more jumping up in the air swinging big mallets to make it boom. There's the Purdue Flag Corps—twenty-seven girls who glitter in game-day silver and black. They carry on a tradition that began way back in 1919 when Purdue was the first to parade Big Ten colors out on the field. There are more girls, more sequins, more sparkle, and more color in the guise of the Goldusters dance line. There are the All-American Twirlers. Eleven girls, a lot of them state and national baton-twirling champions, from all over the United States. There are the four featured twirling positions. The Girl in Black is usually the country's best baton-twirling brunette. The Silver Twins sparkle in silver sequins. And there's the queen—the girl whom ABC cameras always seem to be searching out, the twirler who's glittered the pages of so many magazines, and even the reels of Hollywood—Purdue's famed Golden Girl.

Thursday afternoon, though, all the glitter was gone. All four hundred kids—the twirlers, the marchers, the drum beaters—were just kids in blue jeans and sweatshirts and slippery, shiny raincoats trying to get it together for Saturday afternoon without freezing to death. Marchers, horns pointed at attention up to the tower, tried to march and play and skip the puddles all at the same time. The drummers stood around, guarded Monster, boomed him on cue, but spent most of the day, as one of the guards told me, "checking out the Goldusters." The Goldusters splashed in sweats instead of sequins and the All-American Twirlers just tried to get through practice without bruising their frost-bitten fingers. As for the four featured twirlers, they roamed the muddy field in sweats. And they practiced and practiced and practiced. The four represent the very best in collegiate dedication. They're a colorful side to the pageantry of college football, as significant as any Boilermaker football team that ever hit the field.

Kim Radcliffe, 1988's Girl in Black, is from Zanesville, a tiny town in central Indiana. She's been twirling since she was two. Two years old! Bob Griese probably didn't toss his dad a pass till he was at least three and a half. The Indiana state champion since she was twelve, Kim's won eight national titles, and she's going on three years as the Boilers' Girl in Black. When it's all done, when the glitter and the limelight and the Saturday afternoon games fade, she wants to be an elementary-school teacher. "I love twirling," she bubbled. "I just love it. It's so much fun talking to kids about it. They look at our capes and our crowns. . . . On game day we don't wear this stuff." Kim laughed, modeling her mud-splashed black sweats. "They look at us, their eyes get big, and they say, 'You are queens.' They say, 'I want to be a queen too.' " Girls in Black get asked to do all sorts of fun things—parades and alumni functions and even real important stuff. "For National Book Week, elementary schools around town want me to go in and read for them." She smiled. "They've told the kids, 'The Girl in Black is coming to our school.' " Her smile broke to laughter. "They've even made signs, 'Come and hear the Girl in Black read a book.' "

Lani and Bibi Barnes, junior criminology majors, wear silver sequins on game day. Lani and Bibi look a lot alike—well, actually, exactly alike. They're twins. They're not, however, your average run-of-the-mill twins. Most twins, after all, don't twirl batons. And most didn't grow up in Norcross, Georgia. And most didn't travel eight hundred miles north just to go to college, just to be Silver Twins.

"I think they got 'em lined up for the next ten years," Lani laughed.

Bibi chimed in. "They hunt down twins. If you have little girl twins in Indiana, they say, 'Well, I guess it's time to teach 'em to twirl now.' "

You'd think it was the great twirling reputation of Purdue that lured identical southern belles to the middle of the Midwest.

"Nope. Being from the South, we didn't know much about it."

"We've twirled since we were five. But we didn't know Purdue at all. Even now, back home in Georgia, nobody's really sure where Purdue is at. Everybody's heard of it, but they think of it like Duke or Wake Forest. A school without a state."

"The 1961 Golden Girl recruited us," Bibi noted. "She sent us letters. Called us up. She invited us up to visit."

"We visited," the girls dueted, "and we loved it."

"Plus, it's great for our dad. He's an ex–pro football player, and with two daughters, it's about as close as he could get. Him and Mom drive up for every game! Last week was their first miss in three years!"

Lani laughed. "Sometimes I think it's even more fun for Mom than it is for us."

"Yeah. Everybody knows Mom. She's like a regular. Just ask anybody for Bibi and Lani's mom and they point to the lady with the video camera."

Lani and Bibi do everything together. They practice together. On Saturday afternoon they twirl side by side. They're roommates in the same sorority. After they graduate, both want to head home to Dixie. But for now they love being the Twins at Purdue.

There are, however, a few drawbacks to all the glitter.

"I hate the snow," Bibi laughed.

"Yessir." Lani nodded. "I'm not used to it either. When it snows out, I don't want to twirl. I don't want to go to class. I don't even like to go outside."

But even winter has a "silver lining," as Lani quipped. "At least when it snows in Atlanta we'll know how to drive and nobody else will."

Kim, Lani and Bibi, and the All-American Twirlers are dedicated girls. They've all been working and twirling and competing, often against each other, since they were setting apples on the teacher's desk. Each has persevered to overcome obstacles and grab her moment in the spotlight. But none has weathered such a road, or lived such a storybook tale, as Dawn Beck, Purdue's fifteenth Golden Girl.

Dawn's from Findlay, Ohio, a town of thirty-five thousand in the northern part of the state. She bubbles with enthusiasm. She's pretty, probably as pretty as any Golden Girl has ever been. A senior in prelaw, she carries a 5.85 GPA on a 6.0 scale. She's headed for the University of Michigan's prestigious law school. Best of all, as her director says, "Dawn takes everything in stride. She's in a real star position and a lot of kids might just become prima donnas. But Dawn's really down to earth."

Dawn's Golden Girl dream took root a long time ago, back home in Findlay. "When I was little and had just started twirling, my dad and I used to watch football games on TV. He watched the games; I watched the twirlers. I remember always seeing her—the girl with the gold costume. She was beautiful. And she was always on. And I said to myself, 'That's what I want to be when I grow up!'" Dawn stopped reminiscing and laughed. "I was nine, I think, but I already had my life planned out. Well, a few things kind of fell into place for me. We had a Purdue Golden Girl, Susan Fron, in our twirling association. When I found out, I couldn't believe it. She was a lot older than me at the time, but like a teenager I walked right up to her and said, 'Oh, I'm gonna be the Golden Girl too. Susan really was my inspiration."

It isn't like the nine-year-old twirled for ten more years, pulled onto campus, tried out for for Golden Girl, and magically fulfilled a dream. Far from it! When Dawn arrived at Purdue in 1985, the feature positions Golden Girl and Girl in Black were already locked up. She didn't have a twin sister, but Indiana mothers hadn't raised any twirling twins. Consequently, Purdue had no Silver Twins. So for two seasons she and another girl twirled as "look-alike" Silver Twins. It wasn't the Golden Girl, but it was still pretty exciting for a teenager from a little town in Ohio.

In Dawn's junior year she got her big chance, the one she'd been waiting for ever since she'd dreamed in front of the television set. Golden Girl number thirteen had graduated. Tryouts were that summer. "I practiced so hard. All summer long, and four hours every day, just on my routine." Her routine was the one that all the featured twirlers must do in order to pass. It's a solo full-field strut in front of scores of Boilermaker judges and community members. "I really thought I was going to win. But I did a lot of things wrong. And I got beat. I just fair and square got beat.

"After that I didn't know what to do. I was crushed. Mr. Moffit, the band director, gave me two weeks to think about it. If I came back, he said I could be in the All-American twirling line. But I just didn't know.

"Finally, I told myself, 'I'm not gonna quit.' I loved the band too much. I said, 'I'm not gonna be a sore loser.' So I went into the line"—Dawn burst into a great big grin—"and I had a *blast!* We didn't get as much attention as the featured twirlers, but we had a lot of fun."

The following summer, Golden Girl number fourteen resigned. The position, which usually opens only every three or four years, was available again. "My mind was set. I wasn't going to try out." Dawn shook her head. "It was just too big a disappointment to go through again. Also, they don't usually take seniors." That summer, though, the old dreams took hold. "I gave up and in July I started practicing. But I told myself, 'I'm not going to get my hopes up.' It wasn't important if I made it, just that I tried my best."

In August, Dawn returned to the same place where a year before she'd failed. She'd give it one more shot. "I called my mom three hours before tryouts. I was really nervous. Two or three juniors had dropped out. There were a couple of young girls, freshmen, who were super twirlers, and everybody thought that they were just gonna give it to one of them. Well I called Mom, and she said, 'You know what you always told me, you can't ever give up.' Mom was the last person I talked to before tryout, and of course she had to say that." Dawn beamed thinking back. "But you know, Mom is always right."

And Mom was! Dawn put on a super performance. She beat the odds and earned the twirling position she'd always dreamed of. Dawn Beck became Purdue's fifteenth Golden Girl.

"I love it, I really do. And the kids—that's one of my favorite parts. During the football games little girls will come up and ask for my autograph. Or they'll ask things about twirling. And the parades—they wave at you and they really want you to wave back."

Kind of like a few years ago when a teenager from Findlay, Ohio, told Susan Fron, "I'm gonna be the Golden Girl too."

# MICHIGAN STATE AT PURDUE

*Ross-Ade Stadium,
West Lafayette, Indiana*

| Standings November 5, 1988 | Big Ten | | | All Games | | |
|---|---|---|---|---|---|---|
| | W | L | T | W | L | T |
| MICHIGAN | 4 | 0̄ | 1 | 5 | 2 | 1 |
| INDIANA | 4 | 1 | — | 6 | 1 | 1 |
| ILLINOIS | 3 | 1 | 1 | 4 | 3 | 1 |
| MICHIGAN STATE | 3 | 1 | 1 | 3 | 4 | 1 |
| IOWA | 2 | 1 | 2 | 4 | 3 | 2 |
| PURDUE | 3 | 2 | — | 4 | 4 | — |
| NORTHWESTERN | 1 | 3 | 1 | 1 | 6 | 1 |
| OHIO STATE | 1 | 4 | — | 3 | 5 | — |
| MINNESOTA | 0 | 3 | 2 | 2 | 4 | 2 |
| WISCONSIN | 0 | 5 | — | 0 | 8 | — |

**Other Big Ten Games:**

INDIANA AT ILLINOIS

MINNESOTA AT MICHIGAN

NORTHWESTERN AT IOWA

WISCONSIN AT OHIO STATE

**H**arry's Chocolate Shop sits on the corner of Pierce and State streets. It's *the* place in West Lafayette for folks of all ages. Bob DeMoss, the ex-quarterback and assistant AD, suggested I stop by. "A lot of alums on game day," he promised. Dawn Beck, in between twirling and cartwheeling and working on her Golden Girl routine, bubbled, "Harry's—that's the place!" All week long, all over campus, if I just hinted I was looking for someplace to sip a brew, the one answer that kept popping up was "Harry's Chocolate Shop. It's the neatest place in town."

In 1919 Harry Marack opened a soda fountain in West Lafayette. He called it The Chocolate Shop. A lot of people called it Harry's. Whichever the official name, for fifty-two years until he died in 1971 the place was Harry's. It was run the way Harry wanted it run. And even though the old man's gone, his place hasn't changed all that much. Profs, townsfolk, and students still fill it during the week, and on game weekends alums come drifting back to join them. And everybody always seems to have a pretty good time.

There's not really a lot to the place, which makes it all the homier. Until a side room got tacked on a few years ago, Harry's was just one long room with a bar counter running most of the length of it. Booths, tired wooden pews with tables in between, look like they got plucked out of some Colonial church and wedged against the walls. Carved messages cover them and the wall panels alongside, like notes in a giant high-school yearbook.

Harry's has that warm feel of an old English pub. And stuff clutters every corner of it. Three flags—the United States', Canada's, and England's—hang above the bartender who works the old oak bar. Behind him a huge mirror, a mirror that's been there since the twenties, says "The Chocolate Shop" across the glass. A few stools belly up to the counter. A big open popcorn popper is always filled with freshly popped corn. Customers reach in and grab a handful on their way to a pint of Bass. A couple of TVs hanging in the corner went up before videos and big screens were chic, even before remote control. If you want the channel changed, the bartender has to reach up and do it with a yardstick. Best, though, is the tavern's collection of old photos. Shots of ex–Purdue greats doing their thing hover over the booths. The primo one is of a basketball player in a baggy black-and-white uniform. He's crouched over and dribbling an old leather ball. The ball looks like it's going to deflate when it hits the floor. The kid with the ball looks vaguely familiar, like a face from a different life. That is, until you look at the caption underneath—it reads "Johnny Wooden."

Interesting stories drift through Harry's. Tales swirl about Prohibition bathtub beer and its connection with the cellar trapdoor at the end of the bar. Some guess that maybe it was more than just chocolate sodas Harry peddled back then. And there are stories too about Harry!

"He was a character," one alum recalled. He and his wife were in town for for the game. "Back when I went to school, I bartended here. Back when Harry still ran the place."

"He sure was something." The guy's wife knew Harry too. "He'd stand there at the bar, between the two halves of the bar, with a cigar in the corner of his mouth and just hold court.

"You didn't tell Harry what to do . . . particularly in *his* place."

"I remember," the fella told me, "a guy came in one day. We served ten-ounce Michelob for fifteen cents back then. Well, this guy sat down, said he wanted a draft. So Harry drew him up a draft and sat it on the bar. The guy said he wanted some salt. Harry asked, 'What for?' And the guy said, 'To put it in my beer.' Harry told him if there was supposed to be salt in the beer, they'd have put it in at the brewery. And he took the salt away. He told the guy, 'You can have the beer without salt or not at all.' "

"That was Harry, all right," the lady chuckled. "He did it his way regardless. He even closed the place on game days!"

"That's right—during home games Harry just closed the doors. Could've made a fortune but just shut the place right down. I asked him once why he did it. Harry told me, he said, 'By God, I don't need some guy out of Chicago who borrows enough money to buy a bus ticket and buys some fancy brand-new suit to come in here and tell me how successful he is after he's been out of school for four or five years.'"

"That was Harry, all right."

If the life of Harry is the tavern's oldest circulating story, then it's Indiana Hoosier discussions that are The Chocolate Shop's most emotional ones. I wasn't fully prepared for the IU-Purdue rivalry. Having popped into town with Michigan State, I certainly didn't expect IU to be a main topic of discussion. It's not that I don't know about cross-state villains. As a Spartan fan, living in "Hail to the Victors" country, plenty of days I've skipped right through the sports to the comics. I've come to learn that no sports page is better than one soaked in maize and blue. Wolverine and Buckeye fans, I'm sure, don't see eye to eye either, particularly that last week of the football season. And being a Red Soxer I always love reading about things unraveling around Mr. Yankee—George Steinbrenner. But all that stuff is mild compared to what Boilers feel for Hoosiers. The West Lafayette feeling for Bloomington falls somewhere between contempt and first-class hatred. And it's pretty consistent all over town. In football it whittles the season down into a single game. Start talking Boiler football with anybody, anywhere around West Lafayette, probably any fall weekend, and sooner or later it surfaces that Purdue practically owns the Hoosiers in "the Bucket Game."

"Take a look at the chain," a Boiler told me. He was talking about the chain of brass block P's and I's that hook on to the Oaken Bucket, the Oaken Bucket I'd seen the week before sitting in the IU football offices. "You see a hell of a lot more P's than I's."

"Forty-two to eighteen," his buddy, working on a pint of Bass, reminded him. "We almost own that bucket."

"They got it back last season, but the party's over down there. Mallory hasn't got 'em turned around. You wait and see, they'll stink again in a couple years."

Boilers don't give an inch when it comes to Hoosier football talk. And what's funny is that football doesn't matter all that much. In West Lafayette the Bucket Game is the *second* most important subject for pub discussion. You see, Purdue sits in a state where even in the fall, football's just a passing thought. It's basketball that dominates the state of Indiana. And if there is anything that's despised around Purdue, if there is anything that gets the blood boiling, even in a pleasant little place like Harry's, it's talking about Indiana University basketball. And if you really want to hear a shower of interesting adjectives, just mention a particular Hoosier.

"Bobby Knight's a jerk!" The guy who first let me in on the Bucket Game made the revelation.

His buddy sitting alongside nodded. "Yessir—ain't it the truth."

"He puts himself up like God, country, and flag and all that crap and he's the biggest hypocrite in the world."

"I'll tell you . . ." The fella who had the Bucket numbers memorized was also an expert on Knight's infamous chair toss. "I was at the game. We were kicking his butt on his home floor. I saw the call that he threw it on. It was a good call. I have my videotape. I've watched it over and over. They should've canned him."

The two guys offered up some more Bobby Knight prosecution evidence—lists and lists of reasons why Knight should've been canned. They rolled at least as long as it took to kill a second pint. And people walking by or listening in tossed in on-the-spot evidence to back them up. Nobody, not even the bartender, a guy trained in the art of arbitration, sided with Knight.

"You know"—the Bucket Gamer offered his closing arguments—

"Knight wins despite himself. That's all. He just wins despite himself. And I'll tell you something else—the biggest fluke in the history of sports, *without a doubt,* was when Indiana won the NCAA in '87."

His buddy nodded. "Ain't it the truth. Ain't it the truth."

While Harry's buzzes about Bucket Games and Bobby Knight, the rest of game day West Lafayette lulls. With the stadium a good twenty-minute walk away on the other side of campus, not a lot of folks wander through town. Particularly if the weather's lousy. Oh, you have your basics. The bookstore flies the Big Ten flags, or at least it was flying nine of them. "Not sure what happened to the IU flag." A kid inside shook his head. "Somebody probably ripped it off." He smiled. "But can you blame them?"

Breakfast is a pretty good pregame bet too. Triple XXX, or Tri Chi as the students call it, is your basic twenty-four-hour greasy spoon. It sits off State Street a few blocks down from Harry's. The sign "Famous Chop Steak" doesn't inspire instant mouthwatering, but the place serves up a menu that would lure any respectable semi truck driver. And a lot of people drop by. Assistant football coaches hang out and sip a little coffee before heading over to the stadium. Townsfolk breeze the sports section and wolf down bacon and eggs. It's a good place to take the nip out of a chilly November morning. Breakfast clubs, a student excuse to hammer a few beers, provide an alcoholic wake-up option to Tri Chi. Two bars, Nick's and Edo's, open at 7:00 A.M. on game days. Nick's is quiet and clean, and offers free jelly doughnuts at the door. Edo's is a zoo. Puny plastic pitchers of Bloody Marys and Screwdrivers join AC/DC blaring from dance floor speakers and soundless Bugs Bunny and Roadrunner cartoons on the TV sets. Kids roam around and get a Saturday morning wake-up buzz.

I bounced around town. I got my ears blown off at Edo's and ate a free jelly doughnut at Nick's. I stopped by Harry's and dropped in on the IU-flag-less Purdue bookstore. I also hit up Tri Chi for a good greasy breakfast and the local paper.

On game days only the sports section matters. That morning it filled me in on the Big Ten. The conference race was just about shaped. And once again it looked like the University of Michigan had it in the bag. That is, if they could squeeze by Minnesota and then Illinois, which for a pretty good Wolverine team would be about as difficult as showing up. Still, Bo wasn't taking anything for granted. A thirty-point favorite against the pitiful Golden Gophers, Bo had brought the battle of the Jug into the picture.

"There's no ceremony of turning it over sometime later," the article quoted Bo. "The Jug is right out there on the bench and at the end of the game they just come over and take it! That hurts!" A little psychological pumping-up of his troops. Now instead of four touchdowns, I figured Michigan would win by five.

In addition to the Wolves, other conference teams were getting bowl-game nibbles. Iowa and Indiana looked like shoo-ins. Illinois was somehow still in the Rose Bowl race, and was somehow still in a few other bowl races as well. As for the Spartans, who'd gone almost a month without a touchdown and taken six games to eke out a win, even they were getting whispers. Amazingly, with only one team (Michigan) in the Top Twenty, it looked like the Big Ten would pull five bowl bids. There could be but a single reason—the fans! The best in the world. I can't think of any warm-weather bowl city come January 1 that wouldn't love to be crammed with a townful of Hawkeyes or Spartans or Hoosiers.

But we were in West Lafayette. There were no bowls in the immediate Boilermaker future and probably not a lot more 1988 wins. In fact, Michigan State was a good two-touchdown favorite, which was a pretty big pad considering that the Spartans' offense and the end zone had been season-long strangers. The weather was about as pretty as the Boilers' chances—like it'd been all week long—cold and wet and gray. Not great for the tailgates. But then again Purdue, like IU, isn't great tailgating country. I hit the lots down by the stadium, and found in the West Lafayette rain about the same thing I'd found in the Bloomington sunshine—a bunch of hometowners sitting inside. A few Winnebagos and some black-and-gold vans spattered the lots, but most of their engines were running. Boiler tailgaters stayed warm and toasty inside. And that is not the way to tailgate! Proper tailgating, regardless of the cold, must take place outdoors!

Visiting Spartan fans had the right idea! Probably as many green S flags as old gold-and-black ones dotted the lots. Like little colonies, the State vans bunched together. Eight or ten green flags, zinged by cold, biting winds, stretched out like boards above a fort. I hit the greenest colony. Crammed between a green Dodge van with white trim and a big white Winnebago with green State stuff all over it, some folks were wrapped in winter clothes. They offered me a cup of hot cider and we talked Spartan football.

It'd been a while since I'd been up to East Lansing, and I really wondered how fans were taking the post–Rose Bowl dive. I wondered how they liked dropping back in the pack, and if maybe ole Coach Perles wasn't on the hot seat. I figured, anybody who'd drive to West Lafayette on a shit day like it was, just to catch a blowout . . . well, they must've bled green.

"George is set for life," the guy who poured the cider laughed. "Nine more years on his contract. Hell, he'll be out here with us if they ever do can him. He even said so last year."

I remembered the article. Coach Perles had told *Sports Illustrated* they'd have to kick him out of Michigan State before he'd ever leave. And if they did, well then, George said he'd just head out to the parking lot and drink tomato juice and eat brats with the fans. George is more than the State coach, he's a State fan too. He bleeds green like the rest of us!

"I'll tell you, though"—one of tailgaters shook his head—"Rose Bowl champs or not, we are pathetic this season!"

"God, we're more conservative than last year," another chuckled. "I mean the offense is nonexistent. George makes Bo look like an offensive genius."

"It's pretty sad"—the cider tender poured me a warm-up—"when your whole offense revolves around a left tackle."

One of the ladies popped in a little optimism. "At least the football team's better than the basketball team."

Nobody rushed to the basketball team's defense.

"Yeah, I guess so." The fella shook his head. "Sometimes I think I'm just gonna quit coming. Maybe not renew my season tickets till they learn how to throw a pass." He took a swig of cider. He squinted off into the distance. He smiled. "You know, though, if we win today, and beat the Hoosiers next week, we may just get a bowl bid anyhow!"

After warming up between the Spartan vans, I headed over to the Boilers' one good tailgate spot. It's a place called Slater Hill, an open grassy hillside a couple of blocks from the stadium. Slater Hill has a big outdoor concert stage at the base of it. The hill slopes down and into the stage. Trees line the top of it. Cars pull up on the lawn; folks get out and tip their thermoses. And they wait. I waited with them. And I listened. I squinted way, way off into the distance. Three or four blocks away, across the baseball field and past the outdoor track, out from behind the tennis courts, a long line of bodies snaked toward us. I strained to hear. *Ba ba baboom. Ba ba baboom.* A muffled beat rolled across the fields. I couldn't make out individuals, just a long long line of black-and-gold marchers. It was the queen and her court! Purdue's

All-American Marching Band, and Monster, the big bass drum, bringing up the rear.

The band marched toward us. And the closer it got, the more distinct its music became, and the more people gathered on the hillside. Thick wool blankets were laid out on the ground. Families sat down, or they stood if they couldn't find a dry spot. Moms tapped little ones and pointed to the black and gold. "Here they come! Look, here they come!" The *ba ba baboom* got louder; the band played along. Two Monster beaters even boomed the big drum. They jumped into the air while they swung the mallet. And a couple of seconds later, thunder rumbled across the field.

At the front of the band, ahead of the Goldusters and the twirling line and all the marching musicians, strolled four ladies. The last time I'd seen them they were just kids, sopping wet and sloshing around in the practice field mud. This time, strolling out of the cold gray, ahead of the band, they looked like queens. Lani and Bibi wore sparkling silver warm-ups and were draped in silver fur capes. Kim walked alongside in solid black. And in front, in white with a gold flowing cape, strolled Dawn Beck. Little girls in the hillside crowd grabbed their moms' arms. They pointed; they whispered thoughts and dreamed Golden Girl dreams. The band exploded into "Hail, Purdue" as it hit Slater Field. The hillside clapped along. Band fans, some with their coats unzipped showing off gold "I'm a Band Parent" sweatshirts, settled in for the fifteen-minute show.

After the twirling and music and Slater Hill performance, after a hillside standing ovation, kids mingled with their folks. They had a few minutes to visit before the stadium march.

"I want to be the Girl in Black," Robyn Beck, Dawn's little sister, giggled. "Hopefully in four more years."

"She will," Dawn promised me. "She's a straight-A student! And she was the fourteen-year-old national twirling champion this year. She's a really good kid!"

Robyn giggled. Dawn hugged her little sister. Their mom and dad smiled.

The lady with the video camera who'd driven all the way up from Georgia—Lani and Bibi's mom—did some last-minute primping of her Silver Twins.

"I used to embarrass them," Janice Barnes laughed while she made sure the girls' hair was just right. "But now they're used to it. They let me fool with them and fix their hair."

"Mom, we gotta go!" the twins dueted.

"Good luck, girls!" Mom watched her Barbie dolls, as she calls them, head off to lead the pack. Mom grinned a great big mom grin. "Oh, it's so prestigious up here. The way they treat them, they almost make queens out of them. I'm just so proud of them." She started laughing. "Sometimes I think it's more fun for me than it is for the girls."

Band kids waved goodbye to their folks; boyfriends and girlfriends got one last good-luck kiss; the band assembled and marched off to the stadium. I headed over to the press box. You see, at the beginning of the fall I'd written all the athletic directors, told them what I was up to, and asked for free tickets. All ten came through and some did more. Indiana and Ohio State provided field passes. Purdue did them one better and gave me a press box pass. So I decided, why not check out the Purdue press box? Heck, they'd have free hot dogs and coffee. It'd be warm and dry too. So I hit the press elevator and took it up four flights. But before walking in where the newspaper guys sat, I climbed a little outdoor stairway to the roof. I ended up six stories high on the very top of the press box, the greatest place in West Lafayette to watch the band do its pregame thing.

Cold wind whistled across my flat open perch. I could see clear back across the Wabash River to the Lafayette courthouse. Treetops had given way to November and dropped most their leaves. Concrete campus buildings blended into the gray sky. A cable TV cameraman was the only other guy up there. Snug in a big fat down parka and all sorts of waterproofing, he aimed his camera down at the field. I stood and shivered and looked across the grass. Beautiful, lush, and green, it's what God meant for college football.

A deep voice boomed through the stadium: "PRESENTING THE 1988 EDITION OF THE PURDUE ALL-AMERICAN MARCHING BAND, WITH DRUM MAJORS JIM KOHL AND PAT JONES. FEATURING THE FLAG CORPS, THE TWIRLING CORPS, THE GOLDUSTERS, THE GIANT BASS DRUM, THE SILVER TWINS, THE GIRL IN BLACK, AND AMERICA'S MOST FAMOUS BATON TWIRLER, PURDUE'S GOLDEN GIRL, MISS DAWN BECK!"

The Purdue show unfolded like a flower in bloom. All the groups stretched out from goal line to goal line. The band moved from formation to formation and played along the way. The music rose up to me. Goldusters sparkled in gold sequins. The Flag Corps and Twirlers balanced out the Dusters on the other end of the field. The Silver Twins roamed the green and twirled like the girls in the Doublemint gum commercial, side by side, doing everything exactly the same. Kim Radcliffe, robe gone, down to skimpy black outfit, twirled and spun and threw her baton. And Dawn Beck, with her gold flowing hair, glittered and wowed the crowd. Meanwhile, noisemakers made their noise. The big bass drum boomed. Over on the track the *Boilermaker Special,* an old truck converted to look like an old train, honked its foghorn. And on the tippy top of the scoreboard, a real steamship whistle blew.

The show finished up with Purdue's traditional "I Am an American" speech. The band plays "America the Beautiful" while the PA announcer reads a two-paragraph verse on why it's great to be an American. It's a little hokey, it's a little Midwest-ish, but it's nice, and it's been part of the show since 1969.

The band filed off. Purdue Pete, a kid in a costume with a big plastic head and carrying a hammer, jumped up and down as the Boiler football players huddled on the track. Cheerleaders and Boiler Babes (the pom-pom squad) clapped and cheered and jumped up and down. A baby *Boilermaker Special,* a golf-cart-sized train, the *X-tra Special,* ran circles around the turf. And the Purdue football team broke for the sidelines. The stands, meanwhile, mustered up a cheer. And the game began! Everybody pretty much knew the outcome ahead of time, but when the Boilers took a 3–0 lead, all hell broke loose. The band, sitting in a block on the twenty, played the fight song. The big bass drum boomed. The *Boilermaker Special* hit the horn with a long deep honk. The scoreboard steamship whistle exploded. The Boiler Babes and the cheerleaders, Purdue Pete and fans in the stands, made all sorts of noise. It was enough anyhow to get me just a little nervous, so I climbed the stairway back down into the press box.

It's a good thing press boxes serve free food and are toasty warm, because they rob college football of all its excitement. Small and cramped, they're quiet. Almost library quiet. The only sound inside was the soft hummmmm of a heater. Newspaper guys, some in sports coats, some in sweaters, some just in jeans and T-shirts, crammed tiny seats in front of the big glass windows. They scribbled notes about the game. They wrote that Michigan State had scored two quick touchdowns to answer the Boilers' field goal. They got continual updates on passing yardage and continual updates on rushing yardage. A speaker inside relayed the important stuff like the official time of each score. But nobody sitting there could taste the field. They couldn't hear the pop of the pads. The band, from behind the glass, was like a silent movie. It sat in its twenty-yard-line block, trombone players swung their horns, but no noise came out. Cheerleaders cheered silently. Boiler Babes quietly shook their booties. Crowd roars muffled to a buzz too soft to drown out the heater. And only very faintly could you hear the big bass drum. Only if you saw it smacked, then strained real hard and listened for the boom. Worst of all, nobody cheered. The reporters sat real quietly and wrote real quietly. Michigan State pounced on another Boiler turnover, I pounced on a dog and a cup of coffee and slid outside to the real thing—the cold and wet and noises and smells and tastes of Big Ten football.

The game itself was a blowout. And it got worse by the quarter. The weather got lousier and lousier, for everybody but the guys behind the upstairs glass. The cold and the wet took its toll on everybody but the Spartan defense. They had a ball! On the grass in the rain, they just smeared the poor Boilers. As the gap widened the crowd thinned, and by the third quarter it had dwindled to less than half of the original number. I roamed over to the end of the track, the place where all the noise was coming from. The place where they stationed the big bass drum and the *Boilermaker Special.* I stumbled on the engineer of the *X-tra Special,* the baby Boiler that way back at the start had led the football team to the sidelines. Dave Guarino was a shivering encyclopedia of Boilermaker lore.

"We're in the Reamer Club. The Reamer Club takes care of school mascots and school traditions. That's our job!" Dave, like the other Reamer kids, was freezing his butt off. He rolled on anyhow. "We find out when things were built. The real stories behind the fight songs and cheers. We go to *all* the games. It's a riot!"

"Except for days like today," grimaced another Reamer, one of the six kids covered with blankets sitting in the back of the *Boilermaker Special.*

I nodded that I was freezing too, and mentioned I'd never been to a place with so many firsts and mosts and biggests. It triggered a Reamer Club outbreak.

"We have the world's largest marching band and world's biggest drum," Dave proclaimed.

"... and the world's biggest flag," added a girl in charge of the giant flag they'd unfurled on the field during "I Am an American."

"The *Special* is the world's largest mascot."

"And the turf," somebody in the back end of the world's largest mascot popped up. "Don't forget the turf."

Dave smiled. "I guess you could say we're *Guinness Book* kind of people."

They are! They know everything about Purdue traditions. And Dave Guarino knows the most. Everybody's favorite was the big train. "Yeah, we take this baby to almost all the road games." He slapped the black back end of the *Boilermaker Special* like it was his baby. "Two tons, twenty-three feet long, it's a truck chassis. This is the third version. In 1960 they took it over to General Motors and they hand-built the body!" They did a good job! It has a cowcatcher and a smokestack. Set up on the tracks, it'd probably fool any set of crossing lights. "We just had it appraised for insurance too. It'd cost four hundred eighty thousand dollars to rebuild."

"And that's without the paint!" A girl in the train bed shivered out a little extra info.

Four black speakers perched on the train cab. They were hooked up to the football game's play-by-play. Nobody paid much attention. Not the Reamers shivering in the back bed. Not the three or four Monster guards leaning against the hood. Up by the bell and the light and the catcher and the smokestack. A quiet Monster stood alongside. The Spartans were pushing into the forties. There wasn't a lot to boom about.

"Now this one . . ." Dave, like a used car salesman, moved on to the *X-tra Special.* It was parked right behind the big one. "A Purdue alum had this one hand-built. We can take it inside to the B-ball games too." He stepped back and sized it up. "Yeah, they built it around a golf cart. On a good day going downhill you can get her almost up to thirty-five miles per hour. The copilot and I were even given a four-day vacation in downtown Chicago because of the *X-tra.* There was this business convention going on and their motto was 'I think I can. I think I can.' Well, they had to have a train. The *X-tra Special* was perfect. So they borrowed it, and since we drive it, they put Bill and me up in the Hyatt for four nights! We had a riot!"

"Did you hear that! Did you hear that!" One of the kids in the back of the *Special* was warm all of a sudden.

"I told you they'd choke." Another came to life. "I told you!"

The Purdue broadcast relayed an update from Champaign-Urbana. Illinois had scored again. They had pulled to within a touchdown of the Hoosiers. Monster beaters jumped off the train, hustled over, and hammered the big drum a couple of times. Green-and-white State fans in the stadium corner looked down at the drum and scratched their heads. Up by more than thirty, they probably couldn't figure out why the sudden Purdue celebration.

"Great!" Dave ran over to the speaker.

The kids in the truck listened closely to the two guys on the radio talking about the IU game. Then they buzzed on about the possibilities.

"It's the biggest! The biggest!" Dave was as psyched about Indiana's stumble as he was about Purdue traditions. Everybody was. It was like they'd all shared a caffeine injection.

"You can't believe the Bucket Game. Man, it is crazy! It's even crazy at home. My mom went to Purdue; my stepdad and his whole side went to IU. I'll tell you, when Purdue and Indiana get together for football or *basketball*, especially *basketball*, we split the living room right down the middle. They sit on one side and we sit on the other!"

With the Purdue rout back on the radio, Dave got back into traditions. The whole truck bed listened in, like we were sitting around a campfire. He told about the real steamship whistle atop the scoreboard. He explained the origin of the Oaken Bucket. He told why Purdue was called the Boilermakers. He even revealed that the old brick stack, the one whose days were numbered, was nicknamed Purdue's "Finger to the World."

The other Reamers were mesmerized. One girl shook her head. "I knew he knew a lot! But not all this!"

Dave ran out of traditions and voice at about the same time. But he had to get over to Mackey Arena anyhow. He had to see if they wanted the *X-tra Special* in for the women's volleyball game. I headed back to the field, leaned against the chain-link fence that surrounded the grass, and finished out the game. The 47–3 final was almost already tallied. It was just waiting for the clock to wind down. Cheerleaders and Boiler Babes stood on the sidelines and shivered. Students had booked a long time ago and even diehard alums were trickling out. Only one big square of bodies remained. The band. Cold and wet and loyal till the bitter end, they sat alone on the twenty, a black-and-gold square, surrounded by wet, empty bleacher seats. Sprinkling rain picked up and fired ice darts down from the skies.

Back in the corner, over by the Reamers, the big bass drum boomed and boomed and boomed. I looked out onto the field. The teams were huddled up. I looked across to the band. They sat and shivered and covered their instruments. Purdue hadn't done anything to cheer about. They didn't even have the ball. It was official! The "other game," the one down in Champaign-Urbana, must've ended. All was not lost in West Lafayette. The Hoosiers must've choked.

Besides, there were only two weeks left till the Bucket Game. And it was the only one that really mattered. Best of all, Boilermaker basketball season was just around the corner.

# 9
# NORTHWESTERN UNIVERSITY
## THE WILDCATS

| | |
|---|---|
| Northwestern University Evanston, IL | Dyche Stadium |
| Best Breakfast | Sarki's Grill |
| Best Bar | The Huddle |
| Best Burger | Buffalo Joe's |
| Best of . . . | |

\* tied for best

### The Best in Big Ten Country

#### MASCOT

1. Herky Hawkeye *
1. Bucky Badger *
3. Boilermaker Pete
4. Willie the Wildcat
5. Goldie Gopher

Northwestern football is really what it's all about. Or at least what college football is supposed to be all about! Back when they came up with the term "scholar-athlete," the tiny liberal arts institution just north of Chicago was probably what they had in mind. Unfortunately, good grades don't draw 245-pound fullbacks who can run the hundred in 4.5, nor do they lure fat TV contracts. And those things, nowadays, are what win football games. So Northwestern just keeps plodding along, down at the bottom of the pack, doing things by the old standards, playing the game with scholar-athletes, many of whom are more scholar than athlete. And doing it maybe not with a lot of wins, but doing it with integrity!

Wildcat football has not been a history of success. Heck, you need an Ed McMahon *Star Search* just to dig up some decent moments. As for being a fan—that really takes guts. Northwestern's greatest claim to fame—its thirty-four-game losing streak—must feel like perpetual heartburn. The Cats still wear purple, the closest thing available to black and blue. And again in '88, for the fifth year in a row, they were the Big Ten preseason pick for last place. Still you have to respect the football program! You really do! A private school of fifteen thousand students (only seven thousand undergrads) in the quiet little town of Evanston, Illinois, and it's competing in the biggest conference in the world. It has no Notre Dame fight song or balmy University of Miami breezes or Joe Paterno legacy to lure some superstars and tilt the scales back its way. No TV games. No packed stands. No glitzy glamorous red carpet to the NFL. The people that put on the purple each Saturday afternoon—both the kids on the field and the few folks in the stands—ought to receive a special induction into the College Football Hall of Fame just for showing up.

Northwestern does it the way it's supposed to be done. Books first, square-outs and trap blocks and linebackers filling holes second. A college with integrity, a football program with integrity if nothing else—priorities are secure. And because of that, at least some individuals, it is certain, will never be invited to make Evanston their home. Deion Saunders, the loudmouthed all-everything safety from Florida State, the guy who slugged a cop in preparation for the '89 Sugar Bowl, wouldn't last the slap of a judge's gavel in Evanston. If he goes to graduate school—that is, assuming he ever finishes undergrad school, or ever attended undergrad classes—Northwestern University will not be the place. You'll never find a Wildcat linebacker shaving his head, nicknaming himself the Boz, then writing a book about his teammates firing machine guns off their apartment balconies. Jerry Tarkanean or Jackie Sherrill or Barry Switzer, coaches renowned for their high ethical standards, won't ever be offered head coaching positions with the Cats. Steroids, grade fixing, alumni payoffs are not, were not, and won't ever be a Wildcat problem. And odds are, with only twenty thousand people showing up each Saturday, players don't get illegal kickbacks for their tickets. These are the pluses that come to a program that plays it straight. They may not be enough to offset some pretty dismal win-loss records. But as Sharon Miller, Northwestern's sports information director, said, "Hey, knowing that you didn't cheat, that you did things the right way, that makes the wins all that more special!"

Sports information directors, or SIDs as they're called in the business, run the college sports PR machines. They draw up the game programs that keep fans on top of who came from where. It's their offices that dig up the stats Keith Jackson pulls out of the air each Saturday afternoon, and they're the ones that local sportswriters use to spice up feature stories. They work an unbelievable number of hours. They know more about a university's sports program, past or present, than anybody alive. Except for maybe the folks at the tailgates out in the parking lots.

Can you imagine the nightmares that must filter through the Northwestern sports information office each fall?

Sharon Miller arrived in '82. "My first year here it was a bonanza. We broke the losing streak in football and got our first-ever postseason bid in basketball to the NIT. When we broke the streak, this place went nuts." She thought back and laughed. "So I guess you could say it's been a little anticlimactic since then."

Sharon Miller's different from a lot of SIDs. First off, she's not a he; she's the only woman SID in the Big Ten. Second, she laughs a lot. I guess to get through Wildcat football you'd need a good sense of humor. We talked about the two things that people talk about a lot when they talk Wildcat football: the thirty-four-game losing streak and Northwestern academics.

"There were players here that never won a football game. Students that never saw a winning game!" It really bothered her that thirty-four lost football games might be a kid's most vivid collegiate memory. "Four years is a long time. It really was hard on a lot of people."

In '86, Columbia pulled the monkey off Northwestern's back. They lost thirty-five straight, then went on to forty-four. And while the rest of the country snickered, while Johnny Carson substituted Columbia for Northwestern in the new college football jokes, in Evanston, or at least in the Northwestern sports information office, folks felt a little pity.

"When Columbia was closing in on it, ABC, CBS, *Washington Post, New York Times,* everybody called us. They wanted to talk to people who had played here, or who had coached here during the streak. . . . It really became ridiculous after a while. . . . First Columbia was almost gonna break it. Then they tied it. And then, unfortunately for them, they broke it . . . and it's like the papers thought we were having a party all along the way!" She shook her head. "It's not something you wish on somebody else. You really feel bad for them. For the kids and for the fans. It's too bad there's such a microscope on college athletics. . . . There's so much more to college football than winning and losing. Nowadays, though, I guess there's not allowed to be."

Well, both streaks are over now. Both teams still lose a lot more than they win. And both get hammered pretty badly on occasion. But Wildcat football is no longer rock bottom. At least not three-seasons-in-a-row-without-a-win rock bottom. In 1986 and 1987 the Cats pounded cross-state rival University of Illinois. That had to be sweet. They haven't sat alone in the Big Ten basement since '81. They won their 1988 Homecoming, the first one since 1983. Chalk that up to the schedule makers—Wisconsin was invited. An air of optimism about the Saturday game with Purdue even drifted around the place.

I told Sharon I'd watched Michigan State destroy Purdue the week before. The Golden Girl, I said, was probably the best thing the Boilermakers had going for them. I really thought the Wildcats had a chance.

"Everybody kind of secretly thinks we can win. But I did hear we're four-and-a-half-point underdogs." She sighed. "You know we've only been favored once this year and that was against Wisconsin. And we were only favored by one point! Isn't that great! On our own field, Homecoming, and we were favored by one point. Then again, I guess it's better than being underdogs."

While the football team's win-loss record is something that'd turn even the most loyal Cat fan blush-red, when it comes to integrity, the football team has put together a little bragging material. In Division One, only Duke, Stanford, Rice, and Virginia can claim football programs with as much academic success as the Wildcats'. It's squeaky clean too.

"We have things in perspective," Sharon said. "And I feel comfortable working here. I wouldn't feel comfortable working in an Oklahoma or a Miami. You know, places like that, where kids don't graduate. Or even if they do graduate, they're part of a program that just funnels them through. I work in an atmosphere where there's no cheating, there's no crime, we don't have kids being put in jail. And that really makes the wins all that more special."

That's what Northwestern hangs its hat on, and that's what it stresses to new recruits. And since I was at a place that really practiced what it preached when it came to books and sports, I decided to do a little research. I'd always wanted to know what exactly it took to keep an athletic scholarship. Just how much of a classroom line, if any, a college athlete had to toe. I'd always wondered if the NCAA kept tabs on a place like Miami or Oklahoma or Nevada, Las Vegas. So I asked a lot of questions and did a little reading. Between Sharon and Margaret Akerstrom, director of academic counseling—the office that makes sure athletes are going to class—I got the picture. It's not a pretty one! Particularly outside the Big Ten.

First off, NCAA requirements state that to keep a scholarship the athlete must be "fully enrolled." That, I figured, was a good idea since the university was forking over tuition to keep him. Athletes, by passing Proposition 48, the combination ACT-SAT high-school grade-point minimum, are automatically eligible for their first year of sports. After that, to stay eligible they must complete a certain number of semester credit-hours each year: 24 by the end of the first year, 48 by the end of the second, 72 by the third, and 96 by the fourth. The problem is at most places it takes 120 semester credit-hours to graduate. Which works out all right, since most athletes who plan on graduating are on five-year programs anyhow. Also the NCAA requires that athletes be making "satisfactory progress" toward a major. But guess who determines what satisfactory progress is? The institution that admitted them in the first place! Do you really think Miami or Oklahoma or Nevada, Las Vegas is going to look closely at some All-American's class load?

Semester hours and "progress," according to the NCAA, are it! The kid might have a cumulative grade-point average between a D and an F, but if the twenty-four credits per year are covered, and somebody at the school says, "Yeah, he's making progress towards a major," the kid plays. Oh, I almost forgot. "Always rigid" summer school counts in the total number of credits. So an athlete who's flunked out during the regular year can make it up in June, July, and August, and be eligible again come fall.

Fortunately, the Big Ten Conference is tougher than the NCAA. First the number of required credit-hours is adjusted to 24–51–78–105. Plus, a grade-point requirement's tossed in. Individually, Stanford, Rice, Virginia, and other colleges set their own grade-points, but as major conferences go, the Big Ten is one of the very few with such a requirement. And its petition to the NCAA to adopt a similar standard has twice fallen on deaf ears.

That's too bad. The grade-point's good for kids. It gives them something other than a scrapbook full of football clippings to leave college with. Maybe even a degree! Definitely a good start on the future. And it's not like the standard's impossible. Actually, it's just a breathing-in-the-classroom-and-turning-in-your-papers kind of thing. A grade-point, that shouldn't be too difficult to reach, even considering college football is a full-time job: 1.8 during the first year, 1.8 during the second, 1.9 during the third, and 2.0 after that. If that's accomplished, and if you get your credits, you keep your scholarship and remain eligible. Simple as that!

Northwestern takes things one step further. It puts its athletes on a four-year schedule instead of five. Class loads increase to 30–60–90–120. The academic counseling office plays a major role. Plus, Northwestern University classes are challenging, for all majors. And the school doesn't even offer PE classes, let alone PE majors. Between the demands of the practice field and those of the classroom, athletes coming out of Northwestern are ready for most anything the world can throw at them!

I also found a few other interesting tidbits as well. I grabbed a pile of photocopied articles that Northwestern hands out to recruits, a little PR package that tells the real story never heard during the Saturday afternoon Game of the Week. A couple of *Philadelphia Inquirer* stories were real doozies. "Academic Dodge Ball at UNLV" explained how seven players on Tarkanean's B-ball team had taken care of one quarter of a year's worth of classes with "Contemporary Issues in Social Welfare." They'd taken care of it on a sixteen-day, nine-basketball-game cruise to Tahiti, New Zealand, and Australia. Players earned full credit in three weeks, taught poolside, I guess by Tark the Shark. Another article, "Playing—and Exploiting—the System at Temple," talked about just that. And the most riveting, the one that made my stomach churn: *Sports Illustrated*'s "The Nightmare of Steroids," about how a kid went through hell and the University of South Carolina football program at the same time. It's a good tactic. Use the truth to tell kids what college sports can be like at a place that gives a rip about only one thing. Not you, not your grades, not your life. Just winning ball games!

In the end my research confirmed some things I've always suspected. One, that Bobby Knight is right—the NCAA is hypocritical as hell. If it really cared about the kids more than all the TV revenues, then it'd make sure every school had a grade requirement. And second, that the Big Ten Conference is a step above. That a Big Ten athlete, at least, has some kind of minimal standard to live up to. Mostly, though, after talking and reading and researching, I forgot Northwestern had ever had a losing streak. To me, it's one thing—a school with a lot of class, which once in a while wins a football game, and where those wins really are something a little more special!

Chicago, just a few miles south of Northwestern, is a wonderful city. Every time I go there, I'm overwhelmed. The lights, the Hancock Center, Rush Street, the rush of Lake Shore Drive banked right up against the bright blue waters of the big lake. God, it's exciting! And to reach Northwestern from the south, you drive right through it. Squeezed between the big city and the big lake, Lake Shore Drive turns into Sheridan, slips under the El and up into Evanston—a neighborhood of gorgeous Victorian houses and home of the Wildcats. Just a twenty-minute El ride from the Loop, Northwestern's the only Big Ten university that you don't furrow through the corn to get to.

Evanston and Northwestern go well together. The school looks like a seminary, and the town for a long time almost was one. Dry until 1972, Evanston is the birthplace of the Woman's Christian Temperance Union, which explains why it's still tough to dig up a decent tavern! Downtown, though, is pleasant. Just a five-minute walk from the center of campus, the five or six square blocks temper college town life and college town kids with a quaint, sleepy kind of feeling. Old shops and restaurants blend with bank buildings on a city square. Yuppies and college kids and old retired folks bustle up and down the streets and sidewalks all day long. At dark, Evanston pretty much closes down. Usually that's the time most college towns start kicking into gear. But Evanston's not like most college towns; instead of craziness, it has a normal city spirit. And a whole lot of money too. BMWs, Audis, luxury-model Hondas, more than just an occasional Mercedes—big bucks float all over the place.

Elegant old neighborhoods cradle Evanston. Windy City standbys, brownstones and graystones and ancient red-brick apartment buildings, join the beautiful Victorian homes. Most with quite a few zeros on the price tag. Sheridan Drive, Evanston's link to Chicago, separates the university from the neighborhoods. It runs parallel to the lake and only a block or two from the shore. That block or two is where Northwestern, for nearly a mile, hugs the water. Hanging oaks hover over the neighborhood blocks branching off Sheridan's other side. Tidy lakefront parks run a stretch of green almost all the way back to downtown Chicago. And out beyond, gray November skies and the bright blue waters of Lake Michigan. It's nice, real nice!

So is the campus, which like Evanston is filled with big bucks. A small private school, costing almost twenty thousand dollars a year to attend, it's not your typical humongous state-funded Big Ten university. That is, until you roam the place; then it's pure Big Ten. And along with Indiana, Michigan State, and Wisconsin, one of the prettiest in the conference. Ancient ivy-covered buildings, grassy oak-covered lawns—the campus has a soft quiet look and feel to it. Charming old churches that dot the town nudge up against the campus. Their charm carries over to the school's buildings. Nestled in trees, back off Sheridan, the library's like a cathedral. At night, a faint light glows through its arching stained-glass windows and softens an already soft place.

Daytime, though, Lake Michigan rules. Out behind the main campus stretches the big lake. November waves crash on the shore. A grassy park, sidewalks through pine trees and young maples, and a small pond serve as doormat to the water, a buffer between the lake and classrooms. Joggers and bikers pound against the stiff lake breezes. Golden retrievers strain to break their leashes. Old farts, Old Style in hand, find a few places to cast out a line, and hope to reel in a few more salmon before the winter ice sets in. Big white rocks serve as a break for the pounding waves, and also a spot to look out at swirling waves and get it together for finals week. Or just someplace to stretch out on and catch a little summer sunshine. Poems for secret lovers and "I love you 4-ever" painted messages—some ten years old, some fifteen years old, some still fresh—dot the rocks and serve as college time capsules. Downshore, off in the distance softly jutting out into the water, Chi-town, the Hancock Center lost in fog.

Funny, the heart of such a gorgeous campus is a rock. One single strange-looking rock. A rock that forty years ago used to be a water fountain, until one winter the pipes froze and broke, water stopped coming out, and it went back to being a rock. It sits just a few feet from the steps of University Hall. Another old Gothic building that looks like long ago, it could've been a home for English kings, but now settles for English classes. Steps lead from the doorway down to a small open concrete plaza, where sidewalks empty and trees and hedges and flowers break things up, where a filled bicycle rack sits and a couple of plastic chairs sit around a beat-up elementary-school desk. And where the rock, a big six-foot-tall thing, stands.

"One hundred percent cotton, crew T-shirts. Get 'em while you can. Only ten dollars." A girl was doing the selling from her plastic chair perch. She was holding up a white 100 percent cotton T-shirt. Behind her a big white banner, strung between two trees and hung over the rock. A purple N with crossed oars through it centered the banner, and NW CREW ran down the side.

"Ten dollars, only ten dollars, one hundred percent cotton, Northwestern Crew." Another crew member, a redheaded guy, stood on a chair on the other side of the rock.

The rock's the marketplace. It's the university hub, the place where kids congregate during the day on their way to class. It's the place to vote, to sell doughnuts, to pass out literature, to meet friends, and apparently the place to sell 100 percent cotton Northwestern Crew T-shirts, as well.

"What do you think, want one? One hundred percent cotton." John, the redhead, hustled over. "Come on, they're great!" Sales weren't. Not yet, anyhow; classes hadn't gotten out. I was the only person who paid much attention to the crew, so like at the Chevy dealer's, I picked up all the salesmen at once.

"We're raising money for a new boat. It's a good cause!" Danielle from Pittsburgh, the third seller, approached. Finally, I gave in, forked over the ten dollars, and stuffed my new shirt away in my backpack. The girl on the chair, pleased with the sale, went back to her chair and kept selling. "One hundred percent cotton, crew T-shirts, get 'em while you can. Only ten dollars!"

John and Danielle filled me in on the business venture.

"We're a club sport, so we have to raise all the money ourselves."

"Yeah," John noted, "we used to sell hot dogs at the football games, but . . ."

". . . but nobody came so we didn't make any money," Danielle interrupted. "Besides," she went on, "Northwestern Crew is better than football. It's a hot college thing. *Seventeen* magazine even said so! July issue, I think!"

"June or July. They listed what were the hot college things. And they listed Northwestern Crew."

The girl on the chair stopped selling and leaned over. "It was July."

"July, but it's still a hot college thing!"

"Yeah!" Danielle and John high-fived.

"What about this!" I turned to the rock, the rock that supported the boxes, that the banner hung over. It was a bright, almost gooey red. Names, in white paint, covered it. And a couple of white Greek letters too.

"You don't know about the rock?!" John couldn't believe it. "It used to be a fountain. Back in 1920, I think."

"In 1902." The girl on the chair leaned over again.

"That's what I meant, 1902. The pipes broke in the forties and people have been painting it forever."

"You can stick a screwdriver in it and go down four inches till you hit rock. It's all paint!"

I looked closer. You could. The footholds that covered it were nearly filled in. Just layers and layers and layers of paint.

"It gets painted every night. Well, almost every night. Just stop by about nine o'clock and somebody will be guarding it."

"Guarding it?" I asked. "From who?"

"From anybody else who wants to paint it. If you aren't standing at it, then somebody else will come along and take it over. Then they get to paint it. Everybody does it! Crew team does it, frats and sororities do it, dorms do it. The day before the election, somebody came and did a Bush sign. They painted it Republican! I guarantee you, tomorrow it'll be a different color!"

"Hey, classes are passing!" the girl on the chair announced.

"Just come back tonight. I guarantee you." John backpeddled over to his chair and hopped up. "Check it out!" Danielle caught the hall's steps. John held up a shirt. The treasurer, on the plastic chair next to the rock, called out, "One hundred percent cotton, crew T-shirts. Get 'em while you can. Only ten dollars." The crew went back to work.

I had to see if John was right. So I killed time till the rock painting. I went back out toward the lake and read rock messages for a while. I cruised town, finally found a tavern, and had a beer and a burger. I just moseyed around until the sun went down and Evanston closed its eyes and went to sleep.

It was a cold, wet, windy night. One of those nights when if you weren't wearing gloves your fingers went numb, and if you weren't wearing a hat your ears went numb. It was a night when your nose turned bright red and never stopped running, just one of those typical November Chicago nights. After dark, about 8:30, I cruised back through the empty campus. Under the glow of the library stained-glass windows and the lamplit sidewalks, I headed for University Hall to visit the rock.

The gooey red rock glowed under a shining streetlamp. And sure enough, sitting alongside, all alone, in jeans and a heavy red fall coat, teeth chattering, freezing her rear off, sat Verna.

Verna was a small girl, with a little Oriental in her. When she smiled her whole face smiled, and she smiled a lot. Verna was Delta Theta's pledge trainer. She was a junior. And most important, that Friday night anyhow, she was Delta Theta's rock guard. Next to her sat the work materials: two gallons of "flamingo pink" and "wild lime green" paint, which were close to Delta Theta's house colors; a bunch of newspapers so the paint wouldn't spill all over; and two wooden stirring sticks.

"I'm guarding. I have to be here or some other frat might come and ambush me and capture the rock." She was laughing and shivering at the same time.

"Kind of chilly for rock painting, isn't it?" I wondered at what temperature paint turned to ice. We had to be closing in on it.

"I get relieved at ten. Plus, I can always go stand in the doorway of Harris Hall." She pointed to the hall behind us, the one that along with University Hall surrounded the rock, and provided a funnel for the icy lake wind. "But if I do that"—she shivered on—"I might lose the rock. If somebody came up and tried to sit down, I'd have to run down the steps and beat them to the seat." She was trying not to sound too strange, and to keep from giggling at the same time. It didn't work. She laughed, "So I think I'll just stay here!"

Verna offered me one of the plastic chairs. I sat and asked rock questions. She sat and answered rock questions. The conversation kept our blood circulating and consequently kept us both from freezing to death.

"You see, first you go out and scout. You scout with two people, to see if anybody has the chair. If they don't, you grab the seat and one person runs back to the house and says, *'We're painting the rock tonight!'* She yelled it out like she was rushing through the front door back at the sorority House. She apologized and started laughing again. "It's kind of like your assault plan!"

She'd been guarding the rock for about half an hour, and still no ambush. Things were moving along right on schedule. "We tried last night too. But somebody was already sitting here." The fraternity with gooey red colors, I guessed. "Yeah, Theta Chi. We tried to finagle our way in but couldn't. So we tried tonight, and got it!"

Delta Theta, Verna's sorority, reserves the rock three times a year. Once for the pledges, which was this time, once for initiation, and in the spring to advertise its big philanthropic fundraiser. Since she was the pledge trainer, Verna got to take charge of the pledge paint.

"It'll be all freshmen tonight. Considering how cold it is, probably only ten or fifteen of 'em." I tried to envision a dozen eighteen-year-old girls splashing pink paint all over the rock, at one in the morning, in 20-degree weather. "It'll probably take us 'bout a half hour or so." She stopped and blew on her gloves. "It's so cold, though. You know, we're supposed to paint it at one. That way nobody can paint over us. But maybe we'll cheat a little."

A campus cop car, out on rounds, cruised up. It stopped and a cop rolled down the window. "Everything all right?" We nodded. He drove on.

"They know somebody will be here, so they always check on us. And a lot of people walking home from the bars stop and watch too." "And they shine the light for us too." She pointed up to the streetlamp that was making the gooey red glow.

I asked what the toughest night was to get the rock, knowing for sure Verna had not chosen it.

"Oh, Homecoming! Without a doubt. Nobody gets it on Homecoming! The band comes here at noon. They form a big circle around it so nobody can get through. And that night they paint it purple. With a big white paw print in the middle. It really looks neat!"

"OK, Verna! Everybody knows! We're all set!" One of the pledges shivered up. No gloves, no hat, just a light fall coat. But with a thermos of hot chocolate. It was Verna's relief. The pledge poured out a cupful, steam rose up out of the cup, and we all took a sip.

"Verna, when are we painting it?" This, it was easy to see, was the freshman's first rock paint.

"Probably 'bout one o'clock."

"Verna—why so late? Why don't we just paint it now?"

Verna started to explain that if you painted too early you ran the risk of waking up to somebody else's paint job. But the freshman interrupted.

"What are we painting it with?"

Verna looked down at the two-gallon pails. "With paintbru . . . Oh no, I forgot the paintbrushes!" She tried to be mad, but started giggling again. She rocked back on her chair and busted out laughing. The freshman and I looked at each other and started laughing too. All three of us rocked back on our cheap plastic chairs and laughed till we cried. The wind whistled through the buildings and picked up one of the newspapers and broke it to pages, and carried it away.

"How stupid can I get!" Verna wiped the tears from her eyes. "Well, unless we're fingerpainting it, looks like I better go find some brushes."

One more cupful of hot chocolate and Verna headed back to the house to search for paintbrushes. I left for a warm car heater. And the freshman pledge, with no gloves and no hat, took over guarding. And shivering. Sitting alone in the cold and dark, under the streetlamp, on a little plastic chair, alongside the rock.

# PURDUE
# AT NORTHWESTERN
*Dyche Stadium,*
*Evanston, Illinois*

| Standings | Big Ten | | | All Games | | |
|---|---|---|---|---|---|---|
| November 12, 1988 | W | L | T | W | L | T |
| MICHIGAN | 5 | 0 | 1 | 6 | 2 | 1 |
| ILLINOIS | 4 | 1 | 1 | 5 | 3 | 1 |
| MICHIGAN STATE | 4 | 1 | 1 | 4 | 4 | 1 |
| INDIANA | 4 | 2 | — | 6 | 2 | 1 |
| IOWA | 3 | 1 | 2 | 5 | 3 | 2 |
| PURDUE | 3 | 3 | — | 4 | 5 | — |
| OHIO STATE | 2 | 4 | — | 4 | 5 | — |
| NORTHWESTERN | 1 | 4 | 1 | 1 | 7 | 1 |
| MINNESOTA | 0 | 4 | 2 | 2 | 5 | 2 |
| WISCONSIN | 0 | 6 | — | 0 | 9 | — |

**Other Big Ten Games:**

ILLINOIS AT MICHIGAN

MICHIGAN STATE AT INDIANA

MINNESOTA AT WISCONSIN

OHIO STATE AT IOWA

T he Cats were 1–7–1. Purdue, 4–5. A pretty lousy 4–5. Friday night's cold wind had whipped up a Saturday morning rainstorm, an icy-cold pelting rainstorm. The blue skies and sunshine that had graced Iowa, Indiana, and Illinois were long gone. I had instead classic Chicago November weather, a breeding ground for flu bugs, the type of day when, a week down the road, you just knew that lousy head cold had started. A day when those fashionable pop-up stick-in-your-backpack umbrellas were absolutely worthless. And the football game, no doubt, would pay the price. It'd be an afternoon when tailgates closed up, student sections shrank, and passing yardage took it on the chin. I figured the purple fans who actually showed would have to be the most unbelievably loyal people in the world—while Boilermakers who came all the way up from Purdue, well, maybe they were just a little un-balanced.

But duty called. I pulled out all my warm Spartan wear—a long underwear top, a Rose Bowl T-shirt, a Michigan State hooded sweat-shirt, and a so-called waterproof jacket. I even thought about spraying myself with a can of water-resistant silicone—the kind you cover your boots with. But I didn't have the overnight to dry. So I just layered up, grabbed my green-and-white State umbrella, drank a couple of cups of hot coffee, and headed off for campus in the monsoon.

Football Saturday stop number one—the rock. I wondered if Verna had found the paintbrushes, and if the freshman pledge had stayed at her post or if she'd deserted and lost the rock to some frat. I wondered if maybe their paint had just frozen solid in the pail. I parked on one of the empty Evanston side streets, as close as I could to campus, and sloshed over to University Hall. There between the buildings, next to the plastic chairs that the crew had peddled T-shirts from, the gooey red rock from Friday night had turned to pink. Flamingo pink. With wild-lime-green signatures all over it and a Greek triangle and a Z in the middle. The wind and the cold and the wet beat on the rock, names dripped and ran like they'd been photographed in the middle of a meltdown. *Jojo* and *Tammy* and *Martha, Jill* and *Krista, Shelly* and *Beth,* and in the back, inside one of the last footholds—probably where once upon a time before the pipes froze water had trickled out—*Verna*. They'd done it! And nobody'd painted over 'em, either. Well, if a bunch of freshman girls could suck it up in the cold and do their job on the rock, I figured I could suck it up in the rain and do my job on the football game!

Dyche Stadium isn't really on the main campus. About a mile or so up Sheridan, north of the rock, and another mile away from the lake, it's still in Evanston. And Evanston is good for rain-soaked days. The Woman's Christian Temperance Union may not've cared much for taverns, but I'll bet it had a lot of breakfast meetings. Greasy-spoon hash-browns-and-eggs places are all over town. They dot Central Street, just a few blocks down from Dyche. And on rainy Saturday mornings, they're a great way to get warm. I caught a corner one. I slipped inside, grabbed a counter seat, a *Sun Times,* a plate of over-easies and some hash browns. I killed some time waiting for the rain to stop.

It's tough to show loyalty in lousy weather. Brightly colored sweaters and T-shirts in bright school colors that take on blue skies and sunshine get buried under practical stuff in rainstorms. Everybody, it seems, dresses in school-bus yellow. Ponchos and raingear become fashionable. Warm and dry take over as prime motives. Actually, aside from umbrellas, out in the wet everybody looks pretty much the same. It's not till you peel off the waterproof that you can tell a Wildcat from a Boilermaker. Well, at my "corner spoon," fans had pretty much delayered. Purple, black, and gold reappeared.

A Boilermaker couple sat at a booth next to my counter. They were up to watch the band. Black-and-gold "I'm a Band Parent" sweatshirts gave them away. They were the same shirts I'd seen on band parents at the Golden Girl performance over at Purdue the week before. Since the booths were so crowded, and aisles so narrow, I turned around and said hello.

"You know, somehow we just didn't figure on it raining." Dad, I could tell, was not all that pumped about the game. Something told me a warm fire and a little college football on the tube back in Indiana would've suited him just fine.

"We still have a couple hours, honey—it may clear up."

Mom turned to me. "It's the band's second road trip this season. We've been to all the others all the other seasons. We figured, rain or shine, we'd better not miss this one!"

"I just don't understand. They get the whole year to take a trip and they wait till Thanksgiving in the damn rain. In Chicago! Don't they know it's always like this in Chicago!"

Dad drank coffee, flipped through the sports section, and continued to grumble about the band department's choice of a road trip date. Mom and I talked about the band. The All-American Marching Band, which I'd seen the week before. The Golden Girl, the Girl in Black, the Silver Twins, the big bass drum, and of course the trumpet section. The couple's daughter was a trumpet player.

"Did they bring the train up?" I wondered. The Reamer Club kid I'd met at the game in West Lafayette, the one that knew everything about

Boilermaker traditions, had said they took the big train on road trips. "Wherever the band goes," he told me, "the train goes too."

"Oh yes! You mean the *Boilermaker Special.* It's parked over at the stadium. And they brought the drum too! They always bring the drum."

"Too bad they aren't bringing along a football team." Dad chuckled. His second cup of coffee, a little warmth flowing through the veins, had loosened him up some. He folded the paper and put it away. "You know, they used to be pretty good. I watched 'em back when they had Griese QBing. They weren't bad back then. Phipps and Herman and Everette too. Those guys could throw the ball. But now, well, I wouldn't give you two cents for the team they got now."

"They're not that bad, dear," Mom scolded him. "We've won four games this year. Anyway, we come for the band." She glanced over to me. "You know, they're one of the biggest marching bands in the world!"

"And they're good too," I added.

Mom smiled and thanked me. Dad even nodded a thanks. They were glad somebody who wasn't even a Boilermaker appreciated what their daughter was going to have to march through, and what they were going to have to sit through that afternoon.

"Besides," I said, "if it wasn't for you and me and the bands, there might not be anybody at the game!"

After a little more band talk, and Chicago November weather talk, after the coffee, eggs, hash browns, and the *Sun Times* sports section, after finally giving up on a last-minute blue sky break, I said so long. I relayered and headed out the door over to the stadium. As I hit the sidewalk, I opened my State umbrella. The cold wind whistled through it, the aluminum spindles popped. Again! It inside-outed for the third time since I'd gotten up. This time, though, for good! About a block from the stadium, I tossed it in a Dumpster, and resigned myself to the fact that not even four layers could keep me dry.

Dyche Stadium is classic Big Ten. Built in the twenties, with big old seven-story towers that anchor the ends, it looks like a medieval castle. Someplace where Rapunzel might've let down her golden hair or King Arthur would've held Round Table discussions. Parking lots butt right up against the castle walls. A Chicago neighborhood standard, old red-brick buildings surround the lots like peasant villages. The setting makes for good tailgate land. And Northwestern fans are good tailgaters. Considering what had rolled in off the big lake, they had to be.

Cookout challenges saturated the puddled parking lots. Just lighting the coals was going to be tough enough, never mind keeping them going for the life of a burger. Buns, unless sealed in a leakproof safe, had soggy as their only future. As for anything exotic like steak or chicken or, god forbid, shish kebab, well, this was not the day to get cute.

For the folks that showed up, though, the wet didn't matter. Spirits were high. The parking lots looked like a series of deer blinds. The tailgaters looked like deer hunters. Makeshift plastic tarps ran between cars and, depending on how they were anchored, collapsed at least a couple times in a splash. Primo spots were backed up against trees where you lassoed a limb, then ran the tarp out to some open van door. Other folks, without such luxuries, skipped the food, turned to whiskey and coffee, sat on car bumpers, and said, "To hell with it." Once you reach a certain water saturation point, consume enough alcohol, and talk enough football, the weather just kind of disappears.

I roamed and froze for about a half hour. And made a few discoveries as well. The women's softball field, the biggest and best lot, I found out, had literally washed away. I stumbled on a big circuslike tent, back behind the football center. The Marriott was entertaining guests with caviar, salmon, and a buffet of hot food. I slipped inside, grabbed some hot coffee, stuffed a sandwich into my backpack for a second-half snack, stood around for a while, and warmed up. Back in the lots, I visited with a group experimenting with a new method of roasting turkey in the rain. It was a method that was going to cost them at least the first half, because it wasn't working out so well. I talked with a scalper who swore that regardless the weather, he'd end up in the black. And I caught a Northwestern specialty. Some well-dressed yuppie in a BMW pulled into the lot and asked the rain-soaked attendant if he'd take a fifty-dollar traveler's check. "American Express," the yuppie noted through the rolled-down window. "All right, I guess," the attendant answered and cashed it.

The rain had become a drizzle, the wind and cold kept rolling, and I was finally heading toward the stadium gates when I stumbled across the strangest tailgate setup I'd ever seen. And at it, considering the rain and the importance of the game, what might've been the world's most dedicated tailgaters. Five folks huddled in the grass, fifty feet or so from the sidewalk, alongside the John C. Nicolet Football Center. The spot was just an indent in the corner of a building—two walls and the overhanging roof. But considering the weather, it was primo. All the clan's tailgating stuff—two coolers, a big fat thermos filled with hot chicken soup and another smaller one for coffee, sandwiches and chips and pickles—was plopped out on a little card table. They'd picked up and moved, trading the soggy parking lot for the soggy grass.

"I've never seen a spot quite like this." I squished through the grass, up to the wall, and introduced myself.

"Hey, we saw two dry walls!"

"We dropped Larry off. He ran up and reserved it till we got back." Everybody laughed. The five laughed a lot. In fact, they were having a grand time. Rain, cold, wind didn't even exist. Just coffee—a little juiced up. Some beers, hot chicken soup, and Wildcat football.

"Hey, this is Wildcat Saturday! Nothing ruins Wildcat Saturdays."

"It's a great spot!" Larry turned up his palm and stretched out his hand. "Not a drop!" Dribbling off the roof, water was landing about five or six feet in front of us. It was almost like we were standing inside a waterfall.

"You all Northwestern graduates?" I wasn't sure. Aside from Larry's purple NU ballcap, everybody else had the day's standard on—waterproof yellow.

"Yeah. Go, Cats!"

"Yessiree!"

"Every last one of us!" Every last one of 'em were, Larry Sullivan and John Nichol, Jon, Marilyn, and Jed. And were they Wildcat fans! Big-time Wildcat fans!

"Been season ticket holders since '75." I tried to add up the losses in in my head. It got too high and I gave up.

"We've seen it all! Everything! The good and the bad . . ."

"And the *ugly.*"

"Show him your shirts." Marilyn chuckled. Larry rolled a blue jacket up over his belly. John peeled off a fluorescent-yellow waterproof raincoat. Underneath—the bottom layer—was a purple T-shirt: "I Survived Northwestern Football 1981."

"We saw all thirty-one of 'em."

"All the home games anyhow!"

"How about a cup of coffee?" Jon, in charge of coffee, handed me a full cup. "How about some of this?" Jed, in charge of the Crown Royal, warmed it. The cup toasted up my hands. The Crown Royal toasted my belly. *This* was the *only* way, I decided, to really beat the cold.

"OK." I got down to basics. "What's the best thing about Northwestern football?" It was something they'd never been hit with before. Something I don't think they'd ever consciously taken apart or ever really talked about. The fivesome who had been one nonstop joke-athon looked at each other. And thought.

Jed popped up, "The outcome is seldom in doubt." It brought the house down.

"The problem is . . ." Larry caught his breath and wiped his eyes. And even got a little serious. "When we were in school, all of us, two years in a row, we came in second in the Big Ten."

"Mike Adamle, Eric Hutchinson, Agase was the coach! We were tough!"

"I saw Northwestern beat Ohio State in Ohio Stadium." John said it very slowly, very deliberately, like the victory had been almost a religious act.

"I saw the Cats beat Illinois forty-eight to nothing. Illini fans don't remember that, but I sure do. I won a bet and the bum never paid off!"

"Those were the 'Purple Haze' days!"

Everybody was a fan, but Larry was hard core. That or he'd just had a little more coffee than the rest. Either way, he did most of the reminiscing. The other four followed along with head nods and voiced important additions that Larry might've missed. "Yeah, we tried to get the school to drop 'Wildcats' and change it to 'Purple Haze.' You know—Jimmy Hendrix—'Purple Haze'! Those were the 'Purple Haze' days. And the Cats were awesome."

"How 'bout a little soup?" Tex-Mex chicken soup, John's tailgate specialty, steamed out of the thermos. Big floating chunks of chicken bobbed in and out among the carrots and peas and other veggies. It'd knock out any cold ever manufactured and, along with the Scotch, probably worked pretty well on any flu bugs that happened to be in the area.

"You a Purdue fan?" John asked as he ladled me some of the soup.

"Uh-uh." I shook my head. Put down my coffee, unpeeled a couple of layers, and revealed an '88 Rose Bowl shirt. "Spartans!"

"Boo, boo," the Hazers answered my shirt.

"No, they're all right." Marilyn defended me. "It's those other guys from Michigan we don't like."

I thanked Marilyn for her defense and asked the Hazers if they'd ever road-tripped to East Lansing. I figured they had to have road-tripped somewhere. Anybody who would show up in a monsoon for a

Purdue-Wildcat game, anybody who'd had Northwestern season tickets for thirteen years and wore a T-shirt that canonized the streak, had
to hit the road.

"At least once a year!"

"Where's your favorite place?"

Need I even have asked? "MAD CITY," everybody chorused. Mad
City's everybody's favorite road trip.

"Illinois is good too."

"We went down to Illinois about ten years ago for the famous 'Oh
Bowl.'"

"Yeah, nothing to nothing."

The whole group must've gone, because everybody remembered
and started howling. I got the story in chunks from all directions at
once.

"It was the first game instead of the last. Ninety-five degrees—I'll
never forget it. We just sweltered!"

"Yeah, Frank was passed out in the parking lot. And Duffy's sitting
there sweating."

Larry was crying he was laughing so hard. "We're there in the
ninety-five-degree heat with this poor guy who weighs three hundred
twenty pounds. He's trying just to make it through the pregame and
we haven't even gone inside yet."

"And the game was horrible!"

"Boy, that was something!" They all stopped, looked at one another,
and started laughing again.

Every subject brought on at least a few snickers. That is, every
subject aside from the good stuff—the Northwestern highlights.

"You guys have beaten Illinois two years in a row, haven't you?"

"Yes," they answered together. A very serious yes.

"That's pretty good," I added.

"Yes, it is."

"What about Iowa? You like Iowa?" I told them I'd been roaming all
ten, and I really liked Iowa. In fact, everybody seemed to like Iowa.
Iowa, however, was not a good subject with the Purple Hazers. It got
quiet.

"We don't like Iowa fans." It was the first time I'd heard that.
Usually terms like "loyal" and "friendly" and "cornball" popped up.

John spoke for the group but the rest nodded their approval.

"Bumblebees. That's all they are, is bumblebees. They're obnox-
ious. When they come here, they are. They try to take over. They look

on Northwestern as an easy mark. Let's make it a home-away-from-home game. Let's just go out have a good time and blow away the Cats. We resent it. And I hate their . . . asses!"

I told John I was sorry to hear that. He nodded that that was all right, and promised that one day Northwestern would beat Hayden Fry.

We must've stood there for almost an hour. Chicken soup, whiskey, and coffee. We talked college football and the "Purple Haze" days. The Cat fans lived for more than just purple, though. All but John were hard-core White Sox fans, who, like all good Sox fans, hated the new owners. Marilyn complained, "All they do is raise the ticket costs and give away the good players." John, a Cleveland Indians fan, tried to tell his "longest home run ever" story, about a shot by Frank Howard nearly into the Municipal Stadium bleachers, till all the rest booed him cause they'd heard the same story a hundred times before. We talked about Evanston, about Northwestern, about the rock. Larry's frat had tarred and feathered it. "There are thousands and thousands of layers of paint on that thing." He laughed. "And one coat of tar!"

We drank and ate and laughed right up almost till kickoff. And since we couldn't miss that, the Purple Hazers gave up their spot. They folded up the table and packed up the coolers and thermoses and what was left of the Tex-Mex chicken soup, to drag it back to the cars.

"Come on up!" Marilyn handed me a ticket. They had eleven extras. Normally the group was sixteen. "Best seats in the house. Fifty-yard line. Upper deck."

I promised to drop by in the second half—I had a little stadium roaming to do first. We toasted with one last Crown Royaled coffee. And we parted.

"Go, Cats!" I called to them as I sloshed through the grass to the sidewalk.

"Go, Cats!" the Purple Hazers chorused back.

A high-school football game—that's what it felt like. That's what it looked and sounded like too. There couldn't have been more than five thousand folks inside. Uncovered Boiler fans, dotted with fluorescent yellow and orange ponchos, huddled between the forties on the visitors' side. A couple of hundred at the most. Their cheering wasn't even a buzz. The horseshow end zone was wet and barren. A ghost land of alternating purple and white squares of empty bleacher seats. Even the Wildcat side was just a hit-or-miss splash of purple, most of it tucked up under the overhang. The bands were the loudest cheering blocks. Purdue's sat alone on the twenty, on the Northwestern side of the field, in a huge square under the overhang. Shadows hid their instruments but their tunes rang out across the rain-soaked turf. And the big bass drum pounded away on the track. Down in front, Wildcat marchers put down their horns, pulled up their purple hoods, and cheered along with Willie the Wildcat. As for the game, a battle of first-half punts splashed back and forth. At times, when the ball worked its way inside the twenty, you'd look across the field to absolutely no fans on either side. But in a weird kind of way, it was exciting. If nothing else, I was sure that with the Cats tied at seven at the end of the first half, nobody who'd made it that far was about to go home.

After sitting downstairs for a quarter, after moseying down along the slippery, shiny sidelines, after tramping up into the corner of the lower level and saying hi to the Golden Girl, I headed up to the press box. You see, when I stopped by Sharon Miller's office earlier in the week, I'd asked if there was anybody around who remembered the good ole days. Somebody who'd actually watched Northwestern win on a regular basis. She'd mentioned Bob Voight, the 1947 football coach. He was the only coach who'd ever taken Northwestern to a bowl game. She told me to drop by the box in the second half, which I did. And I sat with Bob and eighty-six-year-old Walter Paulison upstairs in a tiny, unheated old room. A separate box off the newspaper press box. I stayed through the third quarter. It was like watching the game from inside a tree fort.

"Walter's eyes are giving him problems. I announce to him the down and the time. It helps him out." Bob turned to his old friend. "Walter's been here a lot longer than I have. He can probably tell you more about Wildcat football than anybody. Isn't that right, Walter?"

Both guys were good football fans. Both guys caught each game from that cold, cramped booth. Both had seen better Wildcat football days. Bob had coached Northwestern to the '47 Rose Bowl. And he'd won! Walter had been around a little longer. Since 1926. Actually 1921, if you count the four years he attended the school. Walter was the very first SID at Northwestern, although back then it wasn't a fancy position with a fancy name. The Wildcat football publicity man for forty-three years, Walter had pretty much seen everything there was to see. The three of us sat there talking about the old days, questioning the bad calls, pulling for the Cats.

"Walter's never seen a crowd like this. Have you, Walter?"

"Oh, heavens, no."

Bob led the questions and let Walter go from there. It was his way of making Walter feel more comfortable. Both were disappointed in the crowd, which from the box looked more like five hundred than five thousand. Even so, Bob was optimistic about the kids and the university. More than once he mentioned how good it was that Wildcat athletes toed the line in class. He also felt pretty good about the game. So did I. By the middle of the third quarter the Cats were actually taking command. Even if it was still 7–7, a rain-soaked victory looked like a possibility. Walter, on the hand, wasn't so sure.

"Oh, we're playing terrible today." The old guy shook his head. "If this game ends with a tie, it will be less than a defeat."

I suggested Walter go a little easy on the Cats. And during a break in the action brought up a subject that caught his ear. I asked about the Wildcat name and how they'd come up with it.

"Tell him the story, Walter."

The old guy thought back, a long way back, to when he was just a kid. "This would be back in the late twenties. We were playing Chicago. They were still in the conference then. Alonzo Stagg was their coach. It was the period when Chicago was the champion or runner-up. Anyway, we were playing them down there one Saturday. They were supposed to whip us and we damn near won the game. We lost it three to nothing, I think. The *Tribune* writer covering the game wrote his lead: 'It wasn't a football team that came down from Evanston today, it was a band of Wildcats.' " Walter chuckled and paused. "I worked in publicity for the school so I started using the phrase. And sportswriters started using it too. And between us we started using the term 'Wildcats' and it took off right away."

"We even had a live Wildcat at one time, didn't we Walter?"

"We did. For a year or two. The Phi Psi house kept it, I believe."

When you're sitting in a press box, game stats are never more than a typewriter and Xerox machine away. Only moments after the teams traded ends to start the last quarter, the score still knotted at 7, a kid brought the stats around. And scores too. Northwestern was rolling up the yardage and first downs and almost everything. As for the rest of the Big Ten, it was a typical college football Saturday—full of surprises. Ohio State somehow tied Iowa in Iowa, the Hawks' third tie of the season. The Hazers, no doubt, would be happy. Wisconsin was rolling, on its way to a 14–7 rout of Minnesota. Finally, its first win—

and for the Paul Bunyan ax too. And as expected, Michigan had just trashed Illinois by thirty points.

Bob took note of the Wolverine win. "Illinois had no right talking Rose Bowl anyhow." He was right, they didn't. Bo had proved it and was on his way to Pasadena one more time.

I had a date to keep. A seat to find. And hopefully a congratulations to issue. So after the Cats jumped out to a touchdown lead, I thanked the two fellas, told Walter to "go easy on the Cats," and left to find the Purple Hazers.

"IN TO ATTEMPT THE EXTRA POINT, IRA ADLER." The PA announced a third Cats extra-point try. Long and loud and clear.

"Come on, Ira! Kill it, Ira! All right!!!" Up in front of me, Larry was screaming. I was in the walkway, behind the Purple Hazers.

"THE SCORE WITH EIGHT-SEVENTEEN REMAINING IN THE FOURTH QUARTER: NORTHWESTERN, TWENTY-ONE; PUR-DUE, SEVEN."

"Yeah! Oh, yeah! You Cats are awesome!!!"

"Go, Cats, go!"

The "best seats in the house," wooden folding chairs, smack-dab on the fifty, were soaked. And filled with some pretty happy folks—Larry and John, Jon, Jed, and Marilyn, along with only forty or so others, in the whole open upper deck. It was celebration time in Evanston. Crown Royaled coffee was getting toasted. The Cats were up by two touchdowns. And the fat lady was singing!

"Congratulations!" I caught the five by surprise.

"Where you been?"

"Are these Cats awesome or what!"

"We just gotta hold on now."

The rain that'd quieted all game picked up with Ira Adler's third extra point. It started to pelt the open upper deck. Puddles got bigger. A few umbrellas popped.

"That's good," John noted. "Should kill any Purdue comeback!"

"God's just making his presence felt. You know, Notre Dame doesn't have a corner on that stuff!" Larry thrust a number 1 in the air. He yelled again to a chorus of "Purple Haze" hand clappers. "Yeah, oh yeah, you Cats are awesome!"

Yeah . . . awesome . . . *and eligible!*

# 10

# OHIO STATE UNIVERSITY
## THE BUCKEYES

| Ohio State University Columbus, OH | Ohio Stadium |
|---|---|
| Best Breakfast | Holiday Inn |
| Best Bar | Varsity Club |
| Best Burger | Max & Erma's |
| Best of . . . | |

| The Best in Big Ten Country | |
|---|---|
| STADIUM | |
| 1. Ohio | Ohio State |
| 2. Memorial | Illinois |
| 3. Michigan | Michigan |
| 4. Kinnick | Iowa |
| 5. Spartan | MSU |

Archie Griffin never lost to a Michigan team! Probably, in part, because he was always thinking of them. You see, three of those four years the Heisman tailback was a Buck, Woody Hayes reserved every single Monday practice for Michigan. It didn't matter who was next— Iowa, Michigan State, Purdue; Monday was Michigan Monday. And probably somewhere in Woody's gut, each week, each practice, all season long, the Wolverines rumbled. Well, some things have changed since those days. It's not the Big Two–Little Eight anymore! Archie

Griffin's now Mr. Griffin, and he spends his time in business offices instead of end zones. The Woody era is no longer, and Woody's gone too. The Buckeyes, at least for the past couple of seasons, have struggled to reach the .500 mark, let alone the conference championship. But *the game,* as they call it in Columbus, is still *the game.* Regardless of what else happens to be going on in the world, the last Big Ten game of the season, in the minds of those who live for Buckeye football, is still the only real Big Ten game of the season.

There are all sorts of reasons for it. All you have to do is be conscious and in Columbus for an hour, any hour, come "Michigan Week" to notice. The town, even at 4–5–1, is football nuts. The campus is a wealth of little customs and big stories. A lot of them football ones—and a lot of them revolving around Michigan Week. And most are revealed in the *Columbus Dispatch* or the students' daily *Lantern,* almost anyplace on the radio dial or just by a Buckeye fan at a local bar, on the hour, all week, right up till game time.

At the heart of the rivalry are two men—the memory of one and the presence of another. Wayne "Woody" Hayes and Glen "Bo" Schembechler. Their personalities, and "Little Eight domination" back in the seventies, the fact that both usually came into the game as Top Tenners, and that to the winner went a Rose Bowl caught the attention of ABC—and, at least on TV, turned the game into *the game.* But it goes a lot deeper than national TV coverage; it deals with football in a football-crazy town.

It's tough to explain just how much Woody is still loved in Columbus. It's not a Bobby Knight thing, because half of the state of Indiana (the Purdue half at least) despises Knight. Woody adoration is probably closer to what those in Ann Arbor feel for Bo, but with just a little more intensity. He passed away in 1987, but his name lives on all over Columbus. The football practice facility is appropriately titled Woody Hayes Athletic Center. Woody Hayes Drive runs between St. John Basketball Arena and the football stadium. The Woody Hayes Birthday Celebrity Roast, in which 1989's featured speaker is a Mr. Glen Schembechler, raises funds for retarded children. Scholarships and annuities have Woody's name on them. Bars and restaurants feature wall plaques of the man. Bookstores sell Woody everythings—from posters to videotapes. And nobody, but nobody, talks bad about the man.

Ohio State fans also look at Bo a little differently than Little Eight fans do. Maybe it's because Bo was the one guy, the only guy for some time, who could show up in Columbus and beat the Bucks. Maybe it was because he got his ears wet on Woody's staff. Most likely it's because Woody respected him so much, and he let Buckeye fans know it. Regardless of the reason, most Ohio State fans say nice things about Bo. They like what he stands for. They like the Bo-Woody rivalry thing. And more than once, a Buckeye fan hit me with "You know, they're a lot alike, Bo and Woody." You get the idea kicking around Columbus, as big a rivalry as it's been, as strong as the Michigan Week hype is, and maybe as much as they'd never want to admit it, that if it isn't scarlet and gray in Pasadena on January 1, a lot of folks in Columbus would just as soon see maize and blue. And Bo on the sidelines.

Ohio State football is not just Woody and Bo stories, though. It's all sorts of other little traditions as well. One of the littlest is the Golden Pants award—a tiny one-inch gold replica of an old pair of football pants. If the Bucks beat Michigan, the head coach presents each of his players with the Pants. The tradition began back in the thirties when Ohio State Coach Francis Schmidt gave a pep talk to his players. The opponent was a good Michigan team, one that the oddsmakers said was gonna bash the Bucks. Kind of like in '88. Anyhow, Coach Schmidt, in an effort to keep his kids from rolling over and giving up, fired off a memorable pregame pep talk. Nobody, he reminded his Buckeyes, including the Wolverines, was invincible. And everybody, even the Michigan team, puts his pants on one leg at a time. Coach Schmidt was right! The Wolverines weren't invincible, and they really did put their pants on one leg at a time—just like the Bucks. And Ohio State won. Since then, even without a Rose Bowl, there's always been something big riding on *the game*—a tiny golden pair of pants!

Buckeye Grove sits quietly in the shadow of McKraken Power Plant. Two tall red-brick smokestacks hover over it. Across the street is Ohio Stadium. Like a valley between two giant ranges, the tiny plot of trees sits, a reminder of a great football tradition. The story, like the Golden Pants one, is simple. It's told on an iron plaque, based in stone under one of the trees. The plaque reads, "Planted here are eleven Buckeye trees in memory of Ohio State's first football team, spring of 1890." Behind it, only a few feet from one another, stand the eleven Buckeyes—close together, almost in a huddle. The memorial doesn't end with 1890, however—it's ever evolving. For each first-team Ohio State All-American following the "original eleven," a tree is planted in that player's name. The ceremonial planting takes place in May. It's just a simple dedication, a small plaque, on a small stone below a tree, and the Buckeye earns a place forever in the honored grove.

Another great Ohio State tradition is Ohio Stadium. One of the Big Ten's elder statesmen, it went up in 1922. Like Memorial in Champaign, Ohio Stadium drips character. Its architecture conjures up images of Rome and the gladiatorial games. A huge Colosseum-like entrance at the north end, six stories tall, the giant arch—based in two towers, with upstairs columns—roars with power. Groups of arches, smaller than the gigantic one up front, span the concrete facade. Two giant square towers anchor the ends of the horseshoe. In the southeast tower sits the two-ton Victory Bell. Since 1953, every Ohio State victory has been announced by the bell. After each win it clangs once for every point the Bucks scored.

Inside, even empty, Ohio's is the Big Ten's most intimidating stadium. With eighty-five thousand seats, two levels up and around to the open end, it commands the game—yet still allows a view out through the horseshoe to campus. The place just oozes power and history. And yet it is a little quaint too. Four stories' worth of dorm rooms fill the west side. People actually live inside the stadium walls. Studying, however, particularly with the walls shaking to "Beat Michigan," probably isn't recommended.

Best of the Ohio State football Saturday traditions is the Script "Ohio". And it doesn't even involve a football. The Script's a product of the Ohio State Marching Band, and a reason why they nickname themselves The Best Damned Band in the Land (TBDBITL) and don't get much of an argument. I'd always been obsessed by the Script. Each Michigan–Ohio State Saturday when I wasn't at Spartan Stadium, I'd sit in front of the tube and wait for Keith Jackson to marvel at it. I'd wait for the half-time cameras to close in on it. And of course I'd wait for the *i* to be dotted! Since 1936 the Script's been the Ohio State Marching Band trademark. It's one of those things that college football is all about. And best of all, it never changes. The very same march since 1936, the very same number, "Le Régiment de Sambre et Meuse," to march to, and—aside from the first time when a trumpeter began the tradition, 1983 when Woody stepped out and brought down the house, and a few other honorary dotters—a sousaphone (a marching tuba) has always dotted the *i*. To be a part of a tradition as rich as this, to actually be involved, and to be the one who dotted the Ohio *i* would have to be the ultimate dream for all Buckeyes!

At band practice, I found not one but two *i*-dotters.

Jim Kinney, a junior, will have his chance in 1989. It's something he's dreamed about since he was an eighth-grade sousaphone player back in his hometown of Bowerston, Ohio. Cut from the band his first year at OSU, Jim came back, and back again. "I just kept practicing," he told me. "I wasn't gonna give up! It's a real honor to make this band. And tough too! You know, they've cut two hundred before!"

Well, persistence paid off. As a junior, the engineering major is a squad leader. One with a special duty. "I get to blow one of the two whistles when we come through the tunnel. Tomorrow the place will be going crazy. I probably won't even hear it!" And then, next year it all falls into place. Jim will have his sousaphone seniority, and he'll get to dot the *i*. That eighth-grade dream will finally be fulfilled.

As for this Saturday—Michigan and Ohio State, *the game*, national TV, at home in Columbus—Dave Rencehausen, a senior from North Olmsted, Ohio, earned the honor.

"It's awesome! Especially against Michigan!"

Needless to say, Dave was excited about Saturday's dot. "I'm a fourth-year senior and have the most seniority of the sousaphoners." Seniority in OSU band standings is determined by how many times you've actually marched through the game day tunnel. Those seven with the most seniority get to choose in order which one of the seven Scripts (six at home and one away) they want to dot. Not a lot of players march first team, all four years. Dave did. And came into this band season number one on the sousaphone seniority list. The game he picked—Michigan, of course. "If the Michigan game is home, you gotta pick the Michigan game. I never gave it a second thought. The crowd's just so intense!"

Dave might never even have gotten the chance to dot without a few historic decisions way back when. A cymbal-banging sister, who marched the Script when she was a Buckeye, convinced him to switch from the sax to the sousa. And with the switch, provided an opportunity that he had never dreamed of for himself. And one that his mom and dad, grandma and grandpa, and aunts and uncles had never dreamed of either. Which meant that with the honor Dave also needed a whole lot of extra tickets for Saturday.

"The athletic department gives us tickets, two a season, for friends and relatives," he explained. "A lot of the guys don't use them and so far I've got about thirty rounded up. Lots of relatives will be here. My grandma and grandpa are even coming in from Missouri!"

Being an *i*-dotter isn't, however, all extra tickets and grandma hugs. First there are the hours of practice, the talent to make it to the top seven, and there's pain too. Just practicing that strut to the top of the *i*, lugging a forty-pound sousaphone, can take a toll on the legs. Shin splints are an OSU band trademark, and prepractice taping is a must for a lot of the marchers.

But for Dave and for Jim, all the hours, the shin splint taping, the sousaphone seniority, and the waiting and waiting and waiting, it's all worth it. If for nothing else, for that one moment.

"It really is awesome!" Dave lit up. "When you start going around the bottom of the *o* and the drum major picks you up . . . and the crowd starts really going nuts, that's when you really get pumped. That's what it's all about!"

All week long, Michigan Week is one big tradition. Friday, though, Columbus just explodes. All over campus from breakfast on through the night, the BEAT MICHIGAN stew is brewing. During breakfast in the basement of the Union, an FM radio station spent a four-hour morning broadcast interviewing students and ripping the Wolves. Later there was a lunch upstairs at the "Great Debate," a Rotary Club benefit for the severely retarded, where alumni Bucks spent two more hours roasting Michigan fans. And finally at dinner, pizza at the Ohio State alumni hangout, the Varsity Club Pub, was the best place in town to listen to your average Joe Buck rip the Wolverines. To top the night off, I took a cruise of High Street, the wildest stretch of beer taps and T-shirt shops in the Big Ten, and the place where most Bucks get hammered.

But my favorite Friday stop was over at Ohio Stadium for Senior Tackle. It's one of college football's finest traditions. The football team's offering to Michigan Week, the tradition has endured since 1913, the year Woody Hayes was born. It was the end of the 1913 football season, in fact Friday night, at the very last football practice of that year. The Northwestern game was Saturday. Several of the seniors, probably feeling a little sad about the end, asked Coach Wilce if they could go back and hit the tackling dummy one last time. One final stick to go out on a good hit. Coach Wilce obliged, and one of college football's most enduring traditions was born.

Senior Tackle is open to the public. In fact some years when the Bucks have really rolled, the public's flocked to it eight or nine thousand strong. When I got there, the crowd, which probably reached a couple of thousand, was milling around. The sun was going down, blue skies fading to black, and the evening cold was setting in. Stadium lights were on. So was the scoreboard. Most folks wore at least a heavy sweater; others looked like they were socking into a deer blind. The anxious fans accumulated in the far corner of the stadium, in the lower stands, and spilled out onto the red tartan track. At the center of them stood a single microphone. A black guy in a three-piece suit kept asking for everybody to "PLEASE MOVE OFF THE TRACK." His voice boomed out over the stadium speakers; it echoed from the empty upper deck down and across the football field. But nobody paid much attention and the crowd kept milling. Next to the microphone stood a red one-man blocking sled. Taped to the front, the place where you drive the shoulder pad, was that big blue block M on a maize field. A modern-day version of Coach Wilce's 1913 tackling dummy.

All the Saturday afternoon fanfare-makers were present. Cheerleaders, complete with pom-poms, sat and stretched on the track. Brutus Buckeye and his stupid-looking nut-shaped head just kicked around. Down in the far end zone at the closed end of the stadium, the OSU band assembled. Practice was just starting for them. Aside from black game hats with the red plumes, the marchers all wore gray sweats. Everybody waited for the featured show.

Coach Cooper and his staff, followed by the Buckeye players, walked out from the tower, across the track, and onto the field. Cheerleaders cheered. Fans clapped. The black guy in the three-piece suit headed back to the microphone for one last ignored request to "PLEASE MOVE OFF THE TRACK." The players wore red sweats with OHIO STATE in big block letters across the chest. Twelve of them—the seniors—in addition to the sweats had on shoulder pads, jerseys, and helmets. Once all the guys had walked out and gathered with the cheerleaders on the turf behind the sled, and fans had filled in on the track side of the sled, and the man at the mike had given up pushing 'em back, he announced, "THE PRIDE OF THE BUCKEYES, THE OHIO STATE MARCHING BAND." It echoed loud and clear throughout Ohio Stadium. The band, in formation, hummed out "Buckeye Battle Cry" and marched across the field to meet the team. Fans clapped and sang along. The red group of football players turned and clapped. Cheerleaders whirled and jumped and cheered. After two fight songs, for the rest of the show the band stood behind the team in the middle of the field, pretty much at attention.

"And now I'd like to introduce the 1973, '74, '75 All-American"—the black guy was back at the microphone, his voice echoing through the quiet stadium—"who never played in a losing game against Michigan." Everybody cheered. "History's only two-time Heisman Trophy winner." He paused after each of the descriptions like a state rep nominating a presidential candidate. "Ohio State's number forty-five, Archie Griffin." The fans roared. And Archie took the microphone. Ohio State couldn't have a finer representative of what's right with football than Archie—articulate, genuine, dressed to the nines. I don't know it for a fact, but I'll bet under all that respectable dress he's in as good shape as when he used to hammer on Michigan.

Archie welcomed everybody to the 1988 Senior Tackle, and he introduced two Heisman Trophy winners who were on hand. Then to the delight of everybody, he offered an invitation: "I'd like any former Buckeye player who has participated in Senior Tackle to come down here and join us and surround these twelve seniors who are being honored this year." Clapping got louder, and a few "way to go's" shot out of the crowd as fellows slipped through. A handful of them from all different directions, smiling, proud as hell, joined Archie. And with everybody in place, the two-time Heisman trophy winner echoed an introduction of the night's speaker. "He played for Ohio State and earned a varsity letter in 1937, 1938, and 1939. He was an All-American end in 1939. He coached here at Ohio State University from 1946 through 1977." It was Archie's turn for the nomination speech. "He has won more Golden Pants than any other Buckeye. He has seventeen." Archie paused to give his next line a little more oomph. "And that means he was on the winning end of an Ohio State–Michigan game seventeen times." All the Michigan things got a wild round of applause. "I'd like to introduce to you the carrier of the tradition, Coach Esco Sarkkinen."

Esco, seventy years old, is an Ohio State legend. A big guy with a good-sized overhang, untucked plaid shirt under a red windbreaker, and a black Buckeye hat, he faced the mike. And because of an old injury, he leaned on an umbrella. Since so much of Esco's history intertwined with Ohio State football, and since he was so slow and deliberate, you kind of got the idea that Esco could go on and on about the Buckeyes forever. And he pretty much did. Stories about Arch, and about Woody, and about Buckeyes for the last fifty years. The stories were precious, and so was he. He lived for Ohio State football, but he just kept going and going and going. People got a little restless. You could tell by all the moving around that a lot were thinking: What a nice old guy, but how long is he gonna go on? Not Archie Griffin, though. Like a rock, he stood behind Esco with his arms folded, as intent as if it were Woody himself doing the rambling. Esco kept going, till Brutus Buckeye finally came up, lay down against the sled, put his hands together up against the side of his head, and pretended he was going to snooze. The old coach got the hint, took it well, finished up to a round of applause, and handed the rest of the night over to the seniors.

As Esco backed off and the kids took over, folks who had earlier eased up into the seats slid right on down to the field. And sat. An aisle of green turf, big enough for the sled to slide on, opened between them and the team. Behind them, at the middle of the field, the band remained at attention.

Coach Cooper then took the mike. He named each of the twelve seniors. Another player, picked by the senior, would come up to the microphone with him and say a few words—an introduction. The speeches were great. Some of the kids, kids who didn't have a problem lining up across from Michigan's Mark Messner or six-six 315-pound Tony Mandarich, or filling a hole with a 240-pound fullback bearing down on them, trembled while their voices echoed through the stadium. Most gave up being unique and repeated what the previous guy had said, just changing the name: "Greg's my best friend," to "Mike's my best friend," to "John's my best friend." Once in a while, if the confidence was there, they'd add a little something special, even an occasional joke or two. After each intro, fans in the stands would clap, some would call out the player's name, cameras would flash; the senior would strap up his helmet, take a three-point, and crash the sled. They went one after another—each in a manner a little different from that of the player before him. Some just popped it. Others drove it a good ten yards. One, Captain Mike Sullivan, "the toughest nose guard in college football" as Coach Cooper introduced him, and a "short, fat, slow white guy" according to his buddy at the mike, slammed the sled, then threw it to the ground. Those on the track and in the stands yelled their approval. Teammates picked him up and high-fived him. Sullivan jumped into the air, swinging his fists. It wasn't tough to tell where Mike Sullivan would leave his heart on Saturday.

Last of the seniors to hit the sled was number 68, Jeff Uhlenhake.

A three-year letter winner, Jeff, you could tell, was "the man." Cooper called him "the best center in college football." Fans knew him well. When introduced, he got the biggest ovation. But the two who knew him best were sitting right down on the turf just a few feet from the sled, crammed into the middle of a bunch of bigger people. They were two tiny next-door neighbors from back home in Newark, Ohio—a little blond girl probably not much more than seven years old, and her brother, just a little bit taller. Each was wearing a big number 68 Buckeye jersey. The sleeves covered their hands; the jersey bottoms went down past their knees. While Jeff's buddy was introducing him, just as he dropped into the three-point, the two little voices yelled out, "Jeff! Hey, Jeff!" They stood up and waved. Jeff rose up, smiled, and waved back.

He dropped back into his stance, and he drove the big block M. People yelled and clapped, two little people in particular. The football team high-fived and clapped, and the cheerleaders cheered, and the band, which had been behind at attention the whole time, cranked out one more fight song. They all left and headed home or to the Varsity Club, or back to the locker room, wherever they could reach the right frame of mind. But everybody was thinking pretty much the same thing—BEAT MICHIGAN!

# MICHIGAN AT OHIO STATE

*Ohio Stadium,*
*Columbus, Ohio*

| Standings | Big Ten | | | All Games | | |
|---|---|---|---|---|---|---|
| November 19, 1988 | W | L | T | W | L | T |
| MICHIGAN | 6 | 0 | 1 | 7 | 2 | 1 |
| MICHIGAN STATE | 5 | 1 | 1 | 5 | 4 | 1 |
| IOWA | 3 | 1 | 3 | 5 | 3 | 3 |
| ILLINOIS | 4 | 2 | 1 | 5 | 4 | 1 |
| INDIANA | 4 | 3 | — | 6 | 3 | 1 |
| PURDUE | 3 | 4 | — | 4 | 6 | — |
| OHIO STATE | 2 | 4 | 1 | 4 | 5 | 1 |
| NORTHWESTERN | 2 | 4 | 1 | 2 | 7 | 1 |
| WISCONSIN | 1 | 6 | — | 1 | 9 | — |
| MINNESOTA | 0 | 5 | 2 | 2 | 6 | 2 |

**Other Big Ten Games:**

INDIANA AT PURDUE

IOWA AT MINNESOTA

NORTHWESTERN AT ILLINOIS

WISCONSIN AT MICHIGAN STATE

What a lousy day. Maybe, I thought, an omen for the Bucks. You know that overdone saying, "Rain's the great equalizer"? Well, like everybody else I always think about it, and usually agree, but really it's just a bunch of crap. In the end we all know the crummy weather makes the good teams better and bad teams worse. Anyhow, it looked like the theory would get another chance to prove itself. Clouds hugged the ground like they were a part of it. No definition, just white to gray and back to white. The weather report said there'd be more of the same. It was cold too, and when I stepped outside at 6:30 A.M., on my way to High Street, I could see my breath.

All week long folks had prepared me. In one breath they'd reveal, "Well, you can throw the records out for this one." And in the next they'd temper it: "You know, though, the game's not like when Woody was here. Or even a couple years ago, it was big then too." They wanted to believe it'd be like all the others, that even without a Rose Bowl trip as the trophy, a Michigan–Ohio State game was enough to chuck the records. The way the Bucks had been going, though, I could tell they just weren't sure. But I was! After cruising the place for two days, after checking out Buckeye Grove and Senior Tackle, after listening in on the Great Debate and interviewing *i*-dotters past, present, and future, after joining the annual Varsity Club pizza crew on Friday night, and watching scarlet flags in the windows of the Holiday Inn grow in twos and threes and fours as folks from all over Ohio rolled in, after every Columbus radio station had brought up *the game* at least twelve times daily, finally after the arrival of that "great equalizer," I banked on "throwing the records out." This was gonna be a good one!

One thing was for sure, High Street would be "throwing out the records." High Street is a zoo! The loudest, craziest, wildest stretch of college taps in the Big Ten. Maybe the world. It's the place where, if all hell breaks loose in Columbus, it starts there first. It's where back in the sixties the hottest student-police battleground was. It's where in the seventies Buckeye victories over Michigan were celebrated with smashed windows, and where Buckeye losses to Michigan were mourned with smashed windows. It's where a few years ago a maize-and-blue car, one bought and painted for the purpose of destroying it, was overturned and torched. High Street is the place that Friday night of Michigan Week features at least a couple of dozen foot cops, steel cables strung between telephone poles so drunks don't fall into the street, horse cops and horses, lines of loaded students, five lanes of traffic, lights, music, and wild, wild energy.

Papa Joe's is High Street at its craziest. I stopped by on Friday night. During Michigan Week that means Bucket Night. They take a big green or yellow plastic bucket, the kind you wash your car with, stick it under the taps, fill it with Stroh's and charge four dollars a shot. To guzzle, you just bury your arm and a plastic cup in, and fill 'er up. Besides beer splashing all over the tables, there are crunching peanut shells all over the floor. Also at Papa Joe's, no pressure to dance, my collegiate dating downfall. The floor out back, the one that could be used for Friday night dancing, filled up with more bucket-wielding patrons.

Best of all is the layout at Papa Joe's. An open, double-deck, wood-paneled room, it looks like a den at the zoo. The kind that black bears are kept in, while people walk around on top and throw bread down to 'em. The lower level, the bear pit, was a room full of students talking, shouting, and singing over the MTV noise. An iron rail rimmed the upper level and kept upstairs drunks from ending up in the buckets below. It also kept upstairs in tune with downstairs. And Friday night, everybody's favorite fight song was the rearranged "Hail to the Victors." As with the beer band at Iowa, the words to "Victors" and "Conquering Heros" and "Hail, Hail to Michigan" got switched with all kinds of interesting descriptive, rhyming, and degrading phrases.

Well, that was Friday night. Saturday morning I was up at dawn on my way back to Papa Joe's for round two—"kegs and eggs," another Michigan Week ritual.

Things were pretty much what you'd expect from a cold drizzly Saturday morning 7:00 A.M. college main drag . . . empty and quiet. Papa Joe's doors had only been open an hour. I expected at least a touch of sanity. Just a hint that this was planet earth. Fat chance! It was like Friday night déjà vu—only *everybody* was wearing scarlet and gray, and the place was even crazier! Screaming, singing, chanting all sorts of drunken noise. Little plastic plates of scrambled eggs and slivered ham littered the wooden tables. Buckets had more than doubled in price up to nine dollars, but were still cranking off the assembly line and slopping beer all over the place. The front room was bumper-to-bumper bodies. "GO, BUCKS! GO, BUCKS! GO, BUCKS!" chants bounced from table to table in an absolutely unorganized fashion. Then all of a sudden they'd catch on, and the whole place for ten seconds would be screaming out, "GO, BUCKS! MICHIGAN SUCKS!" Upstairs drunks would hang over the rail and entice downstairs drunks into a "Go, Buckeyes" chant. And every so often you'd hear that rewritten "Hail to the Victors" fight song.

Lora Lynn and Kelly, two normal-looking girls, sat at the bar and sipped from their bucket.

"THIS IS GREAT, ISN'T IT! LAST YEAR WAS EVEN BETTER! BY THE END OF THE DAY THEY'LL BE THROWING BUCKETS OF BEER." Lora Lynn revealed the obvious.

"THIS IS OUR FOURTH 'KEGS AND EGGS'!" Kelly yelled. You had to yell or nobody but you could hear you. Lora Lynn echoed, "YEAH, OUR FOURTH! WE'VE GOTTA GRADUATE!"

"BUT WE'LL BE BACK!!!" they dueted. Then they told me the Bucks were gonna win, and why—"THEY HAVE TO, IT'S OUR LAST GAME!" They went back to sipping beer from their bucket and being mellow in a place that overflowed with madness.

"AUGHHHHHH . . . AUGHHHHHH . . . AUGHHHHHH!!!!!" One long continuous scream exploded at a table two down from sweet Lora Lynn. The screaming was so loud it drowned out all the other noise and songs and yells going on. There five frat guys—Delta something—practiced screaming and screaming and screaming.

"HE'S A TELEMARKETER!" Dave, the ringleader, took a breath, turned, and yelled across the table to me. The others, including Ryan, the telemarketer, answered in unison, "AUGHHHHHHH!"

"KICK ASS, KICK ASS, KICK ASS . . . AUGHHHHHH!"

"HE'S GOTTA WORK TODAY AT NINE! . . . WE'RE GONNA KILL HIS VOICE SO HE CAN'T. AUGHHHHHH! THEN HE CAN GO TO THE GAME. AUGHHHHHH!" The table joined him: "AUGHHHHHH!" A couple of guys hanging over the rail upstairs joined in too. Stereo "AUGHHHHHH!" And the "AUGHHHHHH" evolved into "GO, BUCKS . . . MICHIGAN SUCKS! GO, BUCKS . . . MICHIGAN SUCKS!" Half of Papa Joe's joined in.

"WANT A BEER?!" Dave shoved the bucket my way. Chris, whom I was sitting next to, grabbed a spare cup plunged in and plopped it on the table. "A TOAST!" somebody yelled. Everybody's plastic cups were raised and crashed together, splashing most the beer back into the bucket and the rest all over the table. "TO RYAN AND HIS TELEMARKETING JOB! AUGHHHHHH!!! TO THE BUCKS! AUGHHHHHH! GO, BUCKS . . . MICHIGAN SUCKS! GO, BUCKS . . . MICHIGAN SUCKS!"

Rick, Ryan the telemarketer's roommate, added, "THIS IS THE GREATEST RIVALRY OF ALL TIME! WE'LL BEAT THEIR ASS! WE HAVE MORE SPIRIT! WE HAVE PAPA JOE'S! WE HAVE . . ." He thought, lost in the complexity of the moment. "WE HAVE RYAN'S VOICE . . . AUGHHHHHH!"

"BO'S GREAT! HE'S A GREAT GUY!" Dave, who knew his Buck-eye football, was getting philosophical. In fact, for being as hammered as the five guys were, they had a clue when it came to Buckeye stats.

"BO'S A GREAT GUY," Dave repeated. "EXCEPT FOR THIS GAME I ALWAYS PULL FOR BO. HE'S CLASS!"

"JUST LIKE WOODY!" Ed, the last guy, yelled. You had to yell—even if you were sharing a bucket. Or you'd look like a silent movie star—all mouth no sound. "WOODY WAS AN EXCELLENT COACH! MY GRANDFATHER HELPED WOODY RECRUIT RANDY GRADI-SHAR . . . THE BADDEST FUCKING LINEBACKER IN OHIO STATE HISTORY! AUGHHHHHH! AUGHHHHHH!" The upstairs, not knowing it was AUGHHHHHHing the baddest fucking linebacker in Ohio State history, joined in.

"I'M NOT BRAGGING"—he had to turn up the volume—"BUT MY GRANDFATHER KNEW WOODY. HE HELPED WOODY RE-CRUIT. WOODY WAS THE GREATEST COACH OF ALL TIME. AUGHHHHHH!"

Occasionally a maize-and-blue-covered body would cruise the lower level, in front of us. He'd be greeted with an upper-deck shower of half-filled beer cups, boos, and at least a couple of rounds of the reworked "Hail to the Victors." Nobody was really lethal, though, just loaded. Two old guys, the kind you'd normally find flipping burgers up at the Winnebagos, walked in and around. If they hadn't been in their fifties, you'd have thought they were cruising the place for babes. But they were covered in red, each with a Buckeye hat, revealing they were just up for *the game.* Papa Joe's must've been their old stomping ground.

Dave noticed and stopped one of 'em on their way out. "YOU GUYS ARE GREAT! THANKS FOR COMING!" The guy smiled and said something that absolutely nobody could hear. And gave Dave a high five!

"AUGHHHHHH!" The table loved it. "GO, BUCKS . . . MICHIGAN SUCKS!"

"A TOAST!" I offered one on my way out. "FOR WOODY, FOR RYAN'S VOICE, FOR RANDY GRADISHAR!" One last plastic-cup crash and to a good, long, loud chorus of "AUGHHHHHH's" I left the zoo. Outside, High Street was still drizzly, cold, and empty. The rest of the day would seem tame.

I headed back for Ohio Stadium and found a parking spot across the river from the stadium at the Jaffe Center. I locked up and trucked off to the Holiday Inn, "GO, BUCKS" chants from Papa Joe's still ringing in my head, the morning air still cold and damp.

No other Big Ten game day has so much to choose from. It's like the dinner table at Thanksgiving. Dressing, turkey, corn, and sweet potatoes, whatever you pick you can't go wrong. One, two, three in a line, all within a couple of blocks of each other, Ohio's football stadium, St. John Arena and its parking lots, and the Holiday Inn crunch together. During basketball season, basketball teams play in St. John. During football seasons, it's bands. The lots outside get stuffed with Winnebagos and vans, a lot of 'em scarlet and gray. And the Holiday Inn's a constant buzz of energy. And food and music. And Buckeye fans.

A WELCOME TO HINEY GATE banner swung across the drive to the Holiday Inn. Hiney Gate, set up in the hotel parking lot, is a gargantuan party. A bandstand was up in the middle of it and things were just starting to roll. On Michigan Saturday, Hiney Gate's *the* big thing to do. But then again it's *the* big thing to do on Purdue Saturday, and on Wisconsin Saturday and on Indiana Saturday too. Makeshift sales sheds dot the lot. Students work 'em. At each you can get a beer or a brat or a burger in exchange for tickets, tickets that are sold at another stop. The Dangers, a five-man band, kick out fifties, sixties, and seventies tunes. Real, real loud! Their songs and their jokes and the cheers that follow swing into the tailgate lots across Lane Street, which in itself is a bumper-to-bumper accumulation of cars, and people traipsing back and forth. Add to that the parties, a couple of huge souvenir stores within the block, and the Varsity Club forty-five-minute waiting lines, and you have a three-square-block zoo! Kind of a graduated Papa Joe's! Win or lose, it's the wildest game day celebration in the Big Ten.

Behind Hiney Gate hover the ten stories of the Holiday Inn. From the upper floors you can look out over St. John to the stadium. From the stadium you can look back to the Holiday. Windows, beginning Friday afternoon, at least on the weekend of *the game,* fill up with scarlet flags. By 5 P.M. Friday, seven or eight of the windows flagged their colors . . . by Friday night more than a dozen. At game time on Saturday, twenty-three windows boasted the big gray O on a scarlet field. A handful featured maize and blue. Saturday morning, people peppered the windows, looking down and across at the celebrations.

Inside, game day at the Inn is one big food fest. The bar has bar snacks. In the lobby more brats, burgers, chili dogs—cooked, wrapped, and heated. And canned beer on ice. But if you really want to gorge, there's the dining room in back. What a setup! Six-fifty for all you can eat—sausage, bacon, scrambled eggs, potatoes, chicken breasts in gravy, coffee, and an endless flow of different-flavored juices. The place was packed. Lines at the cash register out in the hall, lines along the seven-course smorgasbord, and lines of filled plates at the seat-your-self tables. Scarlet-clothed folks piled in the food and talked Buckeyes. Maize-and-blue Michiganders, a few tables' worth, did a little piling-in of their own as well.

I found a table with an open seat. And as with any open seat, an open Buckeye football conversation. Two guys, a son and his dad, were dressed in appropriate Buckeye garb: Dad in a Buckeye jacket and hat, while his son, a big guy probably about my age, wore a red sweater. And on his finger a Big Ten championship ring. The thing was huge.

"Nineteen seventy-nine." He was referring to the ring. "I played my freshman and sophomore years." I had asked about it. Hell, I was staring at it. My college roommate had gotten one back in '79 for baseball. And I used to stare at his all the time too.

The ex-Buck was big; he must've played the line in '79. I didn't ask why only two years, but it was for sure that his blood still ran scarlet. All three of us shoveled in thirds and talked college coaches. We sized up OSU's new coach, middle-aged George at MSU, and old Bo at Michigan.

"Cooper," the dad told me, isn't the answer. "I don't know, I just don't like him. He rips the kids in the paper too much."

His son nodded. "Earl Bruce wasn't the answer either." The subject was probably one that the two had hashed over quite a few times. Coaching changes always are.

"There's nothing like this game!" Dad changed the subject. And added, "Boy, I'll tell ya, when it was Woody and Bo, this place was a real zoo!" He'd seen his share of *the games,* been coming, he told me, since the middle fifties. "Once, I can't remember the year, I think it was the sixties—it was about twenty minutes or so till game time, the stands were filling up, and a voice came over the PA. They told us there was a bomb threat, that somebody had called and said there was a bomb at the stadium. And you know, I don't think one person got up and left . . . I didn't!"

"I'd believe it." His son laughed. "You're gonna love it. It's some game."

"And don't forget St. John's skull session," Dad reminded me before they took off. "That band's great too!"

Across the street, tailgaters were having a ball. St. John provides plenty of tailgating room. Add to that the grass lots across the river, and there's certainly no reason why anybody who wants to can't pop the hatchback. And while there's too many diversions for massive tailgating, like up in Ann Arbor, those who do it, do it right. Big red flags with that gray O in the middle and a few script *Ohio State*s overpowered the visiting maize-and-blue ones. Cruising down the cold wet happy rows, I bumped into a couple of Wolverines I'd met back in Ann Arbor; I'd had chili and beer with them after the Spartan loss. They recognized me, offered another beer and a little more chili. They wanted to know how my trip had gone, how Michigan Stadium stacked up with the rest of the Big Ten. The football team they knew all about. Rose Bowl tickets, plane reservations, and a New Year's week in Pasadena were already in hand!

It's a good mix, Buckeye and Wolverine fans. And their tailgating. For some reason I thought they'd hate each other. Because of the Bo-Woody rivalry and all those great games, I figured that in addition to a gas grill and a couple of packed-up ice chests, they'd roll out Ollie North security fences. I thought the two sides would spend the whole pregame hurling insults and empty beer bottles at one another. I forgot Columbus and Ann Arbor are in the Midwest.

The St. John Arena is ugly—at least on the outside. A big, tall, boxy thing, it's not much of a match to the football stadium. Inside, two levels of bench seats swing around and hover over the court. With the Wolverines in town, the place was packed. There must've been ten thousand. And they were buzzing. Seated at the center of the floor, dressed sharply in black military-style uniforms with a wisp of red and white, was the OSU Marching Band. Behind them at attention, in an arc, stood the University of Michigan Marching Band. That big block M splashed their chests. You couldn't beat it. Two of the best bands in the country, playing two of the best fight songs in the country, and together for free on Saturday morning. After "The Star-Spangled Banner," and a Buckeye welcoming version of "Hail to the Victors," I got my first injection of "Across the Field." The arena erupted. The band director, Dr. Woods, held a little retarded boy in his arms. The kid gripped the conductor's baton and bounced his hands up and down; the band beat out "Across the Field" again. The arena erupted again, and a great big grin burst out on the kid's face. At the end the child was presented with a Buckeye band sweatshirt, and to clapping hands his mom came up and walked him back to his seat.

Then TBDBITL cut through a repertoire of crowd pleasers. And always, it seemed, every five minutes they threw in another verse of "Across the Field." The Bucks actually have two fight songs—"Buckeye Battle Cry," the official version, which is played after each touchdown, and "Across the Field," an even peppier tune that gets the call all the other times. Each gets the Bucks primed; each is a great Big Ten fight song.

At one point, during a break in the fight song action, before the Wolverines got their chance, band members approached the microphone. Since this was the season's final game, the squad leaders came up and said hi to the crowd. Kids filed up to the microphone and told the crowd their names and their hometowns. Everyone in the stands cheered. Each squad leader carried an instrument in one hand and a folding chair in the other. Kind of neat, I thought, another Buckeye tradition. The place was just loaded with them. Maybe, I guessed, they sat in the same chair each game, each practice, for all four years. And because of their dedication, the chairs served as souvenirs. I liked it. In a way, it was like the Senior Tackle. I asked a band guy standing alongside if I was right.

"Not really." He laughed. "If they don't take it with them, the other guys will pass it back and hide it. Then there's no place to sit."

A big white paper sign in the fifth row announced, CONGRATULA-TIONS, DAVE RENCEHAUSEN. Another one next to it said, TODAY'S I DOT . . . WAY TO GO, DAVE. Dave, down in front, squashed into the chair by his sousaphone between fight songs, nodded to the sign bearers. It was the Rencehausen entourage.

The gang had made it—his mom and dad down from North Olmsted, his grandma and grandpa and cousins and aunts and uncles from Missouri. I found the sign as the concert ended, and with it some pretty happy folks.

"We're so proud of him," Dede, the *i* dot's mom, revealed. "I went to the grocery store to get all the stuff for our party tonight."

"An *i*-dotting party," Dave's sister, the ex-TBDBITL member, added.

"That's right, an *i*-dotting party," Mom continued, "and the lady working the cash register asked me, 'You having a party?' I told her, 'My son's dotting the *i.*' She didn't have any idea what I was talking about. But a lady back in line, an Ohio State alum, heard and she said, *'Your son is dotting the* i. Really—we're going! That's great! It's such a great tradition.'

"Oh, and *USA Today* is taking our picture with Dave; we're gonna be on TV next week!" Mom was beaming.

Grandpa and Grandma smiled and said hello. They were happy but reserved, like most grandmas and grandpas. They were part of the group that had road-tripped over from Missouri. Dad was making sure all the photo equipment was in order: camera set for continuous rapid-fire shots. Mom was in charge of that. The portable VCR was Dad's job—but just to make sure, friends at home were taping the game.

With the signs rolled up, and everybody set, the Rencehausen entourage hustled over for their favorite part of *the game*—the pregame show.

There's about half an hour between the St. John finale and the *i* dot in the stadium. That's if the *i* dot's before the game. Sometimes, if there's no visiting band to share the spotlight, they'll dot at half time. Either way, that last half hour before kickoff, the scarlet flood starts making its way over. Tailgates begin closing up, at least temporarily. Hiney Gate thins. Scalpers get edgy, particularly when it's cold and rainy, the Bucks are 4–5–1, and ABC's in town.

Between St. John and the football stadium, just out in front of the giant arched entrance maybe fifty yards or so, is the Jesse Owens Plaza. A metal sculpture sits in the middle. It's a great meeting place for friends, a final sales spot for scalpers, and a good place for that last beer stockup. Two guys, maized and blue from top to bottom, were doing their best on a couple of twelve-packs of Bud.

"We're gonna get twelve apiece in. All of 'em." Two open cardboard packs of Bud were being emptied.

"Everybody's counting on us," his buddy added.

One per each sock, a couple in each belt, hoods, pockets, sides of the coat when it zips closed. An airport metal detector would've beeped out on metal detection overload. Twenty-four cold twelve-ounce cans between them. They congratulated one another, then, stiff-legged, they walked like unoiled tin men to the gate.

I swung around to the press box side. *I* dotting, I was told, in order to provide its full effect, must be seen from upstairs, press box side. And the "full effect" was something I'd been waiting for.

Underneath the stands, Ohio Stadium is like old Memorial over at Illinois. Puny walkways, old cluttered stairways, concrete ramps circling over and back on themselves again and again. Folks bunch together in a slow awkward flow on their way up to the top. It's like scaling the inside of an old oceanside lighthouse. Game time was still twenty-five minutes away when I found a seat at the open end of the shoe, on the lip of the upper deck, at about the thirty-yard line. Both teams were finishing up end zone plays. The stands were starting to bulge with red. The two huge brick smokestacks, the ones that hovered above Buckeye Grove, rose up above the stadium. The left one billowed gray. I settled in for the show, the Script "Ohio," and Dave's dot.

The Michigan band hit the tunnel. Meanwhile, conversations on *the game* swirled. People who hadn't met for a couple of weeks exchanged hellos and predictions. More "You can throw the records out on this one." The fella I was illegally sitting next to didn't seem to mind. I told him it was just for the *i,* and promised to head downstairs afterward. Lots of folks must sit upstairs for the *i.* People seemed to be plopping on any open plank.

"You know," the fella said, "you can sit next to somebody all season long and not really know them till this game. I've seen some strange things happen to people at this game. I've seen professors lose it up here. Professors!" he emphasized, like professors don't ever lose it.

The crowd roared. A little roar, and an echo like half of 'em had seen something, and the rest tried to catch up. Through the tunnel at a slow cadence, noiseless from my upper-deck seat, the drummers marched in. The rest followed. Slowly, deliberately, a giant rectangle moved out onto the open field. Clapping got a real workout for the first time that afternoon. Out from the rear, kicking through the ranks to the lead column, came the Ohio State University band drum major. Other twirlers followed. The PA boomed, "THE PRIDE OF THE BUCKEYES, THE OHIO STATE UNIVERSITY MARCHING BAND!" And to the approval of a near-capacity crowd, the Buckeye band fired off a rendition of "Buckeye Battle Cry" and marched across the field. For the first time that day, Ohio Stadium really let loose.

After the flag got its salute, another band rectangle formed on the far sideline, about the middle of the field. That same deep voice

boomed through the public address system, "THE MOST MEMORA-
BLE TRADITION IN COLLEGE BAND HISTORY, THE INCOMPA-
RABLE SCRIPT 'OHIO.'" Again Ohio Stadium shook. And the
tradition, the one we were all there to see, the one that Woody had
taken part in, the one that the Rencehausens had a family reunion's
worth of bodies together to celebrate, the incomparable Script began.
"Le Régiment de Sambre et Meuse" rose up from the field. Ohio
Stadium was one big unison clap. Down the twenty-yard line, the
far-sideline rectangle began to break. The huge electronic end-zone
scoreboard square, blank moments before, began to trace the drum
major's march. Behind him like a snake, to the rhythmically clapping
stadium, marchers began the cursive trace. Down the twenty, toward
the press box, a single-file march. The big sweeping *O* flowed into a
little *h*. Where *O* hit *h* and lines crossed, marchers slammed the
instruments to their sides, crossed, and whipped them back up to
attention, then continued playing.

For three and one-half minutes, music and marching and Script
continued. And rhythmic clapping too. I remembered what Dave had
said. When that drum major picks up the dot, that's when the crowd
loses it. That's the time, he told me, when you really get pumped. Well,
some fifty yards away, across the field, trailing Dave and the drum
major, the Script stopped. *Ohio,* big *O* to little *o,* stretched between
the twenties. "Le Régiment" continued. It was show time! The drum
major circled back. He passed the sousaphone dot. Rhythmic clapping
broke to a roar. Dave, still marking time, probably too pumped to play
or even think, followed—the pickup! The drum major turned and
slapped Dave a high five. The scoreboard read *Ohio.* The roar turned
to thunder as Ohio State's drum major strutted out past the *i.* And as
Mr. Rencehausen's VCR rolled, as Dede's camera popped pictures at
a supersonic rate, as the folks back in North Olmsted checked to make
sure their VCRs were working, while the insides of the Michigan
locker room shook, Dave Rencehausen and his sousaphone leaned
back, strutted to the top of the *i,* and finished her off! He grabbed his
hat, snapped a bow to the far side of the stadium. It roared! He clicked
his heels together, turned, and snapped a bow to the press box side.
It roared! The stadium scoreboard dotted the *i!* Ohio Stadium was
primed!

Bring on the Wolverines . . . and let *the game* begin. And what a game
it was—but not for a while. The first half was a blowout. Michigan just

battered the Bucks. National TV, the Woody and Bo showdowns, those 10–7, smash-'em-in-the-mouth, kick-'em-while-they're-down grudge matches were long-gone memories. This Buckeye team, it seemed, didn't belong in the same conference, let alone on the same field with Michigan. Gillette hit one from fifty-two yards out to ice the first half at 20–zip. Both teams retired to lick their wounds. In Ohio's case, major surgery was needed.

"The absolute worse half-time show I've ever seen," some guy in front of me in the half-time coffee line blurted out. He was talking about the OSU band. A salute to veterans of Vietnam—helicopter sounds, voices from the past over the stadium speakers, and the eerie music of the movie *Platoon.* "It was like a goddamn funeral march," he bitched again. "Appropriate," another guy two lines down, referring to the football game, retorted. The folks between nodded or laughed. Then went back to complaining about how bad things were going to get in the second half.

But something must've happened in that Ohio State half-time locker room. Maybe Woody was listening in. Maybe he whispered a little tradition into Coach Cooper's ear. Or maybe Buckeye Grove let loose some magic and it drifted over to the stadium. Archie Griffin might've even recited a mystical "I never lose to the Wolverines" chant. Whatever, when the Bucks took the field, they owned it. The Ohio State funeral procession turned into a point celebration, and on Showdown Saturday in the NCAA—a day when Nebraska squared off with the Switzer machine in Norman, USC and UCLA vied for a January trip to Pasadena, the Fighting Irish and Nittany Lions renewed their rivalry under the Golden Dome, and Harvard and Yale played before a crowd of Izod-sweatered yuppies—it was *the game* that stole the show.

The Buckeyes exploded. Their passing game turned into a Blue Angels aerial show. One touchdown, two touchdowns, three. As the fourth quarter turned, they grabbed the lead. Bewildered Michigan players, coaches on the sidelines, even Bo looked shell-shocked. It kept coming back to me: "You can throw the records out on this one."

If ever a crowd turned a game, it was this one. Ohio Stadium rocked—Michigan quivered, then melted. Everybody, not just the student section, was standing for every play. "AUGHHHHHH" roars in the horseshoe end grew through the stands, and exploded across the field. Michigan players must've thought they'd gone to hell. From my student-crammed horseshoe end, a long loud "O" roared out across the field. At the press box sideline, most everybody with a voice, on both levels, followed it up with an "H." Way down under the scoreboard, "I" thundered in answer. A last "O" boomed from the far side. Like a wave, "O-H-I-O" rolled right through again. The Ohio State band got stuck on a second-half replay of "Across the Field." Meanwhile, "Hail to the Victors," the first-half theme, was muzzled—there was nothing to celebrate. The crowd oozed closer to the field. Back up and behind, people were just plain going nuts. Ohio State snaps and TV time-outs were the only times the noise wasn't deafening. As ABC sold beer and Chevrolets, the band turned and cranked out "Hang on, Sloopy," while the whole corner of the Ohio Stadium end zone rocked back and forth and danced in the aisles—till the Bucks, offense or defense, trotted back onto the field—and again a deafening thunder. All second half, each time the Buckeyes hit the field, that thundering salute would greet them.

Michigan, snakebitten by the noise as much as its foe, recovered with less than two minutes to go. A four-point Buckeye lead vanished—a fifty-nine-yard Kolesar kickoff return, a forty-one-yard diving, twisting, turning catch in the far corner of the end zone, again by Kolesar, an Ohio boy. Six plays later, a last-chance interception of a Buckeye pass, and just like that it was over. Quiet—stunned quiet. That adrenaline that had surged for the whole second half—the energy that'd resurrected the Bucks for 31 second-half points, that had cranked out "Sloopy," the fight song, the "O-H-I-O," the thunder that had greeted every trot of the Buckeye team onto the field—was squelched with twenty-nine seconds to go. For a moment, while Michigan fell on the ball, there was no sound. Not even enough time for seniors on the sidelines to hang their heads and cry. The only noise— down in the Michigan end, a dreamlike replay of the first half, "Hail to the Victors" over and over again.

The time ticked to 0:00 and Michigan celebrated. Teammates grabbed one another and thrust fists into the air. Dazed Buckeyes stood and watched. The two groups of warriors mingled. A string of Wolverines had already started a dance to the locker room. Scarlet shirts got up and dragged themselves across the field toward theirs. The crowd recovered temporarily and provided one last long cheer, a standing ovation, to honor the Buckeye participants. And just like that it was done.

I was as stunned as the other ninety thousand . . . but since my heart wasn't involved, my recovery time was quicker. And while the bands were postgaming it on the field, and folks bottlenecking the exits were trying to figure out just how come the Cinderella shoe didn't fit, I headed over toward the visitors' locker room.

The locker room sat inside the stadium tower on the press box side of the stadium. Earlier in the week, I'd picked up a press conference pass—my first ever! When I got to the door, I was ushered in and up the side stairway with the rest of the newspaper guys. We were to wait upstairs, and when the celebrations down below were over, Bo, I assumed, would come up with all the explanations. Two turns of some rickety stairs emptied at the back of a small room. Wooden chairs organized like a junior-high-school classroom, faced a small wooden table in front. Newspapermen filled the chairs. I was late and slipped in at the back. Every time the steps creaked with another newsman, conversation slowed and heads turned. False alarm, and it was back to getting-the-facts-straight time.

The stairs squeaked again. A cop entered, behind him a guy in a blazer, and behind him was Bo. That same block M cap, the same windbreaker, same clothes he always wears on TV. He stepped around to the front and sat at the little wooden table. Tape recorders clicked on. Notepads opened, pencils primed at a starting point. Bo was calm; he was smiling. I'd never seen him up close and never ever seen him calm or smiling. ABC only closeups the tirades. He really looked happy! For about fifteen minutes, the guys with the pencils trained to the paper asked questions. "What'd you feel when Kolesar caught the pass?" "What'd you feel when Kolesar dropped a pass earlier?" "What'd Kolesar feel when he dropped the first pass?" Bo answered; he smiled some more; he was polite. But you could tell, even before he asked, "OK, has everybody had enough?" that he'd rather have been downstairs, savoring the moment with his boys.

But just before he finished, before the last of the hands went up and the last of the "What were you feeling?" questions was asked, Bo offered up some philosophy. Not really an answer to any particular question, just a little something from the heart. Kind of a look inside the man. A look inside the rivalry.

"The last few years this great classic has swung from defense to offense," he noted. "It used to be, great power defenses would give no quarter in this game. Now it's the offenses that've taken over." Bo paused a moment. He thought about the sixty-five points that had gone on the board that afternoon, and maybe too he reminisced about one of those 10–7 nose-to-nose power defensive struggles. He smiled and added, "I'd like to get it back the way it was."

The way it was when Woody was around.

| Final Standings | Big Ten | | | All Games | | |
|---|---|---|---|---|---|---|
| | W | L | T | W | L | T |
| MICHIGAN | 7 | 0 | 1 | 8 | 2 | 1 |
| MICHIGAN STATE | 6 | 1 | 1 | 6 | 4 | 1 |
| IOWA | 4 | 1 | 3 | 6 | 3 | 3 |
| ILLINOIS | 5 | 2 | 1 | 6 | 4 | 1 |
| INDIANA | 5 | 3 | — | 7 | 3 | 1 |
| PURDUE | 3 | 5 | — | 4 | 7 | — |
| OHIO STATE | 2 | 5 | 1 | 4 | 6 | 1 |
| NORTHWESTERN | 2 | 5 | 1 | 2 | 8 | 1 |
| WISCONSIN | 1 | 7 | — | 1 | 10 | — |
| MINNESOTA | 0 | 6 | 2 | 2 | 7 | 2 |

**Bowl Games**

IOWA vs. North Carolina State—PEACH BOWL

ILLINOIS vs. Florida—ALL-AMERICAN BOWL

INDIANA vs. South Carolina—LIBERTY BOWL

MICHIGAN STATE vs. Georgia—GATOR BOWL

MICHIGAN vs. Southern Cal.—ROSE BOWL

## A Final Thought About the Bowls

Five bowl games. The most of any conference in the country.

Michigan State lost. But it was Vince Dooley's final game, so God probably lent a hand to the Bulldogs. Illinois came up a little short against Florida and the "Let's go, Hawkers" ended up their season on a down note, losing to North Carolina State. Still, I'd bet the farm not a single Iowa fan left early. Indiana buried South Carolina, and can add a little Liberty Bowl hardware to that plumped-up trophy case in the IU football office. And Michigan bashed Southern Cal 22–14. Bo got his second Rose Bowl trophy. The Big Ten got their second straight Rose Bowl win—both of 'em a Michigan school hammering on a California school. I see a definite trend setting in and expect that any day now the Pac Ten will be trying to weasel out of their Rose Bowl agreement.

If they don't, then let's hope the Bowl system stays the way it is. Let's hope that TV doesn't change a good thing just so Brent Musburger can call the final, or so the press can come up with an "undisputed national champion." Because as it stands now, each year thirty-four teams head out to seventeen bowls. Thirty-four alumni groups get together for one last bash, thirty-four marching bands road-trip to someplace sunny and warm, thirty-four versions of school-colors-covered fans get to fire up the cookers in a final foreign parking lot, and they all get to see their team "do it" one more time. If they win, even if it's a Cherry Bowl, then they go out as winners. And those fans have a year to rehash the season, to argue that it was just about bowl time that they'd reached their peak. That the defense was finally starting to jell and the offense was hitting on all cylinders. That now, if their team lined up across from Notre Dame—they'd beat 'em.